Lives of the Mind

ROGER KIMBALL

Lives of the Mind

THE USE AND ABUSE OF INTELLIGENCE

FROM HEGEL TO WODEHOUSE

Chicago

IVAN R. DEE

2002

For John Silber

LIVES OF THE MIND. Copyright © 2002 by Roger Kimball. All rights reserved, including the right to reproduce this book or portions thereof in any form. For information, address: Ivan R. Dee, Publisher, 1332 North Halsted Street, Chicago 60622. Manufactured in the United States of America and printed on acid-free paper.

Library of Congress Cataloging-in-Publication Data:
Kimball, Roger, 1953–
    Lives of the mind : the use and abuse of intelligence from Hegel to
    Wodehouse / Roger Kimball.
      p. cm.
    Includes bibliographical references and index.
    ISBN 1-56663-479-2 (alk. paper)
    1. Philosophy, Modern. I. Title.

B791 .K535 2002
190—dc21   2002073681

Contents

Part Three

Acknowledgments

IN THE PREFACE to part two of *Lives of the Artists* (1568), Giorgio Vasari notes that, like "the best historians," he has endeavored to "point out the mistakes as well as the fine strokes" of the figures he discusses, to provide not simply a "dry, factual account of what happened" but "to show how men have acted foolishly or wisely" in the pursuit of their goals. I harbor a kindred ambition in *Lives of the Mind*. Vasari judged the great artists he discussed with respect to such attributes as *disegno*, *grazia*, and *iudizio*— "design," "grace," and "decorum." I ponder a wide range of figures in terms of their fidelity to the truth and their quotient of what one might call spiritual prudence: their healthy contact with reality.

It is one of the guiding themes of this book that intelligence, like fire, is a power that is neither good nor bad in itself but rather takes its virtue, its moral coloring, from its application. Which is to say that intelligence, like fire, like freedom—like any human grace—can be abused as well as used. The abuse need not be—indeed usually is not—intentional. What the philosopher David Stove said about philosophers is true of intellectuals generally. "Philosophers are hardly ever cynical manipulators of their readers' minds," Stove wrote. "They do not produce delusions in others, without first being subject to them themselves." Since language is one of the primary theaters of intelligence, it follows that anyone curious about the use and abuse of intelligence will endeavor to become a connoisseur of linguistic drama. Accordingly, a large part of *Lives of the Mind* is devoted to savoring certain forms of verbal extravagance. What I have assembled is in part the scrapbook of an intellectual pathologist. But it is also worth noting that the heroes in this book rather outweigh the villains. If there is a moral to be drawn, it is an old and familiar one. From one side, it is an warning about the perils of hubris—the perils of intellectual infatuation. From another side, the moral concerns the virtues of modesty. Anthony Trollope puts it neatly in *Barchester Towers*: "Till we can become divine we must be content to be human, lest in our hurry for a change we sink to something lower."

Intellectual debts, like compound interest, accumulate more rapidly with the passage of time. I wish to register my gratitude to my colleagues, past and present, at *The New Criterion* where much of this book was first published. Christopher Carduff, Erich Eichman, Sara Lussier, Robert Messenger, James Panero, and David Yezzi offered many criticisms and suggestions for improvement: I am deeply in their debt. My greatest debt at *The New Criterion* is to Hilton Kramer, who by precept and example has taught me more than anyone about the vocation of criticism. I am also grateful to James Franklin, John Gross, Alexandra Kimball, and Alain Silvera for many corrections and insights. I dedicate this book to John Silber, Chancellor of Boston University. As a philosopher, Mr. Silber is a model of the responsible use of intelligence; as a friend, he is a model of intellectual generosity, responsiveness, and admonition.

RK *July 2002*

Part One

Raymond Aron
and the Power of Ideas

It is our choice of good or evil that determines our character, not our opinion about good or evil.
—Aristotle, *Nicomachean Ethics*

Despotism has so often been established in the name of liberty that experience should warn us to judge parties by their practices rather than their preachings.
—Raymond Aron, *The Opium of the Intellectuals*

Freedom of criticism in the USSR is total.
—Jean-Paul Sartre, *on returning from Russia, 1954*

S ANTAYANA'S alarming thought that "those who cannot remember the past are condemned to repeat it" has at least as much relevance to the world of ideas as to the world of action. This is one reason that *re*-reading is just as important as reading. Time has a way of blunting the keenness of truth, muting its claim on our attention. The admonition we heeded yesterday we forget today: no emergency intervened to keep its lessons fresh. Human nature is a constant. The temptations and errors it faces do not change. But because circumstances are always shifting, truths need constantly to be restated if they are to maintain the grip, the purchase of truth. Re-reading is one of our richest sources of restatement. Putting us back in touch with what we once knew, what we still half-remember, re-reading can restore us to misplaced convictions, revitalize insights that have fallen fallow. Re-reading reminds us that nothing seems more vital than old truths rediscovered: as with friends, our intimacy is deepened by previous acquaintance.

The obstacles to re-reading are many. Sloth plays a part, of course, as does simple busyness—that curiously modern bane that mistakes movement for progress. There is also the prosaic matter of availability: how many important works are rendered *hors de combat* because they are out of print? There are libraries, yes, but books available only in libraries generally play a diminished role in the contemporary cultural conversation. Which brings me to Raymond Aron's masterpiece, *The Opium of the Intellectuals*.

I would guess that almost everyone reading these words knows something about that book, or at least will recognize the title. Many will have read, or read in, it. First published in France in 1955, at the height of the Cold War, *L'Opium des intellectuels* was an immediate sensation. It caused something of a sensation in the United States, too, when an English translation was published in 1957. Writing in *The New York Times*, the historian Crane Brinton spoke for many when he said that the book was "a kind of running commentary on the Western world today." Aron's subject is the bewitchment—the moral and intellectual disordering—that comes with adherence to certain ideologies. Why is it, he wondered, that certain intellectuals are "merciless toward the failings of the democracies but ready to tolerate the worst crimes as long as they are committed in the name of the proper doctrines"? Aron's title is an inversion of Marx's contemptuous remark that religion is "the opium of the people." He quotes Simone Weil's sly reversal as an epigraph: "Marxism is undoubtedly a religion, in the lowest sense of the word. . . . [I]t has been continually used . . . as an opiate for the people." In fact—and fortunately—Weil got it only partly right. Marxism and kindred forms of thought never really became the *people's* narcotic. But they certainly became—and in essentials they still are —the drug of choice for the group that Aron anatomized: the intellectuals.

The Opium of the Intellectuals was a seminal book of the twentieth century, an indispensable contribution to that most patient and underrated of literatures, the literature of intellectual disabusement. Unaccountably the book was out of print for many years. It was therefore welcome news indeed that Transaction Publishers brought out a new edition of *Opium* in 2001, especially since the new edition has the added attractions of an introduction by the political philosopher Harvey C. Mansfield and, as an appendix, "Fanaticism, Prudence, and Faith," the long response to his critics that Aron published in 1956. As Professor Mansfield notes, *The Opium of the Intellectuals* was a "leading document" of the Cold War—a conflict that was conducted as much with words as with arms—but that does not mean it is primarily a book "about the past." The deformations that Aron analyzed are still very much with us, even if the figures that represent them have changed. Which is one way of saying *The Opium of the Intellectuals* is a book that profits as much by re-reading as by being read.

Aron, who died in 1983 in his late seventies, is a half-forgotten colossus of twentieth-century intellectual life. Part philosopher, part sociologist, part journalist, he was above all a spokesman for that rarest form of idealism, the idealism of common sense. He was, Allan Bloom wrote shortly after Aron's death, "the man who for fifty years . . .

had been right about the political alternatives actually available to us. . . . [H]e was right about Hitler, right about Stalin, and right that our Western regimes, with all their flaws, are the best and only hope of mankind." He was, Bloom concluded, "the kind of man necessary to democracy but almost impossible in it; one who both educates public opinion and is truly wise and learned." Over the course of his career, Aron occupied various exalted academic posts—at the Sorbonne, the Ecole pratique des hautes études, the Collège de France—but he was never merely an academic. He wrote some forty books—on history, on the conduct of war, on the cultural and political prospects of France—and was an indefatigable political commentator, some three decades for *Figaro* and then, at the end of his life, for *L'Express*. (He also wrote for *La France Libre* during the war.)

Although showered with honors at the end of his life, Aron never enjoyed the dazzling celebrity that came the way of Maurice Merleau-Ponty and, especially, of Sartre, his classmates at the Ecole normale supérieure. In part, that was because of his intellectual style, which lacked braggadocio. He also lacked the appetite for celebrity, which is another way of saying he did not prize "brilliance" over truth. He certainly did not lack ability. By many measures, Aron was the most accomplished of his peers, in breadth as well as solidity of knowledge. He took first place at the *agrégation* in that most distinguished class, and it is a nice detail that Sartre humbly presented Aron with a copy of *Being and Nothingness* as an "ontological introduction" to Aron's earlier book on the philosophy of history.

From the 1950s through the early 1970s, Aron was regularly calumniated by the radical Left—by his erstwhile friends Sartre and Merleau-Ponty, for starters, but also by their many epigoni and intellectual heirs. In 1963, for example, Susan Sontag dismissed Aron as "a man deranged by German philosophy belatedly converting to Anglo-Saxon empiricism and common sense under the name of 'Mediterranean' virtue." In fact, it would be difficult to find anyone at once more knowledgeable about and less "deranged" by German philosophy than Raymond Aron. His was a sober and penetrating intelligence, sufficiently curious to take on Hegel, sufficiently robust to escape uncorrupted by the encounter.

The fact that Aron was hated by the Left does not mean that he was a partisan of the Right. On the contrary, he always to some extent considered himself a man of the Left, but (in later years anyway) it was the pre-Marxist Left of high liberalism. (Bloom aptly subtitled his essay on Aron "The Last of the Liberals.") Aron's criticism of the Left was not a repudiation but an extension of his liberalism. As the sociologist Edward Shils noted in an affectionate memoir of his friend, Aron moved from being a declared socialist in his youth to becoming "the most persistent, the most severe, and the most learned critic of Marxism and of the socialist—or more precisely Communist—order of society" in the twentieth century. (Shils, like Aron, was one of a tiny number of sociologists who did honor to the name of his profession.)

Again, this shift tokened not a repudiation of youthful ideals but a maturing recognition that ideals worth cherishing are those that can be fulfilled without destroying what they profess to exalt.

In this context, Shils spoke of Aron's "discriminating devotion to the ideals of the Enlightenment." The ideals in question prominently featured faith in the power of reason; Aron's discrimination showed itself in his recognition that reason's power is always limited. That is to say, if Aron

7

was a faithful child of the Enlightenment—its secularism, its humanism, its opposition of reason to superstition—he also in many respects remained a faithful grandchild of the traditional society that many Enlightenment thinkers professed to despise.

Enlightened thinking tends to be superficial thinking because its critical armory is deployed against every faith except its own blind faith in the power of reason. Aron avoided the besetting liability of the Enlightenment by subjecting its ideals to the same scrutiny it reserved for its adversaries. "In defending the freedom of religious teaching," he wrote, "the unbeliever defends his own freedom." Aron's generosity of spirit was a coefficient of his recognition that reality was complex, knowledge limited, and action essential. Aron, Shils wrote, "very early came to know the sterile vanity of moral denunciations and lofty proclamations, of demands for perfection and of the assessment of existing situations according to the standard of perfection." As Aron himself wrote in *Opium*, "every known regime is blameworthy if one relates it to an abstract ideal of equality or liberty."

THE LEITMOTIF of Aron's career was responsibility. Not the whining metaphysical or "ontological" responsibility that Sartre was always going on about—the anguished "responsibility of the for-itself" burdened by groundless freedom—but the exercise of that prosaic, but indispensable, virtue: prudence. Aron understood that political wisdom rests in the ability to choose the better course of action even when the best course is unavailable—which is always. "The last word," he insisted, "is never said and one must not judge one's adversaries as if one's own cause were identified with absolute truth."

It is worth noting that among Aron's favorite terms of

commendation were "prosaic" and its cognates, while he consistently used "poetry" and its cognates pejoratively. In his *Memoirs* (1983), Aron wrote that in *The Opium of the Intellectuals* he attempted "to bring the poetry of ideology down to the level of the prose of reality." What Aron called the "Myth of the Revolution" (like the "Myth of the Left" and the "Myth of the Proletariat") is so seductive precisely because of its "poetical" charm: it induces the illusion that "all things are possible," that everything—age-old institutions, the structure of society, even human nature itself—can be utterly transformed in the fiery crucible of revolutionary activity. Combined with the doctrine of historical inevitability—a monstrous idea that Marx took over from Hegel—the Myth of the Revolution is a prescription for totalitarian tyranny. What does the liquidation of the Kulaks matter in the face of the necessary unfolding of the dialectic? Like its chemical counterpart, the first effect of the opium of the intellectuals is unbounded exhilaration. Only later does the stupefaction become evident.

Unlike the revolutionary, the reformer acknowledges that genuine progress is contingent, piecemeal, and imperfect. Progress is contingent because it depends upon individual initiative and might be undone; it is piecemeal because ideals are never achieved all at once, but only approached step by faltering step; and it is imperfect because the recalcitrance of reality—including the messy reality of human nature—guarantees slippage, frustration, incompleteness, and sheer perversity.

The ideal of the reformist, Aron noted, "is prosaic," that of the revolutionary "poetic." Equally, one is real, the other fantastical. In his *Memoirs*, Aron acknowledged that "I do in fact think that the organization of social life on this earth turns out, in the end, to be rather prosaic." The rule of law;

economic vitality; respect for tradition; freedom of speech: out of such prosaic elements are the seemingly miraculous successes of Western society forged. (One thinks of Walter Bagehot's observation that "the essence of civilization . . . is dullness . . . an elaborate invention . . . for abolishing the fierce passions." I discuss Bagehot in greater detail below.) The subject of politics, Aristotle noted, is "the good life for man." What constitutes the good life? Aron cannily reminds us that the more extravagant answers to this question are often the most malevolent. They promise everything; they tend to deliver misery and impoverishment. Hence his rejection of Communism:

> Communism is a degraded version of the Western message. It retains its ambition to conquer nature, to improve the lot of the humble, but it sacrifices what was and must remain the heart and soul of the unending human adventure: freedom of enquiry, freedom of controversy, freedom of criticism, and the vote.

Such freedoms may seem pedestrian in comparison with the prospect of a classless society in which liberty reigns and inequality has been vanquished once and for all. But such an idea, Aron noted, is "no more than an illustration in a children's picture book."

To say that Aron was suspicious of the poetical is not to deny that his sober vision of human fulfillment exhibits a poetry of its own. Aron, one might say, was a poet of the realm of prose. Another way of putting this is to say that he was a champion of the real in the face of the blandishments of the ideal. The prospect of ideal—that is, total, complete—emancipation bewitches susceptible souls because "it contains in itself the poetry of the unknown, of the future, of the absolute." The problem is that the poetry of the absolute is an inhuman poetry. As Aron drily observed, in real life ideal emancipation turns out to be "indistinguishable from the omnipotence of the State."

The issue is "not radical choice, but ambiguous compromise." Aron continually came back to man as he *is*, not as he might be imagined. Yes, some individuals are honorable and trustworthy. But, Aron writes, "at the risk of being accused of cynicism, I refuse to believe that any social order can be based on the virtue and disinterestedness of citizens." Following Adam Smith and other classical liberals, he looked to the imperfections of man for the fuel to mitigate imperfection. Unlike the Marxist, the classical liberal regards men as "basically imperfect and resigns himself to a system where the good will be the result of countless actions and never the object of a conscious choice. In the last resort, he subscribes to the pessimism which sees politics as the art of creating the conditions in which the vices of men contribute to the good of the State." Aron acknowledged that this prosaic model lacks the grandeur of utopia.

> Doubtless the free play of initiative, competition between buyers and sellers, would be unthinkable if human nature had not been sullied by the Fall. The individual would give of his best in the interests of others without hope of recompense, without concern for his own interests.

But that "if" issues an unredeemable promise. Aron's twofold task was to remind us, first, that there is no human nature unsullied by the Fall and, second, to suggest, as does orthodox Christianity, that what prophets of the absolute decry as a disaster was in fact a "fortunate fall," a condition of our humanity. The utopian is optimistic about man, pessimistic about particular men and women: "I think I know man," Rousseau sadly wrote, "but as for men, I know them not." The anti-utopian is pessimistic, or at least disabused, about man; this forgiving pessimism frees him to be optimistic about individuals.

In his foreword to *The Opium of the Intellectuals*, Aron noted that he directed his argument "not so much against the Communists as against the *communisants*," against those fellow travelers for whom the West is always wrong and who believe that people can "be divided into two camps, one the incarnation of good and the other of evil, one belonging to the future and the other to the past, one standing for reason and the other for superstition."

Marxism is a primary allotrope of the opium of the intellectuals because its doctrine of historical inevitability insulates it from correction by anything so trivial as factual reality. When Merleau-Ponty assures us that in the modern world the proletariat is the only form of "authentic intersubjectivity" or when he writes that Marxism "is not *a* philosophy of history, it is *the* philosophy of history, and to refuse to accept it is to blot out historical reason," no argument will wean him from his folly. What he needs is intellectual detoxification, not refutation.

It is the same with Sartre, who championed totalitarian regimes from the Soviet Union to Cuba but who exhibited an implacable hatred of America and liberal democracy. ("America is a mad dog," he exclaimed in one effusion; it is "the cradle of a new Fascism.") Sartre's "Ethical radicalism," Aron wrote, "combined with ignorance of social structures, predisposed him to verbal revolutionism. Hatred of the bourgeoisie makes him allergic to prosaic reforms."

In insulating its victims from reality, the opium of the intellectuals at the same time insulates them from the rebukes of contradiction. This has allowed for some peculiar intellectual hybrids. For example, the philosophies of Nietzsche and Marx are diametrically opposed: one celebrates the lonely genius, the other the collective; one looks for a new aristocracy of *Übermenschen*, the other for the institution of the classless society. For any unintoxicated person, such differences are essential: they mean that the philosophies of Marx and Nietzsche are incompatible. But for intellectuals under the influence such distinctions count for naught. As Aron notes, the descendants of Marx and Nietzsche (and Hegel and Freud) come together by many paths. The existentialism of Sartre, the nihilism of Derrida or Foucault, all exhibit a similar intellectual incontinence. What unites them is not a coherent doctrine but a spirit of opposition to the established order, "the occupational disease," Aron notes, "of the intellectuals."

This occupational disease is far from conquered. On the contrary, the *communisants* and fellow travelers that Aron criticized continue to flourish. Consider, to take just one example, the ecstatic reception accorded to the neo-Marxist tract *Empire* in 2001. *Empire* is a five-hundred-page reader-proof tome written jointly by Michael Hardt, an American literature professor at Duke, and Antonio Negri, an Italian philosopher and former member of the Marxist-Leninist terrorist group the Red Brigades. According to one prominent academic, *Empire* is "nothing less than a rewriting of the *The Communist Manifesto* for our time." (This was meant, incidentally, as praise.) According to a writer for *The New York Times*, the book might represent the "Next Big Idea," the successor to structuralism and deconstruction in the halls of literary academia. Updating Marxism with radical environmentalism, the authors of *Empire* hail the growth of a new militancy that "expresses the life of the multitude" and resists the depredations of "Empire," a.k.a. capitalism and the United States. "Militancy today," they assure us, "is a positive, constructive, and innovative activity." As an example, they cite the violent protestors who took to the streets in Genoa and Seattle to protest "globalization." ("These movements," they enthused, "are what link Genoa . . . most clearly to the openness—toward new kinds of exchange and new ideas—of its Renaissance past.") Like all Marxists, Hardt and Negri believe that revolution they herald is not only inevitable but also beneficent:

> This is a revolution that no power will control—because biopower and communism, cooperation and revolution remain together, in love, simplicity, and also innocence. This is the irrepressible lightness and joy of being communist.

George Orwell famously remarked that there are some ideas so absurd that only an intellectual could believe them. *Empire* is a case in point: five-hundred pages of pretentious intellectual drivel and political poison.

The Opium of the Intellectuals provides a kind of aerial survey of the higher gullibility that Orwell disparaged, analyzing its apparently perennial attractions, describing its costs, mapping its chief roadways and pointing out some escape routes. Some readers, as Aron noted in "Fanaticism, Prudence, and Faith," criticized the book for being "negative, for abounding in refutations without providing anything constructive." An especially frequent charge was that the book celebrated "scepticism." The last half-sentence of the book—"let us pray for the advent of the sceptics"—was routinely adduced as evidence.

In fact, as Aron argued, his critics mistook him. In the first place, by lifting his concluding clause out of context, they inverted the meaning of his conclusion. "The man who no longer expects miraculous changes either from a revolution or from an economic plan," Aron wrote, is not obliged to resign himself to the unjustifiable. It is because he likes individual human beings, participates in living communities, and respects the truth, that he refuses to surrender his soul to an abstract ideal of humanity, a tyrannical party, and an absurd scholasticism. . . . If tolerance is born of doubt, let us teach everyone to doubt all the models and utopias, to challenge all the prophets of redemption and the heralds of catastrophe.

If they can abolish fanaticism, let us pray for the advent of the sceptics.

The primary target of Aron's polemic was fanaticism. But he also recognized that the defeat of fanaticism often leads to a contrary spiritual sickness: indifference. Both are expressions of the ultimate enemy, nihilism. Scepticism, Aron wrote, is useful or harmful depending on which is more to be feared at the moment: fanaticism or apathy. The intervening faculty that orients us appropriately is practical wisdom, prudence, "the god" (Aron quotes Burke) "of this lower world." In other words, scepticism for Aron is not the end but a means. "Scepticism," he wrote,

is perhaps for the addict an indispensable phase of withdrawal; it is not, however, the cure. The addict is cured only on the day when he is capable of faith without illusion.

It is also worth noting that the scepticism Aron advocated is not a wholly negative attitude. As T. S. Eliot pointed out in *Notes Towards the Definition of Culture* (1948), scepticism is not necessarily destructive. On the contrary, scepticism is first of all

the habit of examining evidence and the capacity for delayed decision. Scepticism is a highly civilized trait, though, when it declines into pyrrhonism, it is one of which civilizations can die. Where scepticism is strength, pyrrhonism is weakness: for we need not only the strength to defer a decision, but the strength to make one.

Aron would have agreed with Eliot. And he might have pointed out that critics who complained of his being insufficiently "constructive" overlooked the distinctly positive effects that simply telling the truth can have. Hegel was preeminently a constructive thinker; he was also a deeply misguided one. The demand for a "constructive program," for "positive results," etc., often turns out to be a demand for illusion and bewitchment.

At the same time, it is worth stressing that the focus of Aron's criticism was not on "constructive" but on "program." He distrusted the utopian impulse not because he wished to stymie reform but because he saw that extravagant promises generally disappoint. Aron preferred the homely satisfactions of common reality. Thus his celebration of the "modest" ideas underlying American society:

> An empirical success, American society does not embody an historical idea. The simple, modest ideas which it continues to cultivate have gone out of fashion in the old world. The United States remains optimistic after the fashion of the European eighteenth century: it believes in the possibility of improving man's lot; it distrusts the power which corrupts; it is still basically hostile to authority, to the pretensions of the few to know all the answers better than the common man. There is no room there for the Revolution or for the proletariat—only for economic expansion, trade unions and the Constitution.

Aron's indictment of intellectual intoxication is not the

same thing as complacency. Nor is it tantamount to an indictment of intellectuals. Aron was not anti-intellectual or contemptuous of ideas. This was not simply because he was an intellectual himself. He clearly discerned the immense power, for good or ill, that ideas can have. "Intellectuals suffer from their inability to alter the course of events," he noted. "But they underestimate their influence. In a long term sense, politicians are the disciples of scholars or writers."

In an essay called "Utopianism, Ancient and Modern" (1973), the social commentator Irving Kristol underscored this Aronian point:

> For two centuries, the very important people who managed the affairs of this society could not believe in the importance of ideas—until one day they were shocked to discover that their children, having been captured and shaped by certain ideas, were either rebelling against their authority or seceding from their society. The truth is that ideas are *all*-important. The massive and seemingly solid institutions of any society—the economic institutions, the political institutions, the religious institutions—are always at the mercy of the ideas in the heads of the people who populate these institutions. The leverage of ideas is so immense that a slight change in the intellectual climate can and will—perhaps slowly but nevertheless inexorably—twist a familiar institution into an unrecognizable shape.

It was part of Aron's purpose in *The Opium of the Intellectuals* to alert us to the sobering truth that Kristol so eloquently articulated. It is sad to reflect that, nearly fifty years on, many important people in our society continue to dismiss ideas as negligible playthings.

Plutarch and
the Issue of Character

What Histories can be found . . . that please and instruct like the Lives of Plutarch? . . . I am of the same Opinion with that Author, who said, that if he was constrained to fling all the Books of the Antients into the Sea, PLUTARCH *should be the last drowned.*

—Montesquieu, quoted by Oliver Goldsmith

Using history as a mirror I try by whatever means I can to improve my own life and to model it by the standard of all that is best in those whose lives I write. As a result I feel as though I were conversing and indeed living with them; by means of history I receive each one of them in turn, welcome and entertain them as guests and consider their stature and their qualities and select from their actions the most authoritative and the best with a view to getting to know them. What greater pleasure could one enjoy than this or what more efficacious in improving one's own character?

—Plutarch, life of Timoleon

F EW WRITERS better understood the power of ideas and the manifold ways in which intelligence could be used and abused than Plutarch. Of course, like all ancient authors today, Plutarch is at best a name to most people, even—especially?—to most college-educated people. You, dear reader, are of a select group, because you know that Plutarch (*c.* 46–*c.* 120) was a Greek biographer and moral philosopher who wrote, among other things, a famous series of "parallel lives" comparing various Greek and Roman figures. Perhaps, like me, you first learned about Plutarch from reading the notes to *Julius Caesar, Antony and Cleopatra, Timon of Athens,* or *Coriolanus,* the four plays for whose plots Shakespeare drew heavily upon the then-recently translated Plutarch. Perhaps you also, like me, dipped casually into the odd volume of Plutarch now and again, to find out more about Pericles, Cicero, Alexander the Great, or some other antique worthy. Probably, like me, you left it at that.

Literary fashion is a mysterious thing. Why is it that Sir Walter Scott, for example, whom generations of readers found absolutely spellbinding, is unread and, for many of us, unreadable today? Why is it that the Renaissance Italian poet Tasso, who fired imaginations from Milton and Dryden to Shelley, Byron, and Goethe, should now subsist as a decoration in scholarly footnotes instead of as a living presence? Why is it that Plutarch—"for centuries Europe's schoolmaster," as the classicist C. J. Gianakaris put it—should quite suddenly move from center stage to the mental off-off-Broadway of reference books and dissertations? If Plutarch, in Sir Paul Harvey's words, is "one of the most attractive of ancient authors, writing with charm, geniality, and tact, so as always to interest the reader," why does he no longer interest *us*?

Doubtless there are many reasons: the shelf life of novelty, competing attractions, educational atrophy, the temper of the age. It seems clear, at any rate, that wholesale changes of taste are never *merely* matters of taste. They token a larger metamorphosis: new eyes, new

ears, a new scale of values and literary-philosophical assumptions. It is part of the baffling cruelty of fashion to
render mute what only yesterday spoke with such extraordinary force and persuasiveness. It is part of the task of
criticism to reanimate those voices, to provide that peculiar
medium through which they might seem to speak in the
way their best, their most ardent hearers understood them.

Plutarch's best hearers form a distinguished but exceedingly various group. Erasmus, resonating to Plutarch's urbane humanism, translated and broadcast his work. Henri
IV of France, in a letter to his wife, wrote that "Plutarch
always delights me with a fresh novelty. To love him is to
love me; for he has long been the instructor of my youth.
. . . [Plutarch's writing] has been like my conscience, and
has whispered in my ear many good suggestions and maxims for my conduct." Shakespeare, Sidney, Ben Jonson,
Dryden, Milton, and Bacon learned and freely borrowed
from him, as did Shaftesbury, Winckelmann, Lessing,
Hume, and Addison. ("Plutarch," Addison wrote, "has
more strokes of good nature in his writing than I remember in any author.") The nineteenth-century French critic
Brunetière argued that what Homer was to the Greek
tragedians, Plutarch was to the classical French dramatists.
Cotton Mather proclaimed Plutarch necessary reading for
"a person of good sense." Browning drew on his life of the
Athenian general Nicias for "Balaustion's Adventure,"
Wordsworth on his depiction of the death of Dion for his
poem of that name. Emerson adulated him, as, alas, did
Rousseau, who started to read Plutarch when he was six.
(The life of Lycurgus, the legendary tyrant who is said to
have made Sparta spartan, made an especially deep impression on Rousseau.) Boswell, who quoted a few lines
from Plutarch's life of Alexander toward the beginning of
his *Life of Johnson*, called him "the Prince of ancient

biographers." And Montaigne, to end this catalogue of ships, is inconceivable without the example of Plutarch. His essays, which contain more than four-hundred references to Plutarch and his works, are consciously modelled on the Greek's easygoing, discursive inquiries into science, manners, customs, and beliefs. "When I write," Montaigne noted in his essay "On Some Verses of Virgil,"

> I prefer to do without the company and remembrance of books, for fear they may interfere with my style. . . . But it is harder for me to do without Plutarch. He is so universal and so full that on all occasions, and however eccentric the subject you have taken up, he makes his way into your work and offers you a liberal hand, inexhaustible in riches and embellishments. It vexes me that I am so greatly exposed to pillage by those who frequent him. I cannot be with him even a little without taking out a drumstick or a wing.

In short, as the classicist D. A. Russell put it in his book on the philosopher (Scribner's, 1973), Plutarch's works "are among the formative books of western civilisation."

Plutarch's writing divides into essentially three parts. One part is the *Lives*. Extant are twenty-three pairs of lives (including one double pair) and four singletons. Scholars believe that we have between a third and one half of Plutarch's corpus; missing are not only the companions to the four solo biographies but also the lives of such important figures as Augustus, Claudius, and Nero, and other works. The dual biographies begin, in the traditional order, with the mythological figures of Theseus, supposedly an early king of Athens, and Romulus, the legendary founder of Rome; they conclude with lives of Dion, the philosopher and brother-in-law of the Syracusan tyrant Dionysius, and

Brutus. The lives were written late in Plutarch's career, probably between 105–115. His general procedure was to write the life of a prominent Greek, then cast about for a suitable Roman parallel. In the text that we now have, nineteen of the parallel lives end with a brief comparison; probably they all once did.

Some of the comparisons are distinctly more compelling than others. There are obvious parallels between the orators Demosthenes and Cicero, for example, or the conquerors Alexander the Great and Julius Caesar. But many of Plutarch's pairings seem arbitrary—or, if that seems too severe, let us say "merely convenient." One often feels, in any event, that he was more interested in the exhibition than the analysis of character. Reflecting on his task at the beginning of his life of Alexander, Plutarch tells his readers that

> I am not engaged in writing history, but lives. And the most glorious exploits do not always furnish us with the clearest discoveries of virtue or vice in men; sometimes a matter of less moment, an expression or a jest, informs us better of their characters and inclinations, than the most famous sieges, the greatest armaments, or the bloodiest battles. Therefore as portrait-painters are more exact in the lines and features of the face, in which character is seen, than in the other parts of the body, so I must be allowed to give my more particular attention to the marks and indications of the souls of men, and while I endeavor by these to portray their lives, may be free to leave more weighty matters and great battles to be treated by others.

It was the bit about "a matter of less moment, an expression or a jest" that Boswell quoted to help justify his own procedure in dealing with Dr. Johnson. Both biographers rely of the friction of anecdote—the arresting detail, the turn of phrase, the private manner of public men—to elicit the moral bearing of their protagonists.

The second part of Plutarch's work are several volumes of "symposia" or table talk, occasional pieces that he wrote up following spirited after-dinner-party conversations at his home or the homes of friends in Athens, Eleusis, Corinth, Delphi, Thermopylae, Rome, and elsewhere. These bagatelles are usually light, sometimes trivial, but are always entertaining. Plutarch begins by indicating the topic and the speakers—which often included Plutarch himself—who debate it: "Whether it was a good custom to deliberate over wine" (yes); "Whether the hen or the egg came first" (probably the hen); "Why old men hold writing at a greater distance for reading" (he got this one wrong); "Why we take pleasure in hearing actors represent anger and pain but not in seeing people actually experience these emotions" (complicated: you will have to read this one to learn his answer).

Some of the issues raised in the table talk have a distinctly contemporary relevance. Item: "That one should guard especially against the pleasures derived from degenerate music, and how to do so." One of the guests recalls another dinner at which the host provided an elaborate musical entertainment. It seemed a fine performance—"at first."

But then, shaking the hall and filling it with resounding noise, when [the performer] perceived that most of the auditors were so overwhelmed as to allow him, under the spell of pleasure, to do with them what he pleased and hypnotize them with his piping or even with licentious movements, he cast off all disguise and showed that music can inebriate, more effectively than any wine, those who drink it in as it comes, with no restraint. For the guests were no longer content to shout and clap from their places, but finally most of them leapt up and joined in the dancing, with movements disgraceful for a gentleman, though quite in keeping with that kind of rhythm and melody.

It is a pity that one cannot enlist Plutarch to report on the next big rock concert.

The third part of Plutarch's work consists of somewhat more formal essays, many of which began life as lectures. Like the table-talk, these pieces betray a hearty, somewhat garrulous curiosity. Several are in the form of a dialogue. Begun in the 80s, most were written before Plutarch embarked on the *Lives*. Although today the *Lives* are far and away Plutarch's most popular work—insofar as any of it can still be said to be popular—at one time his essays exercised a nearly equal claim to attention. Many bear dedications to Plutarch's friends; some were written on request for guidance or information. They range over a wide number of topics, moral, cosmological, etymological, hortatory, and numerological. There are treatises on love, on education, on whether animals have reason, on superstition, on Plato's philosophy, on Stoicism, on Epicureanism. (Plutarch was sound on Epicurus, as you can tell from this title: "You Cannot Live a Happy Life if You Follow Epicurus.")

Although generally moderate in tone, Plutarch could be a severe critic. In "On Herodotus' Spite," which has been called the "first instance in literature of the slashing review," he takes the historian to task for all manner of prejudice and misrepresentation. He makes some palpable hits, catching Herodotus out in various errors. But as the Plutarch scholar R. H. Barrow observed, Herodotus' real failing in Plutarch's eyes was to advance any criticism at all of those states that saved Greece from Persia. "Plutarch," he concluded, "is fanatically biased in favor of the Greek cities; they can do no wrong."

Plutarch does not often wander into purely literary terrain, but when he does he lets you know where he stands. In the fragmentary "Comparison of Aristophanes and Menander," he clearly awards the palm to the decorous New Comedy of Menander. "The witticisms of Aristophanes," he wrote,

> are bitter and rough and possess a sharpness which wounds and bites. And I do not know wherein his vaunted cleverness resides, whether in his words or his characters. Certainly even whatever he imitates he makes worse; for with him roguishness is not urbane but malicious, rusticity is not simple but silly, facetiousness not playful but ridiculous, and love not joyful but licentious.

Menander, by contrast, is said to bring us a "polished diction" whose ingredients are "mingled into . . . [a] consistent whole." Yes, well . . . but is Menander as funny as the scabrous, politically incorrect Aristophanes? I suspect that is not a question Plutarch would wish us to entertain.

Some of Plutarch's essays sound a more personal note. There is, for example, a touching letter of consolation to his wife on the occasion of the death of their only daughter. (Plutarch wrote beautifully on the *philia* that animates married love.) Plutarch also had some useful things to say about how one can distinguish between a flatterer and a genuine friend (for one thing, a true friend is willing to disagree and criticize one) and how to turn the hatred of others to good account (like fire, the enmity of others keeps one alert and on one's toes). In "How a Man May Become Aware of His Progress in Virtue," we find a superb compendium of common sense. The habit of translating words into deeds, Plutarch observes, is one good mark of moral progress. "An indication of this is, in the first place, the desire to emulate what we commend . . . and, on the other hand, unwillingness to do . . . what we censure." The single longest essay in the *Moralia* is devoted to - the Egyptian gods Isis and Osiris, an historical-anthropological work full of arcane information and conjecture that is still often referred to by Egyptologists.

Plutarch's essays and table-talk are published together and are generally known by their Latin title, *Moralia*, "moral matters." As for translations, there were early on various translations into Latin (by the Italian humanist Guarinus, for example). But the person who really brought Plutarch to Western Europe was Jacques Amyot, who published a French translation of the *Lives* in 1559 and of *Moralia* in 1572. Amyot's translations swept educated Europe. In a way, they made as deep an impression in England as France, for Thomas North, who published an English translation of the *Lives* in 1579, based his work not on Plutarch's Greek but on Amyot's French. It was North's Plutarch that Shakespeare, for example, absorbed and refigured to such happy effect. Here is Plutarch, in North's translation, on Antony's first glimpse of Cleopatra:

> [S]he disdained to set forward otherwise, but to take her barge in the river of Cydnus, the poop whereof was of gold, the sails of purple, and the oars of silver, which kept stroke in rowing after the sound of the music of flutes, howboys, citherns, viols, and such other instruments as they played upon the barge. And now for the person of herself: she was laid under a pavilion of cloth of gold of tissue, apparelled and attired like the goddess Venus commonly drawn in picture; and hard by her, on either hand of her, pretty fair boys apparelled as painters do set forth

Cupid, with little fans in their hands, with the which they fanned wind upon her.

And here is Shakespeare:

The barge she sat in, like a burnished throne,
Burned on the water; the poop was beaten gold,
Purple the sails, and so perfumed, that
The winds were love-sick with them, the oars were silver
Which to the tune of flutes kept stroke, and made
The water which they beat to follow faster,
As amorous of their stroke. For her own person,
It beggared all description; she did lie
In her pavilion—cloth-of-gold of tissue—
O'er-picturing that Venus where we see
The fancy outwork nature; on each side her
Stood pretty dimpled boys, like smiling Cupids,
With divers-coloured fans, whose wind did seem
To glow the delicate cheeks which they did cool.

North's translation was more inspirational than accurate. In 1683, John Dryden began a life of Plutarch and oversaw a translation of the *Lives* by several hands and based on the original Greek. This translation has been reworked and revised several times, most recently in the nineteenth century by the English poet and classicist Arthur Hugh Clough.† There have been other translations of the *Lives*, but Clough's edition (available in two vol-

---

† I believe that the only complete edition of Plutarch's *Moralia* available in English is in the indispensable Loeb Classical Library, published by Harvard University Press. Most of the translations—the work of several hands—were done between the 1930s and the 1960s. There is also a Loeb edition of the *Lives*, translated by Bernadotte Perrin in the 1910s and 1920s.

umes from The Modern Library) remains the handiest complete edition.

IT IS a curious irony that Plutarch, who expended so much energy bringing other people to life in his biographies, should himself remain a somewhat shadowy figure. We have some of the standard externals. We know that he was born to a prominent family in Chaeronea, Boetia, a town about twenty miles east of Delphi. He studied philosophy in Athens and emerged a worldly and undoctrinaire Platonist. Like Plato, he believed that to know the good was tantamount to following it. That is one reason Plutarch is often described as "naïve"—a diminishing adjective that, like "charming," one finds regularly employed to describe him. Identifying evil with ignorance, Platonists unwittingly discount the reality of sin. (As Coleridge observed, sin consists in seeing the good, understanding it, and then choosing evil anyway.) But Plutarch did not share Plato's systematizing ambitions or his contempt for the flesh. He entertained often. He was happily married—his wife, Timoxena, peeks glancingly through at us from his table talk, a dignified, hospitable presence—and had at least five children.

Plutarch was officially critical of Stoicism, but the scholar who refers to his "recessive stoicism," "poised between the pessimism of stoicism and the optimism of humanism," has it about right. He was above all a proud, civic-minded Greek at a time when Greek power was definitively eclipsed by Rome. Historical marker: Plutarch wrote most of his work during the reigns of Domitian (81–96), Nerva (96–98), and Trajan (98–117); his contemporaries writing in Rome included Tacitus, Martial, Pliny the Younger, and Juvenal. If there is a current of pathos in Plutarch, it has to do with the recognition that his world

—the world of the Greek gods and Hellenic culture—had declined into a sort of posthumous existence. What were living realities to him in his relative backwater had long since become museum pieces to the world at large. As Sir Paul Harvey observed, much of Plutarch's work was "an attempt to satisfy the demand for moral guidance in an age of reaction against the decadence of the Roman world, when the faith in the old gods and philosophies was failing."

Plutarch himself helped to extend that spiritual autumn by serving for many years as a priest at the Delphic Oracle. Delphi, as one commentator noted, was "almost a second home to Plutarch." His interventions helped to restore the oracle's outward fortunes for a time. Although his own commitment seems never to have wavered, there are many suggestions that he understood he was tending a guttering flame. "The power comes from the gods and demigods," he wrote at the end of his essay "On the Obsolescence of the Oracles," "but, for all that, it is not unfailing nor imperishable, nor ageless." Still, Plutarch's life and writings continually bore witness to the famous maxims inscribed at Delphi: "Know Thyself" and "Avoid Extremes."

Plutarch traveled extensively. A long trip to Alexandria stocked his mind with material for his monograph on Isis and Osiris. He was clearly in Rome, though how often and for how long is not known. His knowledge of Roman literature was poor; he acknowledges in his life of Demosthenes that he did not know much Latin until he was "well into middle age." He never mentions Ovid or Virgil; when he cites a passage from Horace, it is in a Greek translation. Nevertheless, Plutarch's lectures in Rome were popular— so popular, indeed, that his friend Sosius Senecio, to whom the *Lives* are dedicated, seems to have procured him an honorary Roman citizenship from Trajan. Many ancient sources—Plutarch's works prominent among them—provide a tolerably detailed picture of the stage set upon which Plutarch performed. What we are missing, by and large, is the actor himself. Plutarch exists as a genial but disembodied authorial presence, a courteous ghost. Over the centuries, there have been several lives of Plutarch, but nothing that gives us a Plutarch's life of Plutarch.

It is pretty clear that Plutarch regarded himself first of all as a philosopher. But posterity has tended to regard him more as a kind of moral compendium: a repository of vivid characters, arresting anecdotes, dramatically engaging conflicts—the drumsticks and wings to which Montaigne refers. This has encouraged some modern commentators to tincture their admiration with condescension. R. H. Barrow, for example, while noting that Plutarch was deeply immersed in Greek philosophy, concluded that he

> originated nothing. His mind was not adventurous; it did not use its accumulated knowledge as a springboard to make a leap; it may have lacked imagination. Yet in one particular realm Plutarch was a man of genius. For he had a supreme gift of sensitiveness to religious and moral values which was acutely alive to inconsistency and was profoundly disturbed by it. It would be wrong to say that this sensitiveness issued in a passion for truth; for 'truth' is apt to be lifted to a metaphysical plane. Plutarch's mind worked on lower levels. It would be better therefore to say that he had a passion for sincerity, and was able to discriminate values with precision and delicacy.

Barrow's diminishing assessment prompts the question whether being "adventurous" is necessarily desirable in a moral philosopher. It is certainly adventurous of the ethicist Peter Singer to advocate euthanasia and infanticide; is it also commendable? In his essay on how one can discern progress in virtue, Plutarch observed that "those who do not adjust their tenets to fit the facts, but rather try to force the facts into unnatural agreement with their own assumptions, have filled philosophy with a great number of difficulties." How many volumes of highfalutin' metaphysics is that penetrating observation worth?

Clough, in his introduction to the Lives, offered a more balanced account of Plutarch's achievement:

> In reading Plutarch the following points should be remembered. He is a moralist rather than an historian. His interest is less for politics and the changes of empires, and much more for personal character and individual actions and motives to action; duty performed and rewarded; arrogance chastised, hasty anger corrected; humanity, fair dealing, and generosity triumphing in the visible, or relying on the invisible world.

In short, Plutarch regarded history as a moral theater whose performances it was his task to recapitulate for the edification of himself and his readers. "The most important questions for Plutarch," D. A. Russell notes, are naturally the practical ones."

> How can the *mesotes* [the mean] be secured? Not only many of the treatises in the *Moralia* but in a sense the *Lives* as a whole are concerned with this. The biographer provides documented and instructive case-studies of the play of reason and emotion. The more we know of the detail of a life, the more clearly we can see the process and effect of the moulding of the one by the other.

Considered as a "mirror" for the soul (as Plutarch says in

his life of Timoleon), history provided a series of cautionary tales, of virtue compromised and virtue salvaged.

Plutarch did not go in for salacious details about his subjects as, for example, did his younger Roman contemporary Suetonius (*c.* 70–*c.* 160) in his *Lives of the Caesars*. But his biographies, though sometimes rambling, are nonetheless powerfully entertaining and informative. How could they fail to be? Plutarch had assembled some of the most extraordinary personalities of antiquity, and he endeavored to portray not so much what they did but who they were.

Consider Alcibiades, one of the most gifted and treacherous figures in history. The Roman biographer Cornelius Nepos (*c.* 99–*c.* 24 B.C.—Plutarch knew some of his work) begins his chapter on Alcibiades by noting that "it is agreed by all who have written his biography that he was never excelled either in faults or in virtues." Immensely rich, he was also widely reckoned the handsomest man of his times. A skilled orator, he seemed to be able to talk his way out of, or into, anything. Alcibiades was also a military genius of sorts: as able leading an army as commanding a naval assault. If, like Emma Woodhouse, he was "handsome, clever, and rich," he was unlike that heroine in that his vanity and hubris were never checked. Chameleon-like, he *displayed* character without ever possessing one. "At Sparta," Plutarch tells us, "he was devoted to athletic exercises, was frugal and reserved; in Ionia, luxurious, gay, and indolent; in Thrace, always drinking; in Thessaly, ever on horseback; and when he lived with Tissaphernes the Persian satrap, he exceeded the Persians themselves in magnificence and pomp."

Educated in part by Pericles, Alcibiades (as readers of Plato's *Symposium* will remember) became an intimate of Socrates. Boundless narcissism combined with extravagant gifts of fortune made Alcibiades a prodigy of ambition. When he decided to enter public life, Plutarch notes, "his noble birth, his riches, the personal courage he had shown in many battles, and the multitude of his friends and dependents, threw open, so to say, the folding-doors for his admittance." During the Peloponnesian War, he was one of Athens's greatest assets; he was also her most horrible liability. It was Alcibiades who helped destroy the so-called Peace of Nicias and masterminded the disastrous Sicilian Expedition. He undertook the risky expedition solely for his own greater glory; its failure would eventually cost Athens her empire.

"Traitor" does not encompass Alcibiades' perfidy. Virtually on the eve of the Athenian fleet's departure to Sicily, many sacred statues were mutilated in Athens. It is likely that Alcibiades, on a drunken rampage with friends, was guilty of the outrage. He was allowed to set sail, but was later called back to Athens to stand trial. He then went over to Sparta. Learning that his property had been confiscated and that he had been condemned *in absentia* to die, he remarked: "I will make them feel I am alive." As indeed he did. For his advice to the Spartan forces was directly responsible for the defeat of Athens in Sicily. Probably the Spartans would never have completely trusted Alcibiades; but he sealed his fate with them by seducing the wife of a Spartan general and having a son by her. He then fled to Sardis where he was taken in by Tissaphernes. In short order, he betrayed him as well. Briefly imprisoned, he managed to escape and offered his services once again to Athens as the war dragged on. He won some brilliant victories for his native city. But the end came after his good advice was ignored by the Athenian commander at Aegospotami. The Athenian fleet was utterly destroyed and Athens was at the mercy of Sparta. Alcibiades fled to

Phrygia, but a Spartan condemnation followed him. The assassins did not dare confront him face to face. But one night as he lay sleeping with a mistress—"a young lady of a noble house," Plutarch comments, "whom he had debauched"—he woke to find his house on fire. He managed to escape, but was felled by a cataract of darts and arrows.

I have always been surprised that more is not made of Alcibiades today. He seems the perfect contemporary hero: rich, handsome, brilliant, amoral: he had it all. He was even bisexual, virtually a prerequisite for appearing well-rounded these days. Plutarch notes that when it came to "temperance, continence, and probity," Alcibiades must be judged "the least scrupulous and most entirely careless of human beings." But he forgives him a lot, not least because "he was often of service to Athens, both as a soldier and a commander."

In fact, Plutarch nearly always attempted to accentuate the positive. Again and again he stresses that his overriding purpose is to edify. In his life of Demetrius, one of the bad hats who scrambled for power after the death of Alexander the Great, Plutarch acknowledges that evil men must be discussed. Just so,

> [m]edicine, to produce health, has to examine disease, and music, to create harmony, must investigate discord; and the supreme arts, of temperance, of justice, and of wisdom, as they are acts of judgment and selection, exercised not on good and just and expedient only, but also on wicked, unjust, and inexpedient objects, do not give their commendations to the mere innocence whose boast is its inexperience of evil, and whose truer name is . . . simpleness and ignorance of what all men who live aright should know

In other words, Demetrius and other villains are worthy of

our interest not for themselves but because "we shall be all the more eager to watch and imitate the lives of the good if we are not left without a description of what is mean and reprehensible."

Still, notwithstanding a few exemplary cases of evil, it was Plutarch's general policy either to winnow out what was disreputable or to surround it with exculpating extenuations. Since, he writes in his life of the Athenian commander Cimon,

> it is difficult, perhaps impossible, to exhibit a life which is blameless and pure, . . . we must select its good elements and in these we must satisfy truth and present a likeness. The shortcomings and faults which run through a man's conduct owing to individual passion or political necessity we should regard rather as the defects of goodness than the misdeeds of wickedness; these our narrative should not display eagerly or gratuitously; rather it should show restraint out of regard for human nature, which produces nothing of unalloyed nobility, no character beyond the criticism of goodness.

Plutarch pursued this high-minded procedure not out of primness or timidity but because he thought it the most effective propaganda for virtue. There is something about the display of virtuous character, Plutarch believed, that inspires emulation. In a famous passage in his life of Pericles, Plutarch notes that there are many things which we admire that we do not seek to imitate or emulate. When it comes to "perfumes and purple dyes," for example, we may be "taken with the things themselves well enough, but we do not think dyers and perfumers otherwise than low and sordid people." The fact that we admire a statue by Phidias does not mean that we admire Phidias himself. But the spectacle of virtue in action is different. The "bare statement of virtuous actions," Plutarch wrote,

> can so affect men's minds as to create at once both admiration of the things done and desire to imitate the doers of them. The goods of fortune we would possess and would enjoy; those of virtue we long to practice and exercise: we are content to receive the former from others, the latter we wish others to experience from us. Moral good is a practical stimulus; it is no sooner seen, than it inspires an impulse to practice.

We sophisticated moderns tend to chalk up Plutarch's belief in the magnetic properties of the moral good to his "charming naïveté." It is significant that today we are much more apt to emulate what pleases us than what we approve. Hence it is that the contemporary equivalents of Plutarch's perfumers and dyers are among our most prominent culture heroes, as of course are celebrity artists of all sorts. What does this change tell us about ourselves? What does it mean that a rock star or television personality is adulated by millions? The issue of character, in both senses of "issue," was at the heart of Plutarch's teaching. It was also at the heart of Western culture for the centuries in which Plutarch was accounted an indispensable guide. Countless people turned to Plutarch not only for entertainment but also for moral intelligence. He was, as one scholar put it, "simply one of the most influential writers who ever lived," not because of his art but because of the dignity he portrayed. Until the events of September 11, it seemed as though we had lost our taste for that species of nobility. Character no longer impressed us. Has that changed? Perhaps. A good test is the extent to which Plutarch and the humanity he championed once again resonate with our deepest concerns.

"Strange Seriousness":
Discovering Daumier

He was naked, and he saw man naked, and from the centre
of his own crystal. . . . He approached everything with a mind
unclouded by current opinions. There was nothing of the
superior person about him. This makes him terrifying.
—T. S. Eliot on William Blake

Celui dont nous t'offrons l'image,
Et dont l'art, subtil entre tous,
Nous enseigne à rire de nous,
Celui-là, lecteur, est un sage.

C'est un satirique, un moqueur;
Mais l'énergie avec laquelle
Il peint le Mal et sa séquelle
Prouve la beauté de son coeur.
—Baudelaire on Honoré Daumier

There is surely no great point in this; the only point is life, the
glimpse of the little snatch of poetry in prose.
—Henry James on Honoré Daumier

FAMILIARITY is soul fat: it insulates and cushions, dockets the uncanny, translates every tomorrow into a rerun of yesterday. Do not scorn such anodynes. Be grateful for

37

them. They help us negotiate a world that, when not actively hostile, is often the next worst thing: unexpected. Humankind, T. S. Eliot observed, cannot bear very much reality. Familiarity populates the unknown with hints of habitation. It reassures us with bulletins about the *déjà vu*, the *déjà vécu*. How beguiling of Plato to suggest that all knowledge is really an *anamnesis*, a recollection, a recalling to mind something that, deep down, we already possess. It would be pretty to think so.

We could not manage without familiarity. But our humanity cannot manage without continually defeating it. Art, like love, is a prime resource for perpetuating that antiphony. Art, like love, resists novelty with the gorgeous artifice of tradition: a bible of patterns and conventions that predate and outlive us, guiding practice with the gift of shared form. At the same time, art, like love, invests every pattern with a disarming, absolute "yes" to experience. That is part of its lure, its power, its majesty.

There are few artists whose raids on the familiar are more cunningly executed than those of Honoré Daumier. Each of us, probably, has a dozen or so caricatures by Daumier in his head: send-ups of kings, emperors, politicians, lawyers, doctors, blue stockings, art collectors, mythological personages, and the good, self-satisfied bourgeois citizens of nineteenth-century Paris: which are your favorites? Most of Daumier's caricatures are funny: they are also by turns sad, poignant, unflinching, and above all memorable.

The famous *Rue Transnonian* (1834) commemorates senseless slaughter as chillingly as Goya but without Goya's bombast or obscenity. The lithograph portrays a poor, working-class family mistakenly shot in its stark, disheveled flat by jittery troops from King Louis-Philippe's army. The image of the dead father lying spread-eagled on his back, half-naked, crushing the corpse of his infant into the floor boards, is a howling indictment of royal injustice. No wonder the king attempted to have all copies of the print confiscated and destroyed. (Daumier's employer, Charles Philipon, said of the print that it was "not a caricature . . . [but] a page of our modern history bespattered with blood.")

Daumier met brutality with exposure, folly with laughter, pomposity with a twinkling prod. His astonishing lack of sentimentality made him accurate; his unfathomable humanity preserved him from savagery. One critic called him "Molière with a crayon." Daumier could be amused, sorrowful, indignant, sharp: he was never vicious. Noting that the primary impulse behind caricature is "doubt or despair concerning man as such, a denial of the goodness or beauty of human nature," the German art historian Hans Sedlmayr nonetheless went on to observe that in Daumier the "lack of confidence in man is outweighed by a recognition of his greatness. Daumier saw the grandeur of man as did scarcely any other artist of the nineteenth century. Grandeur and absurdity are merged in him and so beget the tragicomic."

Many will be surprised by the extravagance of Sedlmayr's praise. What, after all, has a caricaturist—a satirist in ink—to do with "greatness" or "grandeur"? Caricature, as Henry James said in his essay on Daumier, is a kind of "journalism made doubly vivid." If Daumier makes us see the ways in which journalism "touches the fine arts, touches manners, touches morals," still "journalism is the criticism of the moment *at* the moment"—that is to say, occasional and hence generally ephemeral. Most of us will recall the several prints by Daumier we have encountered in histories of art or as illustrations for miscellaneous books (how often we see Daumier thus, "in service" as a prop to narrative) and wonder whether Sedlmayr's words are themselves a kind of caricature, exaggeration in the service of irony. Daumier's work is entertaining, yes; memorable, certainly; but most of it is so familiar, so accessible, so tied to particular occasions: how can we reconcile our deflationary if affectionate recollections with Sedlmayr's superlatives?

In fact, the more deeply we look into Daumier, the more apposite Sedlmayr's judgment appears. The large retrospective of Daumier's work that was on view at the Phillips Collection in Washington, D.C., in the fall of 1999 was an effective antidote to diminishing presumption. In this exhibition, familiarity bred consequence. Daumier the commentator and Daumier the comic quickly recede before Daumier the artist. It took only a short while in this exhibition before we understood why Daumier's friend Delacroix should have written to him to say "There is not a man I value and admire more than you." Or why Balzac (who met Daumier in the early 1830s) exclaimed, "This chap has Michelangelo in his system." As it happens, Michelangelo, an important model for Daumier, is also a frequent touchstone for those who seek to understand Daumier's work. In 1867, discussing *The Legislative Belly* (1834), one critic wrote that the celebrated lithograph was "a masterpiece of the same order as the Sistine Chapel." Like caricature itself, perhaps, this was an exaggeration that makes a point, a point reinforced by Daumier's friend Charles Daubigny when first he visited the Sistine Chapel: "Why, this is Daumier!"

Just about every aspect of Daumier's art elicited superlatives. In 1878, a year before Daumier's death, Degas declared him the equal of Delacroix, remarking that to draw a leg as Daumier did required forty years of study. The young Rodin, when he saw Daumier's statuette *Rata-*

poil (1850)—a caricature of Louis Napoleon—contented himself with an admiring, "What a Sculptor!" Writing about Daumier in 1922, Duncan Phillips—an avid early collector of Daumier's work—ranked him with "the greatest of the great." He acknowledged the many ways in which Daumier's work resembles that of Goya and Hogarth, and then astutely pointed out that "Goya's satire was a matter of satanic hate and morbid revery and Hogarth's of didactic discourse on the frailties of human nature, whereas Daumier, like Balzac, was conscious always of having to do with the epic of facts and with the beauty of truth." Phillips dilated on Daumier's mastery of tonal harmony, above all his exquisite deployment of "velvety" black—"the queen," as Renoir put it, "of colors." (Sooner or later, almost everyone who writes about Daumier has recourse to the adjective "velvety" to describe his blacks; of particular note, however, is the way that Daumier's sumptuous blacks often stand in ironical contrast to his pedestrian or woebegone subject matter.) Even Velázquez, Phillips wrote, "never surpassed Daumier in revealing the sensuous colorfulness of blacks and ivory whites, nor are the shadows of Rembrandt more mysterious or marvelous as envelopment for figures."

High praise, this. Daumier's friend Baudelaire concurred. In his 1857 essay "Some French Caricaturists," Baudelaire expatiated on Daumier's "wonderful understanding of portraiture":

> While exaggerating and burlesquing the original features, he remained so soundly rooted in nature that these specimens might serve as models for all portraitists. Every little meanness of spirit, every absurdity, every quirk of intellect, every vice of the heart can be seen and read in these animalized faces, and at the same time everything is

broadly and emphatically drawn. Daumier combined the freedom of an artist with the accuracy of a Lavater.

Baudelaire concluded that Daumier was "one of the most important men . . . in the whole of modern art":

> What completes Daumier's remarkable quality and renders him an exceptional artist who belongs to the illustrious family of the masters, is that his drawing is naturally color-ful. His lithographs and his wood-engravings awake ideas of color. He evokes color, as he does thought.

It wasn't only Daumier's lithographs and woodcuts that sparked such enthusiasm. His paintings—which even today are much less well known—elicited similar encomia. For the great German critic Julius Meier-Graefe, Daumier was "a painter so mighty, that no terms can exaggerate the greatness of his importance." In *The Development of Modern Art* (1908), Meier-Graefe noted that although Daumier's palette tended to be subdued, he

> could be a great colorist upon occasion. He substituted a fluid strawberry red for his usual brown, painted blue at-mosphere like Velázquez, pale golden backgrounds like the most refined of the Dutchmen, and invented contrasts of pink and orange which recall the Venetians.

Meier-Graefe also put his finger on an element that made Daumier so important for the artists who were his peers or followers, a roster that includes Manet, Van Gogh, Cézanne, Degas, Rouault, Giacometti, and Picasso. (How much of Daumier there is in Picasso's bittersweet clowns!) "A new art-language arose from Daumier's sketchiness," Meier-Graefe wrote, "at the syntax of which we are still working." Just as Daumier's caricatures laid bare with a few deft strokes the personalities and pretensions of their subjects, so his paintings conjugated a mood, an emotional reality with subtly modulated lozenges and triangles of color. The sketchy, "unfinished" quality that typifies Daumier's painting is not the sketchiness that aspires to but fails to achieve photographic exactitude but rather that articulate aesthetic precision that subsists on the far side of a merely tabulating delineation.

Daumier's measure is hard to take. This is partly because his work simultaneously caters to and exceeds our expectations. One of Daumier's lightest, most amusing series is *Ancient History*, which appeared in Philipon's satirical sheet *Le Charivari* in the early 1840s. (*Le Charivari* proved to be Daumier's chief outlet: he provided the magazine with some eight lithographs a month from its inception, in 1832, until 1860, and then again, after a three-year hiatus, until 1872.) A pompous, pot-bellied Menelaus leading a plump, shrewish Helen away from the smoldering ruins of Troy; a scrawny Narcissus leering goatlike at his reflection in a pool; a moronic Pygmalion, rapt that his new statue should bend down to share his snuff—the series presented the modern repetition of classical mythology, not (to paraphrase Marx) as tragedy but as farce. As Baudelaire noted, *Ancient History* was Daumier's answer to the great question posed by the vogue for neo-classicism: *Qui nous délivera des Grecs et des Romains?*—Who will deliver us from the Greeks and Romans? Daumier, Baudelaire wrote,

came down brutally on antiquity—on false antiquity, that is, for no one has a better feeling than he for the grandeurs of antiquity. He snapped his fingers at it. The hot-headed Achilles, the cunning Ulysses, the wise Penelope, Telemachus, that great booby, and the fair Helen, who ruined

Troy—they all of them, in fact, appear before our eyes in a farcical ugliness which is reminiscent of those decrepit old tragic actors whom one sometimes sees taking a pinch of snuff in the wings.

Daumier parodies, punctures, and delights with *Ancient History*. But the art historian Howard Vincent is surely correct that we return to those prints not primarily because of their satirical point but because of their aesthetic excellence. "The essential reason," Vincent wrote in his study *Daumier and His World* (1968), "that these cartoons endure repeated study, yield increasing pleasure, lies not in their parodic gaiety but rather in the high quality of their draughtsmanship."

Daumier is enigmatic because he delivers so much more than he promises. He is enigmatic also because he is largely unknowable. He wrote almost nothing except letters, precious few of which survive; the testimony of friends and associates is vague and often inconsistent; and Daumier's quiet temperament—he was, Vincent says, essentially "a spectator, not a participant"—does little to aid the biographer. About Daumier the man we have some scraps of fact, a number of charming but only intermittently reliable anecdotes, and a large province of conjecture.

As to the facts: Daumier was born on February 26, 1808 in Marseilles, the third child and first son of Cécile-Catherine and Jean-Baptiste Daumier, a glazier. Daumier *père* had unfulfilled literary ambitions. He wrote verse, managed to get some of it published, but was grieved that his genius was insufficiently recognized. He died insane in 1851. Some writers have conjectured that his father's literary aspirations helped young Honoré to set his sights beyond Marseilles and the glazier's trade. Perhaps so. In any event, the boy arrived in Paris with his family at the age of eight and at twelve was engaged as a notary's errand boy, a *saute-ruisseau*, which gave him a first taste of law courts and the "men of justice" he would later caricature to such profound effect. (The black gowns and hats of the French lawyers, punctuated by white cravats, must have been as irresistible to Daumier's eye as the proverbial lawyerly self-importance was to his sense of humor.) Daumier had little formal education. "The streets of Paris," Howard Vincent wrote, "were his school and college, his occupation and pastime. They were his career. They formed him, made him aware, and out of this awareness he himself shaped Paris and her people into the thousand forms of his prints and painting, a devoted record of his city." In 1821, Daumier took a job as a clerk at a bookstore in the Palais-Royale, near two important printsellers and the Louvre, where he undoubtedly busied himself making copies. His artistic ambition began to flower, and in 1822 he became a pupil of his father's friend, Alexandre Lenoir, a painter, archaeologist, and art collector.

We know little about Daumier's subsequent studies. He soon grew dissatisfied with Lenoir's training, which emphasized color and drew heavily on the examples of Rubens and Titian, and enrolled at the Académie Suisse and the Académie Boudin. By the age of fourteen, Daumier had begun experimenting with the new process of lithography, an inexpensive printing technique discovered by a German actor and playwright named Aloys Senefelder in 1798 and only lately come to Paris. In 1825, Daumier apprenticed with one Zéphirin Belliard, who specialized in lithographic portraits. He later worked with other artists. But it was not until about 1829, when he encountered Charles Philipon, that Daumier began to come into his own.

Philipon (1800–62)—described by one admirer as "le

journalisme fait homme"—was an extraordinary figure. Together with his brother-in-law, he operated the Véro-Dodat Gallery, which specialized in satirical caricatures. But that was only a small part of his enterprise. The indefatigable entrepreneur, artist, journalist, and wit founded two of the leading satirical magazines of the nineteenth century, *La Caricature*, a weekly, and *Le Charivari*, a daily. In 1832, he started "L'Association mensuelle lithographique," a print-of-the-month club whose proceeds helped pay for the fines exacted by the censor for material that appeared in his other magazines. Some of Daumier's finest prints appeared in "L'Association mensuelle." It was Philipon who first fully exploited the potential of lithography for the popular press. It was he who devised the "Pear": the image of King Louis-Philippe that, in the hands of Daumier and his other artists (including Grandville, Gavarni, Decamps, and Monnier), came to epitomize the sovereign and his regime for the entire country. And it was he who wrote almost all of the captions for Daumier's early lithographs. Philipon collaborated with Daumier; he directed, incited, instructed, and—last but not least—paid him (though modestly). "If it had not been for Philipon," Daumier later acknowledged, "who goaded me like a driver his oxen, I would have done nothing."

Daumier was the perfect lieutenant for Philipon's assaults. Graced with an extraordinary visual memory, he never bothered with models. Graced with abundant technical fluency, he rarely bothered with preliminary studies: his touch was rapid, sure, and deadly. Philipon's implacable opposition to political injustice earned him the enmity of the censor, whoever happened to be in power. Louis-Philippe or Louis Napoleon: it didn't matter—Philipon's magazines were regularly raided by the police. He and his artists were repeatedly fined and even, on occasion, imprisoned. Daumier had some share in this glory. At the end of 1831, he created his famous lithograph *Gargantua*. It portrays a bloated, pear-headed Louis-Philippe perched on a commode. The starving citizens of France struggle up a plank to deposit the country's treasure in his gaping maw. Down below, ministers and favorites scurry about eagerly with the sundry writs, honors, and ribbons that the king obligingly excretes. This ferocious sally in Philipon's philippic against Louis-Philippe was instantly proscribed. A six-month sentence against Daumier and others was initially suspended, but further outrages in *La Caricature* led to the reimposition of the sentence a few months later. In August, 1832, Daumier was arrested and incarcerated in Sainte-Pélagie prison: "a charming resort," he wrote to a friend, "where not everyone enjoys himself."

Largely because of *Gargantua*, Daumier is often compared to Rabelais. But, notwithstanding the scatological motif in that lithograph, Daumier's humor—indeed, his entire sensibility—is distinctly un-Rabelaisian. As Duncan Phillips observed, "of his four thousand cartoons, there is not one that is unclean, an amazing record for a French humorist." Daumier's work was often pointed; some of it was instinct with wounded righteousness; but throughout it all there is a current of affirmation and, ultimately, of serenity. By all accounts Daumier himself was a quiet, self-effacing man. His abiding sadness was a coefficient of his talent; excelling at caricature, he became its slave: first at *Charivari*, then at other satirical magazines. Time and again he attempted to get his work as a painter taken seriously. The Salon was frosty, the public uninterested. Caricature paid the bills, though barely. Still, cheerfulness kept breaking through. When a friend expressed concern about his parlous financial situation, Daumier replied, "What more do I need? Two fried eggs in the morning, and in the evening a herring or a cutlet. To that add a glass of Beaujolais, some tobacco for my pipe, and anything more would be superfluous." In 1870, the last year of the Second Empire, Daumier was offered the Legion of Honor, which he refused. He was not about to accept honors from a government he detested. But unlike Courbet, who was offered the same award, Daumier did not make a public drama out of his refusal. When Courbet asked him why he did not use the occasion to generate publicity, Daumier replied: "I did what I thought I ought to do. I am content, and it is no concern of the public."

It is peculiar how indistinct an image we have of Daumier. He had many friends, was reasonably social, but somehow his personality remains inaccessible. In 1846, Daumier married Marie-Alexandrine d'Assy, a dressmaker fourteen years his junior. The marriage was childless but was said to be happy—though in fact, as Vincent remarks, "about Daumier's family life virtually nothing is known." From 1863, Daumier and his wife rented a house in the summer in Valmondois, a village twenty miles north of Paris. One of the most charming anecdotes about Daumier is that his friend Corot eventually bought the house for him—a story that unfortunately turns out to be false. By 1872, when he retired from *Charivari* for good, Daumier's eyesight was failing from cataracts; by 1877, he was nearly blind. Two years later he was dead.

Daumier's output was prodigious: four thousand lithographs, one thousand woodcuts, almost three hundred paintings, nearly a thousand drawings, dozens of sculptures. In 1878, several friends organized a large retrospective of Daumier's work at the Durand-Ruel Gallery in Paris. Victor Hugo served as honorary chairman. It was a great moment for Daumier. Having just suffered through an unsuccessful operation on his eyes, he was unable to attend the exhibition. But at last he was beginning to receive notice not just for his clever caricatures but also for his paintings. Indeed, the exhibition—carefully designed to highlight Daumier's achievements as a serious painter—came as a revelation. Daumier the caricaturist the world knew or remembered. Daumier the artist was something else. One critic, after praising the exhibition, referred to Daumier as "This Titan who used all his strength against the pygmies." The show was a rousing critical success; financially, it was a disaster. The masses whom Daumier had pleased, goaded, and amused for decades stayed away *en masse*. According to one account, the exhibition recorded receipts of some 3,000 francs and expenses of nearly 13,000.

The Phillips exhibition did not suffer that ignominy. It was a hit, and rightly so. Including some 250 works, it amply displayed every facet of Daumier's *oeuvre*. There was only one thing to be lamented. In 1831, Philipon asked Daumier to make clay busts of the "celebrities of the *juste milieu*," the thirty-odd ministers and propagandists for Louis-Philippe's "middle course, as far," the newly crowned king promised, "from the excesses of the power of the masses as from the abuses of royal power." The painted busts were then made available as "clay snapshots" for the artists of *La Caricature*. Fashioned of unfired clay, the sculptures (now at the Musée d'Orsay) were too fragile to make the trip across the Atlantic. Instead, bronzes of the figures Daumier made are on view at the Phillips. They are no substitute for the clay originals. Still, assembled in a large vitrine, they make an impressive rogues' gallery, a phrenologist's delight, a psychologist's wonder.

Making one's way through the exhibition, one was struck again and again by Daumier's sheer deftness. With what remarkable *economy* he conjured up character! All of Daumier's most famous caricatures are here: the early *Masks of 1831*, a selection from the *Robert Macaire* series on which Philipon collaborated with Daumier, *The Physiology of the Bourgeoisie*, *The Men of Justice*, *Parisian Sketches*, *Theatrical Sketches*, *Ancient History*, *Ratapoil*, and others. Particularly amusing are two plates from 1862: *Nadar Elevating Photography to the Height of Art*—which portrays the famous photographer ascending over Paris, camera in hand, in his balloon—and *In the Studios*, which shows a group of critics or art lovers assembled in front of a painting: "Wow! . . . Amazing! . . . Gosh! . . . Superb! . . . it speaks!"

There is plenty to admire in Daumier's caricatures. But as at the 1878 retrospective, the real revelation here is Daumier's painting. Caricature is fundamentally an illustrational art. It exaggerates a physical quality in order to reveal an underlying moral or emotional reality. In the best caricatures, exaggeration evaporates in the light of a higher realism. Daumier was a master of this process. But his paintings, far from being caricatures in another medium, exist in an entirely different spiritual and aesthetic register. Discussing Daumier's painting, Duncan Phillips observed that although Daumier was celebrated as a caricaturist, "he was just as much a mystic." What Phillips meant, I think, is that Daumier's paintings inhabit a realm of feeling far removed from the hurly-burly of social and political satire. This is not to say that Daumier was a religious painter. He made a few paintings with religious themes—a Magdalene, a Saint Sebastian. But his best paintings—some family scenes, *Third-Class Carriage* (1862–64), *The Uprising* (1852–58), *The Fugitives* (1865–70), and several paintings of Don Quixote—are secular. Nevertheless, they possess rare depths of solitude and melancholy tenderness. This is true even of *The Fugitives*, which portrays the deportation of Republicans in the aftermath of the 1848 revolution, and *The Uprising*, a haunting, mysterious painting whose exact subject remains indeterminate.

Technically, Daumier's paintings were ahead of their time. The compression of pictorial space and simplifying expressiveness of his modelling look forward to Cézanne, the elongation of Don Quixote looks forward to Giacometti. Daumier's technique—his unwillingness to sacrifice aesthetic weight for superficial "finish"—is part of what makes his paintings seem so modern. I am not sure exactly what it is that makes them linger hauntingly in one's memory. Daumier's paintings are curiously beguiling. They exert a large immediate appeal, but their full force becomes evident only in retrospect. Only then do their margins of articulate silence become fully present.

Daumier presents us with innumerable aesthetic delights. He also presents us with a curious conundrum. There is a delicate but ineradicable sadness infusing many of his paintings. There is also, seemingly inseparable from that sadness, an inveterate joy. This paradoxical combination is perhaps most evident in his paintings about Don Quixote, the deluded apostle of chivalry. Daumier's great achievement is to make us see past the delusion to the human grandeur that inspires it. Noting that caricature explored "the innumerable different ways in which the human subject may *not* be taken seriously," Henry James went on to puzzle over the "strange seriousness" that characterizes Daumier's work. It is significant how many critics have paused to underscore that seriousness. Meier-Graefe did, as did Baudelaire. Ultimately, perhaps, it is Daumier's seriousness that so moves us and that led one admirer to remark that Daumier had Don Quixote's soul in Sancho's body.

Walter Bagehot:
The Greatest Victorian

There are few ways in which a man can be more innocently employed than in getting money.
—Samuel Johnson

The essence of civilization, as we know, is dullness. In an ultimate analysis, it is only an elaborate invention . . . for abolishing the fierce passions, the unchastened enjoyments, the awakening dangers, the desperate conflicts, . . . the excitements of a barbarous age, and to substitute for them indoor pleasures, placid feelings, and rational amusements. That a grown man should be found to write reviews is in itself a striking fact. Suppose you asked Achilles to do such a thing, do you imagine he would consent?
—Walter Bagehot, on Matthew Arnold

Only a blockhead can fail to realize that our characters are the result of our conduct.
—Aristotle, *Nicomachean Ethics*

IN THE large catalogue of half-forgotten Victorian masterpieces, Walter Bagehot's *Physics and Politics* (1872) occupies a distinguished place. Like its author, this short book is difficult to categorize. Informed by the burgeoning science of ethnology and the reinvigorated science of natural history, it belongs to neither. It might be described as a work of political psychology, but it is better written, rhetorically more astringent, and possessed of greater common sense than most works belonging under that rubric. Bagehot himself—part professional banker, part magazine editor, part cultural and political commentator—was also more than the sum of his parts. He once enjoyed a justly deserved reputation as a canny student of human nature. For many readers today, however, he is little more than an historical worthy: a name attached to a handful of epigrams. The historian Jacques Barzun, who introduced an edition of *Physics and Politics* in 1948, got it exactly right when he noted that Bagehot is "'well-known' without being known well."

In fact, Bagehot is one of those distinguished literary figures who seems to have been embalmed by his own distinction. There are no doubt many reasons for this. In his essay "Bagehot as Historian" (1968), Professor Barzun mentions two: he bore a name that was "puzzling to pronounce"—this made people shy about quoting him—and he made the mistake of dying at the inconsiderate age of fifty-one, before his idiosyncratic genius could take firm root in the popular imagination. Bagehot—the first syllable is pronounced like "badge," the second like "it": "badge-it"—has consequently had the misfortune to become more celebrated than he is read and discussed.†

The misfortune affects the reading public as much as it

---

† One occasionally hears "Bagehot" pronounced with a hard "g." But as the scholar Norman St. John-Stevas observes in *Walter Bagehot: A Study of His Life and Thought Together with a Selection from His Political Writings* (1959), "this is mistaken. It should be pronounced soft as in *badger*, which was indeed a fifteenth-century variant of the family name." Citing local and family testimony, St. John-Stevas is right that evidence for the soft "g" is "overwhelming."

does Bagehot's posthumous reputation. To miss out on Bagehot is to miss out on one of the great triumphs of English prose. It is a light, champagne prose: sparkling but not facile, broadly allusive but never pedantic, witty and epigrammatic but shrewd, strong, and sober enough to treat an extraordinarily wide range of serious issues. And treat them it does. Bagehot's prose is more than an aesthetic delight: it is a repository of uncommon wisdom about the common realities of life. The excellence of his writing, in other words, is an excellence of substance as well as style, matter as well as manner. What he says, he invariably says well; but one generally also finds that it is well that he said what he did.

During his brief lifetime, Bagehot's essays exerted an enormous influence. He had keen and original things to say about literary figures from Shakespeare and Milton to Shelley and Henry Crabb Robinson, the eccentric friend of Goethe, Schiller, Wordsworth, and Coleridge. Bagehot wrote penetrating essays on Adam Smith, Macaulay, Gibbon, Disraeli, Sir Robert Peel, and the English reformer John Bright. His speciality, as one critic observed, "was the human element in all the affairs and institutions of life, whether it relates to literature, history, politics, economics, sociology, religion, or science."

Talent has a way of commanding opportunity. At the end of 1851, the young Bagehot went to Paris to escape a bout of melancholy and indecision about his future career. Louis Napoleon just then embarked on the *coup d'état* that marked his elevation from president of the Second Republic to Emperor Napoleon III. Bagehot's eye-witness dispatches to a London newspaper on the *coup* and its aftermath turned out to be a classic of pugnacious political reporting.

In 1867, Bagehot published *The English Constitution*

(serialized the preceding two years in Anthony Trollope's *Fortnightly Review*), a work that is still regarded as an indispensable account of the workings of the English government between the first and second Reform Bills (1832 and 1867). Like many of Bagehot's works, *The English Constitution* is about much more than its announced subject. This gives it a relevance far beyond its time. Indeed, parts of the book might be even more pertinent now, 130 years later, than they were when first published. One cannot help thinking that the current Prime Minister and what remain of the Windsors could profit greatly by meditating on Bagehot's reflections on the importance of preserving the charm and mystery—what Bagehot referred to as the *impressive* as distinct from the *effective* aspects—of the monarchy. "We must not let in daylight upon magic," he wrote in a famous passage. "We must not bring the Queen into the combat of politics, or she will cease to be reverenced by all combatants; she will become one combatant among many." *Autres temps, autres moeurs*—or should one say, *plus ça change. . .*?

Bagehot seems incapable of writing a dull sentence—a somewhat paradoxical fact, perhaps, since dullness was a virtue that he much applauded. Whether the subject was the American Civil War—about which he wrote nearly forty articles—parliamentary reform, or the workings of the London money market, he was sure to be bold, memorable, and pertinent. He was particularly pertinent when reflecting on the psychology of politics: the lineaments of leadership and motivation. Bagehot pondered deeply on the human requirements of civilization. He understood that personality often counted more than policy. "It is the life of teachers which is *catching*, not their tenets," Bagehot noted in *Physics and Politics*. The influence of personal example is one reason that what we have come to call the "character issue" has always been so important in government: "In political matters, how quickly a leading statesman can change the tone of the community! We are most of us earnest with Mr. Gladstone; we were most of us *not* so earnest in the time of Lord Palmerston. The change is what everyone feels, though no one can define it." Bagehot's observation remains as true today as it was when he wrote it.

Bagehot did not simply comment on events from afar. As editor of *The Economist*—a position he held from 1861 until his untimely death—his advocacy of free trade helped to shape the financial policies of England at the zenith of her power. Gladstone was one of many politicians from both parties who sought his counsel. He became, it has been frequently observed, a kind of "supplementary Chancellor of the Exchequer." In an essay published in 1948, the eminent Victorianist G. M. Young, after duly reviewing the obvious candidates for the title of "The Greatest Victorian," finally awarded the palm to Bagehot. "One needs a man, or woman," Young wrote, "who is typical of a large and important class: rich in the abilities which the age fostered: one who made a difference, and under whose influence or direction we are still living." George Eliot, Tennyson, Arnold, Ruskin, or Darwin may each have made greater contributions in his own line; the title *Victorianorum maximus*—greatest of the Victorians—may belong to one of them. But Bagehot's all-round genius, Young concluded, entitles him to the title *Victorianum maxime*, "The Most Victorian."

Many distinguished personages have agreed. Woodrow Wilson, for one, was smitten with Bagehot, calling him "a seer" and "one of the most original and audacious wits that the English race has produced." Of course, it would be unfair to hold Bagehot accountable for all of his enthusiasts. But it is remarkable how intense his appeal has sometimes been. The first collection of his works was issued not by a university or a commercial press but by an American corporation. In 1889, at the direction of its president, the Travelers Insurance Company published *The Works of Walter Bagehot* in five volumes and sent copies to its policyholders—the idea being, perhaps, that imbibing Bagehot's common-sense reflections on the human condition would make people better insurance risks.

Bagehot possessed abundantly a gift he discerned in Shakespeare: an "experiencing nature." He delighted in what he called "the grand *shine* on the surface of life." A central word for him is "enjoyment." Keenly moral, he abominated moralism: "Nothing is more unpleasant," he wrote, "than a virtuous person with a mean mind." Likewise, though formidably learned himself, he regularly cautioned against bookishness. "He wrote poetry . . . before breakfast," Bagehot wrote of Robert Southey with undisguised contempt; "he read during breakfast. He wrote history until dinner; he corrected proof sheets between dinner and tea; he wrote an essay for the 'Quarterly' afterwards; and after supper by way of relaxation composed the 'Doctor.'" Bagehot's sense of ironical contrast was indefatigable. Comparing Gibbon's ornate style with the world-shaking events he described in *The Decline and Fall of the Roman Empire*, Bagehot observed that perhaps "when a Visigoth broke a head, he thought that was all. Not so; he was making history: Gibbon has written it down." In a biography published in 1915, Mrs. Russell Barrington, Bagehot's sister-in-law, frequently remarks on his boyish sense of fun. At breakfast once with a young nephew struggling to open an egg, Bagehot advised: "Go on, Guy, hit it hard on the head. It has no friends."

In politics Bagehot was a conservative Liberal. He supported a robust military but was broadly anti-imperialist. Unlike many conservatives today, in Bagehot's time Tories tended to favor economic protectionism and oppose free trade. A student of David Ricardo's and Adam Smith's writings on economics, Bagehot understood the important role that free trade played in fostering general economic prosperity. Consequently he was an enthusiastic supporter of policies that encouraged free trade. But even here he was the opposite of doctrinaire. He understood that a policy of "free trade" was one thing in the economic sphere, quite another when generalized to the whole of life. Writing in 1848, he noted that the principle of *laissez-faire* is "useful and healthy when confined to its legitimate function, *viz* when watching that Government does not assume to know what will bring a trader in money, better than he knows it himself; but it is a sentiment very susceptible of hurtful exaggeration: in the minds of many at this day it stands opposed to the enforcement of a moral law throughout the *whole* sphere of human acts susceptible of attestation."

In the end, Bagehot is probably best described as a Whig with Tory leanings. How significant were those leanings may be gleaned from his observation (in the context of a discussion of the "Cavalier mind" and Sir Walter Scott, one of his favorite authors) that "the essence of Toryism is enjoyment." Bagehot gloried in the pulse, the vitality of life; he had little time for people or policies "sicklied o'er with the pale cast of thought," or with anything else, for that matter. The other side of this heartiness was an impatience that could sometimes border on callousness. "Ugly men," he wrote in his essay on Milton, "are and ought to be ashamed of their existence." Bagehot was loath to entertain, let alone dwell on, life's failures. Poverty, he remarked in a prickly essay on Dickens, is "an unfit topic for continuous art."

It is in this sense that Bagehot represents what the critic John Gross called "a standing temptation to indulge in selective Victorianism," accentuating the positive and—though not ignoring the negative, exactly—tending to dismiss it as a regrettable necessity. "The best history," Bagehot wrote in *Physics and Politics*, "is but like the art of Rembrandt; it casts a vivid light on certain selected causes, on those which were best and greatest; it leaves all the rest in shadow and unseen." And again: "The difficulty in truth is in the existence of the world. It is the fact, that by the constitution of society the bold, the vigorous, and the buoyant, rise and rule; and that the weak, the shrinking, and the timid, fall and serve." True enough; indisputable, even: but not calculated to appeal to sentimentalists.

In a biographical sketch published in 1963, Norman St. John-Stevas noted Bagehot's unusual capacity to "bridge the gulf between the practical and intellectual worlds." One suspects that Bagehot's upbringing had something to do with this amphibious talent. He was born in Langport, Somerset, to parents whose families dominated the town. Bagehot's father, Thomas—an earnest, pragmatic man—was a partner in the Stuckey Bank, a famous West Country bank that his wife's uncle had founded. (The bank issued its own notes until 1909 and it is said that many Somerset men, suspicious of bank notes issued by a "foreign" London bank, would demand payment in "Stuckeys.") It seems fitting that Walter, who would later join his father in business, was actually born in the bank, in the upstairs living quarters occupied by his parents. Edith Stuckey, ten years Thomas's senior, was a widow when he married her. Of the three children from her first marriage, one was an imbecile and two died in childhood. Walter was the second of two children from her marriage to Thomas, the first of whom also died in childhood. Perhaps in response to these

59

multiple tragedies, Edith Bagehot suffered from periodic bouts of insanity. After her brother died in 1845, Walter became her chief emotional support. As many commentators have noted, the "dark realities" to which he alludes in several essays undoubtedly refer in part to his mother's dementia. "Every trouble in life," he later remarked, "is a joke compared to madness." Despite, or perhaps because of, this mental custodianship, Walter was always extremely close to his mother and was devastated by her death in 1870.

Bagehot's lifelong friend Richard Holt Hutton (1826–1897)—with whom he founded the *National Review* in 1855 and who went on to become editor of the *Spectator* —described Bagehot as "a thorough transcendentalist" but not a "dogmatist." As with many Victorians (and not only Victorians, of course) it is difficult to ascertain all that much about Bagehot's religious convictions. His father, a Unitarian, presided over Sunday morning services at the family house. Walter regularly attended these services—and then accompanied his mother, an ardent Anglican, to the parish church in the afternoon. Bagehot, it is worth remembering, lived at a time when doubt had become an animating principle of faith for many serious people. (As T. S. Eliot said of Tennyson's *In Memoriam* [1850], it is religious not "because of the quality of its faith, but because of the quality of its doubt.") Bagehot flourished just after the time when, as G. M. Young put it in "Portrait of an Age," "one undergraduate has to prepare another undergraduate for the news that a third undergraduate has doubts about the Blessed Trinity." By the time Bagehot came of age, the sea of faith was on the ebb, its "melancholy, long, withdrawing roar" (in Matthew Arnold's famous phrase) a taken-for-granted supposition of educated debate. Whatever the exact nature of Bagehot's doctrinal commitments, he belonged to those determined to preserve the echoes of that retreat, confident, perhaps, that as a tide ebbs so it invariably flows. Alluding to St. Paul, he wrote that

> We know that we see as in a glass darkly; but still we look on the glass. We frame to ourselves some image which we know to be incomplete, which probably is in part untrue, which we try to improve day by day. . . . This is, as it seems, the best religion for finite beings, living, if we may say so, on the very edge of two dissimilar worlds, on the very line on which the infinite, unfathomable sea surges up, and just where the queer little bay of this world ends.

In his article on Bagehot for the *Dictionary of National Biography*, Hutton noted that his friend's "great characteristic as a writer, whether on economic or literary subjects, was a very curious combination of dash and doubt, great vivacity in describing the superficial impressions produced on him by every subject-matter with which he was dealing, and great caution in yielding his mind to that superficial impression." This characteristic acted as a prophylactic against dogmatisms of doubt as well as dogmatisms of credulity.

Thomas and Edith Bagehot were both conscientiously solicitous about Walter's education. At thirteen, after grammar school in Langport, he was sent to school in Bristol, where Dr. James Cowles Prichard, Edith's brother-in-law and the founder of the science of anthropology in England, took him under his wing. Prichard's interests made a lasting impression on Walter and echoed in many later works, not least in *Physics and Politics*. University posed a problem. A fervent Nonconformist, Thomas objected to Oxford and Cambridge because of the religious tests that were still in force there. So when he was sixteen,

Bagehot went up to University College, London, which had been recently established at the site of a disused garbage dump in Gower Street. Though dogged by ill health—at one point he had to take five months off to recuperate—Bagehot was a brilliant student. He studied mathematics with the eminent, idiosyncratic mathematician Augustus De Morgan, and took a first in classics followed by a first in philosophy and the gold medal in intellectual and moral philosophy. Bagehot met and became friends with R. H. Hutton directly he went up in 1842. In 1848, the year he took his M.A. degree, he met and came under the influence of the poet Arthur Hugh Clough (1819–1861), then principal of University Hall. Clough rather specialized in cultivating intellectual and spiritual impossibilities—Bagehot later criticized his "fatigued way of looking at great subjects"—but, according to Hutton, the poet's adamant negativity exerted a "greater intellectual fascination for Walter Bagehot than any of his contemporaries."

After leaving university in 1848, Bagehot read law. He was called to the bar in 1852, but had by then decided against a legal career and returned to Langport and his father's shipowning and banking business. Banking suited Bagehot. When depressed, he found it cheering to go down to the bank and run his hands through a heap of sovereigns. It was around this time that Bagehot began writing in earnest, contributing literary and biographical articles to *The Prospective Review* and other journals and newspapers. At Clevedon, Somerset, in 1857, he met and was befriended by James Wilson, financial secretary to the Treasury, who had founded *The Economist* in 1843. At the same time he met and befriended Eliza Wilson, the eldest of Wilson's six daughters, a handsome, somewhat neurasthenic woman who outlived Bagehot by forty-four years. The two soon became engaged and were married the following year. It was an advantageous as well as an affectionate match. At the Wilsons' London house in Belgravia, Bagehot met many prominent contemporaries, including Gladstone, Thackeray, Matthew Arnold, and Lord Grey. In 1859, James Wilson went as a financial adviser to India, where he died from dysentery the following year. Meanwhile, he had made Bagehot a director of *The Economist*, which was then being edited by Hutton. After Hutton left to edit the *Spectator*, in 1861, Bagehot took over the editorship of *The Economist*. (The paper was owned by Eliza and her five sisters, who paid him £800 a year for his services.) Bagehot regularly contributed two—and sometimes three or four—articles a week to *The Economist* for the rest of his career.

Bagehot was both intensely social and intensely private. He had, Mrs. Barrington says in her biography, "no enemies but few intimates." Outwardly, the balance of Bagehot's career was uneventful. By all accounts, his childless marriage was extremely happy. He stood for Parliament four times and four times lost, once by seven votes. His always delicate health took a decided turn for the worse in 1867 when he caught pneumonia. He never fully recovered. There followed a succession of chills, colds, and other pulmonary complaints, cheerfully borne but increasingly enervating. In March 1877, Bagehot contracted his last illness: a cold that quickly worsened and within a few days proved fatal. He spent his last hours reading a new copy of Scott's *Rob Roy* (1817) while his wife sat by him, cutting the pages.

IT SHOULD BE noted that Bagehot's magic does not work on everyone. One who is conspicuously resistant to his spell is the English poet and critic C. H. Sisson. In *The Case of Walter Bagehot* (1972), Sisson assembled what amounts to a brief for the prosecution. Sisson's objection to Bagehot is twofold. On the one hand, he sees him as "a founding father of the apologetics of 'fact,'" a skeptical, even cynical, force bent on exploding inherited values. On the other hand, Sisson regards Bagehot as "a moneyed provincial pushing his way in a conventional society." ("Cynical" is a word that often crops up in discussions of Bagehot. Leslie Stephen—in *Studies of a Biographer*—was one of many commentators who discerned a cynical streak in his writing and character, but noted admiringly that "the cynic's merit is to see facts.") "What we get from Bagehot," Sisson wrote,

is not so much a theory as a position, and not so much a position as a form of tactics. It is Walter Bagehot whom the successive positions are intended to protect—the Walter Bagehot who slipped down the crack between Unitarianism and Anglicanism; who was the child of the Bank House as some are sons of the manse; whose money was better than that of the squire's but did not produce better effects on the locals; who should have been educated at Oxford but was above that sort of conformism; who conformed instead to the world of business but was cleverer than its other inhabitants; who was all the time worried about the sanity of his stock and did not have any children; who distrusted hereditary powers and owed all his opportunities to family influence.

And so on.

There is probably no antidote to the allergy that Sisson has to Bagehot. It is the revulsion of one sort of temperament to another that seems antithetical. What Sisson objects to—a large part of it, anyway—is the very thing that makes Bagehot Bagehot. Not his subtlety, exactly, but his deployment of subtlety. Bagehot seldom runs on one track. Whatever topic he is pursuing, he habitually manages to look behind it as well. It is not irony, precisely, for although he *uses* irony, Bagehot is too earnest to be described as ironical.

The same goes for "cynicism." Bagehot could be sharp; he could be startling; he could be dismissive; but he was too aware of possibility to rest in cynicism. Jacques Barzun referred in this context to Bagehot's "binocular vision," his habit of taking "double views." The historian Gertrude Himmelfarb, in "Walter Bagehot: A Common Man with Uncommon Ideas," observes that "he was that rare species of the twice-born who could give proper due to the rights and merits of the once-born. And he did so not by a denial of his own nature but by virtue of the very subtleties, complications, and ambiguities that informed his nature."

What another critic has dubbed Bagehot's "duomania" shows itself even in his methods of analysis. Bagehot is fond—perhaps overly fond—of breaking his subjects into two categories. When he talks about genius, he begins by discerning two types, regular and irregular; religion comes in two flavors, natural and supernatural; biography is selective or it is exhaustive; fiction is either ubiquitous or sentimental; goodness is sensuous or ascetic. Writers, he says, like teeth, "are divided into incisors and grinders." A rare exception to this law of pairs is found in Bagehot's famous essay on Wordsworth, Tennyson, and Browning (1864), which unfolds a tripart division of "Pure, Ornate, and Grotesque Art in English Poetry."

In fact, the duality one sees in Bagehot's work reflects a duality in his character. On the one hand, we have Bagehot the apostle of "dullness," extolling stolidness in individuals and governments alike. On the other hand, we find him (in an essay on the eighteenth-century wit Lady Mary Wortley

LIVES OF THE MIND

Montagu) noting how easy it is to dull the mind "by a vapid accumulation of torpid comfort."

> Many of the middle classes spend their whole lives in a constant series of petty pleasures, and an undeviating pursuit of small material objects. The gross pursuit of pleasure, and the tiresome pursuit of petty comfort, are quite suitable to such "a being as man in such a world as the present one." What is not possible is to combine the pursuit of pleasure and the enjoyment of comfort with the characteristic pleasures of a strong mind. If you wish for luxury, you must not nourish the inquisitive instinct.

Again, we have Bagehot the banker and man of affairs—the man St. John-Stevas describes as "a sardonic, no-nonsense, experienced man of the world," and, opposing him, we have "the passionate, mystical Bagehot" who understands that what really matters in life is not calculable in terms of a profit-and-loss ledger. "No real Englishman, in his secret soul," Bagehot observed, "was ever sorry for the death of a political economist: he is much more likely to be sorry for his life." The "mystical" side of Bagehot peeks out most conspicuously in some of his literary essays. In "The First Edinburgh Reviewers" (1855), one of his most celebrated essays, Bagehot writes that "a clear, precise, discriminating intellect shrinks at once from the symbolic, the unbounded, the indefinite." He then goes on—it is the quintessential Bagehot touch—to observe that "the misfortune is that mysticism is true."

> There are certainly kinds of truth, borne in as it were instinctively on the human intellect, most influential on the character and heart, yet hardly capable of stringent definition. Their course is shadowy; the mind seems rather to

have seen than to see them, more to feel after than definitely apprehend them. They commonly involve an infinite element, which of course cannot be stated precisely, or else a first principle—an original tendency—of our intellectual constitution, which it is impossible not to feel, and yet which it is hard to extricate in terms and words.

The real motor for Bagehot's "duality" was his inextinguishable sense of the incongruous. "How can a soul be a merchant?" he asks. "What relation to an immortal being have the price of linseed, the fall of butter, the tare on tallow, or the brokerage on hemp? Can an undying creature debit *petty expense* and charge for *carriage paid*? . . . The soul ties its shoe; the mind washes its hands in a basin. All is incongruous." One of the things that makes Bagehot's writing so tonic is his refusal to resolve such incongruities. A more pedestrian writer, contemplating the absurdity of the soul tying its shoe, would dispense with the soul and come down firmly on the side of the footwear. It is part of Bagehot's genius to preserve the extravagance—not because it is startling but because it is true to our experience of the world.

Bagehot's greatest achievement was in applying his "binocular vision," his incorrigible sense of the incongruous, to the realm of politics and social life. His talents in this regard were already fully developed in the seven letters that he wrote about Louis Napoleon's *coup d'état* for *The Inquirer*, a Unitarian paper of abundant goodwill and characteristic shallowness. Bagehot was only twenty-five in December 1851 when the *coup* began. But the letters show that he was already a master of controversy and in full possession of several themes that would occupy him later.

Bagehot certainly knew how to get his readers' attention. Noting that "the first duty of a government is to ensure the security of that industry which is the condition of social life," he went on cheerfully to defend Louis's use of force and approve his curtailing the French press. The effect of Louis's intervention, Bagehot wrote, "was magical. . . . Commerce instantly improved," the boulevards were once again "gay and splendid; people began again to buy, and consequently to sell." Not that Bagehot was surprised by Louis Napoleon's appeal; after all, he was bold; he had "never been a professor, nor a journalist, nor a promising barrister, nor, by taste, a *littérateur*."

These were powerful, if negative, recommendations for leadership in Bagehot's view. Besides, the French people had time and again shown that they were too clever to be trusted with political liberty. "With a well-balanced national character," Bagehot argued, "liberty is a stable thing." "Stupidity," he wrote in a famous passage, is "about the most essential mental quality for a free people, whose liberty is to be progressive, permanent, and on a large scale." Stupidity was "nature's favorite recourse for preserving steadiness of conduct and consistency of opinion." But a Frenchman, according to Bagehot, is constitutionally incapable of stupidity: "*esprit* is his essence, wit is to him as water, *bon-mots* as *bon-bons*." Liberty is pleasant; but "the best institutions will not keep right a nation that *will* go wrong."

ALL THIS, of course, outraged the good readers of *The Inquirer*, who detested Louis Napoleon, were aghast at his dictatorial pretensions, and regarded any infringement on British-style liberty (at least in Europe) as unconscionable. Then, too, there was the embarrassing syllogism that if "stupidity" was a prerequisite for political freedom, and if the English were peculiarly suited for liberty, then the English must be mired in stupidity. Well, Bagehot would not have said "mired." But he claimed early and often that stupidity was an Englishman's birthright. "A great part of the 'best' English people," he wrote in *The English Constitution*, "keep their mind in a state of decorous dullness. They maintain their dignity; they get obeyed; they are good and charitable to their dependents. But they have no notion of *play* of mind; no conception that the charm of society depends upon it." Even worse, perhaps, than Bagehot's praise of stupidity and dullness were the kind things he found to say about the reactionary behavior of the French Catholic Church, an unpardonable abomination to many of his readers. "Tell an Englishman that a building is without use and he will stare," Bagehot wrote elsewhere; "that it is illiberal, and he will survey it; that it teaches Aristotle, and he will seem perplexed; that it don't teach science, and he won't mind; but only hint that it is the Pope, and he will arise and burn it to the ground."

Naturally, a good deal of Bagehot's outrageousness in his missives to *The Inquirer* was calculated; but this was small comfort to its owners, who found that his contributions almost ruined the paper. The sober backdrop to Bagehot's rhetoric was the Burkean theme that stresses the importance of "sense and circumstance" in politics. Above all, Bagehot was writing against "the old idea which still here creeps out in conversation, and sometimes in writing," that

> politics are simply a subdivision of immutable ethics; that there are certain rights of men in all places and all times, which are the sole and sufficient foundation of all government, and that accordingly a single stereotype government is to make the tour of the world—and you have no more right to deprive a Dyak of his vote in a "possible" Polynesian Parliament, than you have to steal his mat.

Here again, we see that the pertinence of Bagehot's political reflections is by no means limited to the nineteenth century.

The difficult insight that Bagehot is everywhere at pains to communicate is that not all things are possible at all times and all places. If political liberty is a precious possession, it is forged in a long, painful development of civilization, much of which is distinctly, and necessarily, illiberal. Hence the advantage of binocular vision, which allowed Bagehot, even as he was extolling Louis Napoleon's *coup*, to risk his life helping the republicans build barricades. This was not an expression of irony or inconstancy on Bagehot's part; it was an expression of political realism. As he put it later in "Caesarism as It Now Exists" (1865), the Second Empire was "an admirable government for present and coarse purposes, but a detestable government for future and refined purposes." One can help prepare for the future; one must live in the present.

The ideas that found preliminary expression in Bagehot's letters on Louis Napoleon's *coup* recur again and again in his writings. They received their most complete development in *Physics and Politics*. Of the six essays that compose the book, five were serialized in the *Fortnightly Review* beginning in 1867. A bad bout of pneumonia interrupted his work, but Bagehot added the final essay, "Verifiable Progress Politically Considered," when he published the book version in 1872.

The notion that human beings—and, by analogy, that advanced human societies—had developed out of more primitive forms had been in the air for decades by the time Bagehot began *Physics and Politics*. Evolution—often called "descent with modification" or simply "development" in the early nineteenth century—was, as the philosopher David Stove pointed out in *Darwinian Fairytales*, an

Enlightenment idea par excellence. Darwin's theories about the place of natural selection in biological evolution, published in 1859 in *On the Origin of Species*, gave the idea of evolution new scientific authority. But the basic idea of evolution—minus the explanatory motor of natural selection, which Darwin adopted from Thomas Malthus's *Essay on Population* (first published in 1798)—was part of the mental furniture of the age. Robert Chambers's *Vestiges of the Natural History of Creation*, published in 1844, was one of several books on the subject that influenced Bagehot. The crudities of "Social Darwinism," put forward most famously in the writings and speeches of Herbert Spencer (1820–1903) and T. H. Huxley (1825–1895), were a natural outgrowth of this constellation of ideas. (Huxley earned the sobriquet "Darwin's bulldog" for his tireless advocacy of Darwinism.)

The long subtitle of *Physics and Politics*—"Thoughts on the Application of the Principles of 'Natural Selection' and 'Inheritance' to Political Society"—certainly suggests that it belongs to that unpromising genre of muscular Darwinism. As always with Bagehot, however, things are not as straightforward as they at first seem. To be sure, by "physics" Bagehot meant "science," more particularly "Darwinism." (Perhaps a more accurate title would have been *Biology and Politics*, though doubtless Bagehot had in mind the etymology of "physics," i.e., the Greek word φύσις, which means "nature.") He approvingly quoted various works by Spencer and Huxley, and indeed such passages are among the most dated in the book. He referred on and off to the "transmitted nerve element" and other Lamarckian museum pieces. (Gregor Mendel's discoveries in what we have come to call genetics were published in 1866 but remained unrecognized until this century.)

The point to bear in mind is that Bagehot early on made

it clear that in invoking the idea of natural selection he was merely "searching out and following up an analogy." As Crane Brinton put it in his chapter on "The Prosperous Victorians" in *English Political Thought in the Nineteenth Century*, Bagehot "is never dogmatic, never desirous of proving too much, even to himself. He merely examines, with due regard for the limitations of logic, some of the implications of the doctrine of the survival of the fittest applied to human society. He is concerned with the nature and survival of what common sense calls a 'national character,' and which exists for every group." The great theme of *Physics and Politics*, Bagehot writes in his last chapter, concerns "the political prerequisites of progress, and especially of early progress." Just how far Bagehot's use of the term "natural selection" is from Darwin's stricter signification is shown by the way he links its operation to the operation of Providence—an agency conspicuously missing from any orthodox Darwinian account of evolution. "By a law of which we know no reason," Bagehot notes, "but which is among the first by which Providence guides and governs the world, there is a tendency in descendants to be like their progenitors, and yet a tendency also in descendants to *differ* from their progenitors. The work of nature in making generations is a patchwork— part resemblance, part contrast."

As usual, Bagehot has two main ideas. The first concerns the enormous difficulty our forefathers must have faced in establishing *any* political order or rule of law, benevolent or otherwise:

> In early times the quantity of government is much more important than its quality. What you want is a comprehensive rule binding men together, . . . What this rule is does not matter so much. A good rule is better than a bad one,

but any rule is better than none; while, for reasons which a jurist will appreciate, none can be very good. But to gain that rule, what may be called the impressive elements of a polity are incomparably more important than its useful elements. How to get the obedience of men is the hard problem; what you do with that obedience is less critical.

Bagehot's second idea concerns the similarly difficult task later ages always face in advancing beyond the order that made their own existence possible. The first step—inaugurating law, custom, and habit—is the hardest; but history proper begins with the next step: "What is most evident is not the difficulty of getting fixed law, but getting out of a fixed law; not of cementing . . . a cake of custom, but of breaking the cake of custom; not of making the first preservative habit, but of breaking through it, and reaching something better." In his second chapter, "The Use of Conflict," he sums up "the strict dilemma of early society."

> Either men had no law at all, and lived in confused tribes, hardly hanging together, or they had to obtain a fixed law by processes of incredible difficulty. Those who sur-mounted that difficulty soon destroyed all those that lay in their way who did not. And then they themselves were caught in their own yoke. The customary discipline, which could only be imposed on any early men by terrible sanc-tions, continued with those sanctions, and killed out of the whole society the propensities to variation which are the principle of progress.
>
> Experience shows how incredibly difficult it is to get men really to encourage the principle of originality. They will admit it in theory, but in practice the old error—the error which arrested a hundred civilizations—returns again. Men are too fond of their own life, too credulous of the

completeness of their own ideas, too angry at the pain of new thoughts, to be able to bear easily with a changing existence; or else, *having* new ideas, they want to enforce them on mankind—to make them heard, and admitted, and obeyed before, in simple competition with other ideas, they would ever be so naturally. At this very moment there are the most rigid Comtists teaching that we ought to be governed by a hierarchy—a combination of savants orthodox in science. Yet who can doubt that Comte would have been hanged by his own hierarchy?

Bagehot traces the vicissitudes of this dialectic through various stages from "The Preliminary Age"—that is, the rude time of prehistory when (he says with some exaggeration) "the strongest killed out the weakest as they could"—to modern times and "The Age of Discussion." Along the way Bagehot discusses the civilizing—or at least order-inducing—effects of violence ("The Use of Conflict") and the hard road any population faces in forging a national identity ("Nation-Making"). The perennial problem —and the admonitory theme of *Physics and Politics*—is that man, the strongest and smartest of the animals, "was obliged to be his own domesticator; he had to tame himself." Consequently, "history is strewn with the wrecks of nations which have gained a little progressiveness at the cost of a great deal of hard manliness, and have thus prepared themselves for destruction as soon as the movements of the world gave a chance for it."

THERE IS a great deal in *Physics and Politics* to shock readers inclined to a pacific view of human development or a politically correct understanding of life. About philanthropy in general, Bagehot shared the suspicions of many nineteenth-century conservatives:

The most melancholy of human reflections, perhaps, is that, on the whole, it is a question whether the benevolence of mankind does most good or harm. Great good, no doubt, philanthropy does, but then it also does great evil. It augments so much vice, it multiplies so much suffering, it brings to life such great populations to suffer and to be vicious, that it is open to argument whether it be or be not an evil to the world, and this is entirely because excellent people fancy they can do much by rapid action—that they will most benefit the world when they most relieve their own feelings.

Bagehot was even more controversial in other areas. "Let us consider," he writes in a famous passage toward the end of *Physics and Politics*,

in what sense a village of English colonists is superior to a tribe of Australian natives who roam about them. Indisputably in one, and that a main sense, they are superior. They can beat the Australians in war when they like; they can take from them anything they like, and kill any of them they choose. As a rule, in all the outlying and uncontested districts of the world, the aboriginal native lies at the mercy of the intruding European. Nor is this all. Indisputably in the English village there are more means of happiness, a greater accumulation of the instruments of enjoyment, than in the Australian tribe. The English have all manner of books, utensils, and machines which the others do not use, value, or understand. And in addition . . . there is a general strength which is capable of being used in conquering a thousand difficulties, and is an abiding source of happiness.

In fact, the importance of military prowess in binding a population into a society is a leitmotif in *Physics and*

Politics. In "The Use of Conflict," Bagehot notes that the progress of the military art is the "most conspicuous, I was about to say the most *showy*," fact in human history. "All through the earliest times," he writes,

> martial merit is a token of real merit: the nation that wins is the nation that ought to win. The simple virtues of such ages mostly make a man a soldier if they make him anything. No doubt the brute force of number may be too potent even then (as so often it is afterwards): civilization may be thrown back by the conquest of many very rude men over a few less rude men. But the first elements of civilization are great military advantages, and, roughly, it is a rule of the first times that you can infer merit from conquest, and that progress is promoted by the competitive examination of constant war.

Bagehot is undeceived about exigencies that face a nation at war. "So long as war is the main business of nations, temporary despotism—despotism during the campaign—is indispensable. Macaulay justly said that many an army has prospered under a bad commander, but no army has ever prospered under a 'debating society.'"

The point is, Bagehot argues, that "war both needs and generates certain virtues; not the highest, but what may be called the preliminary virtues, as valor, veracity, the spirit of obedience, the habit of discipline." That is to say, war, and the martial virtues it requires, makes certain valuable things possible, including civilization itself: "Civilization begins," Bagehot writes, "because the beginning of civilization is a military advantage"—an unflattering thought that many will find shocking.

Even more shocking is the similar argument that Bagehot makes regarding slavery:

> Slavery, too, has a bad name in the later world, and very justly. We connect it with gangs in chains, with laws which keep men ignorant, with laws that hinder families. But the evils which we have endured from slavery in recent ages must not blind us to, or make us forget, the great services that slavery rendered in early ages. . . . Refinement is only possible when leisure is possible; and slavery first makes it possible.

Perhaps the only thing more difficult than accepting this contention is coming up with convincing arguments against it.

All such "hard" observations constitute as it were the strophe of Bagehot's argument. The antistrophe, the opposite movement—the movement toward which *Physics and Politics* as a whole tends—is that "the whole history of civilization is strewn with creeds and institutions which were invaluable at first, and deadly afterwards." Slavery is one such institution. And ultimately the martial sensibility may be as well.

> Life is not a set campaign, but an irregular work, and the main forces in it are not overt resolutions, but latent and half-involuntary promptings. The mistake of military ethics is to exaggerate the conception of discipline, and so to present the moral force of the will in a barer form than it ever ought to take. Military morals can direct the axe to cut down the tree, but it knows nothing of the quiet force by which the forest grows.

Savages, Bagehot writes with cool dispatch, prefer "short spasms of greedy pleasure to mild and equable enjoyment." Thus it is that progress in civilization is measured by increasing deliberateness. Government—the institutional distillate of progress in civilization—is valuable not only because it facilitates action but also, and increasingly, because it retards it:

> If you want to stop instant and immediate action, always make it a condition that the action shall not begin till a considerable number of persons have talked over it, and have agreed on it. If those persons be people of different temperaments, different ideas, and different educations, you have an almost infallible security that nothing, or almost nothing, will be done with excessive rapidity.

It is naturally "the age of discussion"—the age of "slow" government and political liberty—that Bagehot ultimately extols in *Physics and Politics*. "Nothing," he notes, "promotes intellect like intellectual discussion, and nothing promotes intellectual discussion so much as government by discussion." But Bagehot is ever at pains to remind his readers of the harsh prerequisites of civilization, which include war, slavery, and gross inequity. Government by discussion, Bagehot is quick to acknowledge, is "a principal organ for improving mankind." At the same time, he insists that "it is a plant of singular delicacy." The question of how best to nurture this delicate plant is Bagehot's final problem. Part of the answer is in facing up to the unpalatable realities about power that make civilization possible. The other part lies in embracing what Bagehot calls "animated moderation," that "union of life with measure, of spirit with reasonableness," which assures that discussion will continue without descending into violence or anarchy. It seems like a small thing. But then achieved order always does—until it is lost.

Part Two

What's Left of Descartes?

C'est le privilège du vrai génie, et surtout du génie qui ouvre une carrière, de faire impunément de grandes fautes.

It is the privilege of true genius, and above all genius that opens up a new path, to commit great errors with impunity.
—Voltaire

Bene vixit, bene qui latuit.

He lived well who concealed well.
—Descartes' motto

ONE EVENING many years ago, when I was in graduate school, I somehow found myself in conversation with a group of graduate students who were studying political science. Almost everything about that conversation is now lost in the mists of time, except one detail. The conversation had turned to the nature of modernity. I brought up Descartes, and was probably just about to utter the word "dualism" or "technology" when a vivid young man who tabulated election results interrupted: "I really don't see what someone who lived in the seventeenth century could possibly tell us about the modern world."

The reply, if any, is not recorded. But the incident

remained with me as a sort of cautionary tale. Notwithstanding the indifference with which that tabulator of election results regarded the seventeenth century, it is difficult to name an individual whose thinking did more to pave the way for modernity than René Descartes—born though he was in 1596. Everyone is familiar with Descartes' famous formula *Cogito, ergo sum*: "I think, therefore I am." Almost everybody knows—or supposes he knows—that Descartes espoused a relentlessly dualistic philosophy that made an all-but-impermeable distinction between mind and matter. Of course if this were the whole story, my tabulator would have been right to shrug.

But it is not the whole story. Nor is it simply that Descartes was, as textbooks invariably put it, "the father of modern philosophy": that he was, in the words of a typical encomium, "one of the founders of modern thought and among the most original philosophers and mathematicians of any age." True, without Descartes' contributions to mathematics, it is not clear that our tabulator of election results could have done much with his tabulations. Every time that a student of algebra calculates the square root of $a + b$ or refers to x^3 he uses a notation pioneered by Descartes; when someone wishes to plot a curve on a graph, he is likely to do so using the co-ordinate system invented by Descartes and that still bears his name.

But Descartes' influence goes far beyond algebraic notation, analytic geometry, and other mathematical innovations. For better or worse—quite possibly for better *and* worse—the modern world is in a deep sense a Cartesian world. To appreciate the extent of Descartes' continuing presence, one need only consider the triumph of scientific rationality and its handmaiden, technology. Descartes did not single-handedly invent these defining features of modernity, the foundations of which belong to an even earlier era. But along with Copernicus, Galileo, Bacon, and others, Descartes was one of the key figures in the formulation of the so-called "New Science" that was destined to replace the contemplative model of science inherited from the Greeks.

To an unprecedented degree, Descartes understood that the citadel of nature could be successfully stormed only by redescribing reality in the language of mathematics—thus purging the visual world of all that was merely visual—and then by testing those descriptions in experiment. In the *Discourse on Method* (1637), justly one of his best-known books, Descartes boasted that his philosophy, in contrast to that taught by the Schools, is fundamentally a "practical philosophy" whose precepts yield "knowledge which is very useful in life." By following his methods, Descartes wrote, we could discover the basic mechanical principles of natural phenomena and then, like skilled craftsmen, intervene and put those principles to work in the world. By so doing, he promised in one of his most striking phrases, we could *"nous rendre comme maîtres et possesseurs de la nature,"* "render ourselves the masters and possessors of nature." Medicine was only one field in which he expected great strides to be made on the basis of his philosophy.

Looking back from the beginning of the twenty-first century, when technology—including medical technology—has transformed the world, it is difficult not to acknowledge the power of Descartes' vision. Perhaps less obvious, however, is that fact that underlying Descartes' "method" was a fateful new attitude toward both the self and the world. As the image of rendering man the master and possessor of nature suggests, physical reality was henceforth to be seen not as a divinely ordered creation but as a homogenous field for human experimentation, manipulation, and reconstruction. We get a clue about Des-

83

cartes' attitude toward the self in his famous method of systematic doubt: his resolve to "reject as if absolutely false anything as to which I could imagine the least doubt, in order to see if I should not be left at the end believing something that was absolutely indubitable."

If traditionally philosophy began in wonder, as Aristotle said, after Descartes it would begin more darkly with doubt. (In this context, it is significant that Descartes hoped to explain extravagant natural phenomena such as meteors and lightning in such a way that "one will no longer have occasion to admire anything about what is seen": for Descartes, wonder was an impediment to knowledge.) Never mind that Descartes himself embraced what he was careful to call "hyperbolic"—i.e., deliberately exaggerated—doubt chiefly because it guaranteed (as he thought) an invincible certitude: his heirs found that certitude plenty fragile. And they seized upon the turn inward that such doubt presupposed not as a preliminary to more certain affirmation but as an invitation to explore the newly emancipated self that was thereby revealed.

Thus it was that Descartes' efforts to achieve certainty by withholding assent from everything susceptible to doubt instigated a revolution not just in philosophy but in the whole tenor of intellectual life. There are perhaps few thinkers less "Cartesian" than Marx, Nietzsche, or Freud. Yet even such paradigmatic modern figures continued to move on a map drawn by Descartes, partly in their very opposition to the Cartesian view of man (opposition being a common token of intellectual debt), partly in their determination to subject every accepted opinion to the corrosive scrutiny of doubt.

Whether Descartes, devout Catholic that he was, would have welcomed this development is a good question: almost certainly he would have deplored it. In the *Discourse on Method*, he warns that the "resolution to get rid of all opinions one has so far admitted to belief is in itself not an example for everybody to follow." For one thing, he explains, it is just the sort of thing to tempt those many people "who think they are more clever than they are, and cannot help forming precipitate judgments." That is one reason that at the beginning of his revolutionary intellectual journey he attempts to indemnify himself against a corresponding moral revolution. Wherever his speculations may lead, Descartes explained, he began by resolving "to obey the laws and customs of my country, adhering to the religion in which by God's grace I had been instructed since my childhood, and in all other things directing my conduct by opinions the most moderate in nature, and the furthest removed from excess." Michel Foucault, where are you?

Given the extent of Descartes' influence, it is perhaps not surprising that his legacy should be fraught with ironies, misunderstandings, and various intellectual perversities: fame multiplies the opportunity for misapprehension. As Stephen Gaukroger notes in his biography of Descartes (Oxford University Press, 1995), "more than any other modern philosopher, he has been fashioned according to the philosophies of the time and interpreted accordingly." Gaukroger, who teaches philosophy at the University of Sydney, proposes to extract the "real" Descartes from the integument spun by his multifarious interpreters. Whether what we actually get is an unencumbered Descartes, or only one bedecked with Gaukroger's preoccupations, is an open question. His reference early on to "Simone de Beauvoir's incomparable intellectual autobiography" will hearten or dismay readers according to their feelings about this one-time idol of *gauchiste* feminism. His evident fondness for psychoanalytic interpretations occasionally insinuates a slight psychologizing haze into the biographical portions of the book, though this rarely becomes downright disfiguring. Gaukroger several times refers, somewhat anachronistically, to occasions when Descartes may have suffered a "nervous breakdown"; he makes much of the facts that Descartes' mother died a little more than a year after he was born and that his father was distant and cold. (Actually, he seems to have been distinctly hostile. When Descartes published the *Discourse on Method* in 1637, his father is reported to have remarked: "Only one of my children has displeased me. How can I have engendered a son stupid enough to have had himself bound in calf?")

In any event, the real meat of this book lies elsewhere. It is often said that with Descartes philosophy abandoned or at least discounted metaphysics for the sake of epistemology. The prime exhibits for this contention are the *Discourse on Method* and the *Meditations on First Philosophy* (1641), works that set forth Descartes' experiments in systematic doubt and that put the question of justifying knowledge center stage. (Gaukroger is right that "the *Meditations* read like an account of a spiritual journey in which the truth is only to be discovered by a purging, followed by a kind of rebirth.") These are the books by Descartes that every beginner in philosophy is invited to ponder and that most philosophers have made the center of their interest in Descartes. So it is not surprising that the most engaging pages of Gaukroger's book are those dealing with these two books.

Descartes specialized in unsettling intellectual complacency. In a famous passage in the second Meditation, he recalls sitting berobed in his study next to a fire, contemplating a ball of beeswax fresh from the honeycomb. What a familiar object—or is it? The wax has a certain shape, size, texture; it is hard and will give off a sound if you rap it; it is milky white and retains a certain floral scent and sweetness. Yet if the wax is put next to the fire it quickly loses what flavor and scent it still possessed; its color changes; it loses its shape and texture and hardness. Is it, then, still the same wax? In that most venerable of philosophical replies, Descartes answers, "Yes, but . . .". Yes, but it is not the wax I just saw, for it now looks different. Yes, but it is not the wax I just heard, for it no longer makes the same sound when rapped. Yes, but it neither smells nor feels the same is it did fifteen minutes ago. Neither the senses nor the imagination, Descartes argues, comprehends the essence of the wax: on the contrary, I really know the wax only through an act of "purely mental perception." And what is the wax thus perceived by the mind?

> It is the very same wax as I see, touch, and imagine—that in whose existence I believed originally. But it must be observed that perception of the wax is not sight, not touch, not imagination; nor was it ever so, though it formerly seemed to be; it is a purely mental contemplation, which may be either imperfect and confused, as it originally was, or clear and distinct, as it now is, according to my degree of attention to what it consists in.

As Descartes noted, such speculations produce a kind of intellectual vertigo, removing the firm foundation that common sense obligingly furnishes. "Yesterday's meditation," he concludes, "plunged me into doubts of such gravity that I cannot forget them, and yet do not see how to resolve them. I am bewildered, as though I had suddenly fallen into a deep sea, and could neither plant my foot on the bottom nor swim up to the top."

The *Meditations* trace a movement from unexamined

confidence, through a series of trials by increasingly radical doubt, to a certainty chastened by reflection.

> I decided to feign that everything that had entered my mind hitherto was no more true than the illusions of dreams. But immediately upon this I noticed that while I was trying to think everything false, it must needs be that I, who was thinking this, was something. And observing that this truth "I am thinking, therefore I exist [*je pense, donc je suis*]" was so solid and secure that the most extravagant suppositions of the sceptics could not overthrow it, I judged that I need not scruple to accept it as the first principle of philosophy I was seeking.

Although he was clearly a virtuoso of doubt, Descartes did not distract himself with bootless speculation about the definition of truth. In an important letter of 1639, he notes that he has never had any doubt about "what truth is" for the simple reason that

> it seems a notion so transcendentally clear that no one could be ignorant of it. There are many ways of examining a balance before using it, but there is no way to learn what truth is, if one does not know it by nature. . . . Of course, it is possible to tell the *meaning of the word* to someone who does not know the language, and tell him that the word *truth*, in the strict sense, denotes the conformity of thought with its object, and that when it is attributed to things outside thought, it means only that they can be the objects of true thoughts, whether in our minds or in God's. But we can give no definition of logic which will help anyone discover its nature. And I believe that the same holds of many other things which are very simple and known naturally, such as shape, size, movement, place, time and so on. For if

you try to define these things you only obscure them and cause confusion. For instance, a man who walks across a room shows much better what movement is, than a man who says "it is the act of a being in potency, in so far as it is in potency" and so on.

Similarly, Descartes had little patience with the intellectual autism of those who feign ignorance about the basic building blocks of knowledge. "My method cannot," he writes in a posthumously published work, "go so far as to teach us how to perform the actual operations of intuition and deduction, for these are the simplest of all and quite basic. If our intellect were not already able to perform them, it would not comprehend the rules of method, however easy they might be." It is a great pity that such eminently commonsensical passages—full of mental sanity and mental sunshine—did not make a greater impression on the philosophers who came after Descartes. What a lot of murky disputation—not to say bad philosophy—might have been avoided!

GAUKROGER DEALS at length with Descartes' metaphysics and speculations about knowledge. He also spends a great deal of time explicating Descartes' more strictly scientific and mathematical works. This makes some parts of his book quite technical and even—since much of Descartes' science is chiefly of historical interest—a tad antiquarian. Gaukroger's mastery of this material is impressive. But I think it fair to say that most readers, asked if they were interested in detailed discussions of Descartes' theory of vortices or the function of the pineal gland, would respond in the spirit of Salter in Evelyn Waugh's *Scoop*: "Up to a point, Lord Copper."

Gaukroger's focus on Descartes' scientific works is part

and parcel of his mildly "revisionist" view of the philosopher's accomplishments. Gaukroger, who duly acknowledges three grants from the Australian Research Council, informs readers that "it is not the Descartes from whom philosophers have made such a good living for decades that they will find here." Well, yes and no. There are not really that many surprises in this book, though Gaukroger does emphasize elements of Descartes' work that generally get shorter shrift. In his view, Descartes was first of all committed to making advances in natural science, not to immunizing philosophy against the virus of scepticism. Among the most explicit items he advances to support his case is the note that Descartes wrote toward the end of his life to one of his admirers:

> You should not devote so much attention to the *Meditations* and to metaphysical questions. . . . They draw the mind too far away from physical and observable things, and unfit it to study them. Yet it is precisely physical studies that it is most desirable for men to pursue.

Accordingly, perhaps the chief intellectual interest of this book is Gaukroger's effort to rescue Descartes from the philosophers and set his work in the context of seventeenth-century scientific speculation, especially the daring —and heterodox—cosmological theories of Copernicus.

Like all biographers of Descartes, Gaukroger is constrained to depend rather heavily on Adrien Baillet's life of the philosopher that appeared in 1691. Although obviously "out of date," Baillet's book is still the only source we have for certain quotations and anecdotes about Descartes, parts of whose life are rather sketchily documented. For example, I believe that Baillet is the only contemporary source for the story that Descartes fought a duel over a lady in 1628; likewise, it is from Baillet that we learn that Descartes said, apparently around the same time, that he had never found a woman whose beauty was comparable with that of truth. (For what it is worth, I note that Descartes claimed to have been particularly attracted to women who were slightly cross-eyed.) In the biographical parts of his book—which probably amount to no more than a tenth of his text—Gaukroger is also indebted to the very readable biography of Descartes by Jack R. Vrooman that appeared in 1970. He leaves earlier useful but somewhat pious efforts such as Elizabeth S. Haldane's *Descartes: His Life and Times* (1905) entirely out of account.

Descartes was born in La Haye, a small town in Tours that is now called "Descartes." The third of three surviving children, he was precocious but sickly. His father, Joachim, was a councillor of the Parlement of Brittany and a man of moderate landed property. After Descartes' mother died, he and his siblings were sent to live with their maternal grandmother. Joachim remarried and in due course fathered an additional four children. In 1607, when he was ten, Descartes was sent to the new Jesuit *collège* of La Flèche in Anjou, where he spent the next eight years absorbing the classical curriculum as set forth in the *Ratio Studiorum*, the comprehensive prescriptions for study and behavior followed by all Jesuit colleges. Sometime in 1615, he went to study law at the University of Poitiers, where he took his baccalaureate and license in civil and canon law in 1616.

When he was in his early twenties, Descartes seems to have contemplated a military career and over the next decade or so was attached to several armies. He enlisted in the Dutch army as a gentleman soldier under Prince Maurice of Nassau in 1618. Later that year, he met and collaborated with Isaac Beeckman, a scientist and mathematician who, eight years Descartes' senior, acted as a kind of mentor and rekindled Descartes' interest in science. Descartes presented his first work, *Compendium Musicae*, as a gift to Beeckman on New Year's Day 1619. (Beeckman was an interesting figure: among other things he set up the first meteorological station in Europe in 1628.) In 1619, as the Thirty Years War was beginning, Descartes left Maurice and enlisted in the Bavarian army.

It was while he was stationed at Neuburg in northern Bavaria on November 10, 1619, that Descartes had the famous series of three dreams (or nightmares) that, he believed, revealed to him the *"mirabilis scientiae fundamenta,"* the foundations of a marvelous knowledge. (Tradition places this episode in Ulm, but Geneviève Rodis-Lewis corrects this in *Descartes: His Life and Thought* [Cornell University Press, 1998].) According to the French Thomist philosopher Jacques Maritain, these dreams (the details of which we know about from Baillet) contained "in embryo the whole of cartesian rationalism." For his part, Gaukroger is "very pessimistic" about what can be achieved by interpreting the dreams. Noting how "stylized" and literary they are (in one part of the dream, Descartes recalls seeing a fragment from an ode by Ausonius: *"Quod vitae sectabor iter?"*—"What road of life shall I follow?"), Gaukroger concludes that "it is quite possible that Descartes was suffering a nervous breakdown, almost certainly not his first." Be that as it may, Descartes regarded the dreams as "the most important thing in my life" and vowed to make a pilgrimage of thanksgiving to Our Lady of Loreto, a vow he apparently fulfilled five years later.

Descartes' movements in the early 1620s are not well known. In 1623, he visited Italy, and he was settled in Paris in 1625–26. He sold the property left to him by his mother, losing the title "Seigneur du Perron" but gaining a modest regular income. During this time he met the Jesuit priest Marin Mersenne, one of his most important correspondents, worked intensively on geometrical problems, and began working on the book (which was left unfinished) that became the *Rules for the Direction of the Mind* (posthumously published in 1701). Around 1626, he discovered the law of refraction, which describes the behavior of light rays as they pass from one medium to another. In 1628, at a meeting on Aristotelian philosophy at the residence of the papal nuncio, Descartes had a famous public confrontation with a certain doctor Chandoux, a chemist/alchemist who argued against the dominance of scholastic philosophy and in favor of a science based on merely probable knowledge. His training in rhetoric standing him in good stead, Descartes gave a dazzling public refutation, arguing that only absolute certainty could serve as a basis for knowledge. (It is a nice detail that Chandoux was later executed for counterfeiting.)

Cardinal Bérulle, an important figure in Parisian intellectual and political circles, was in the audience and encouraged Descartes to develop his insights into a comprehensive system. Descartes still lived at a moment when it was possible—just—for an individual to aspire to a kind of universal knowledge. This Descartes certainly did. In the *Principles of Philosophy* (1644), he assures his readers that "there is no phenomenon in nature which has not been dealt with in this treatise." He had originally intended to call the *Discourse on Method*, which was published as an introduction to three essays on mathematics, *Project of a Universal Science Destined to Raise our Nature to Its Highest Degree of Perfection.*

In 1628, Descartes joined the army that was besieging the Huguenot stronghold at La Rochelle. This was to be his last association with the military. In 1629, Descartes retired to

Holland, where he remained, with brief interruptions, until 1649. In part, Descartes went to the Netherlands in search of greater seclusion; he was an intensely private, indeed secretive, man, and he moved often to avoid the importunities of friends and admirers. The 1630s found him in Amsterdam, Deventer, Leiden, Utrecht, Haarlem, Endergeest, and the Hague. The Netherlands were attractive also as an oasis of (relative) liberty and freedom. As Bertrand Russell wrote in his history of philosophy,

> it is impossible to exaggerate the importance of Holland in the seventeenth century, as the one country where there was freedom of speculation. Hobbes had to have his books printed there; Locke took refuge there during the five worst years of reaction in England before 1688; Bayle (of the *Dictionary*) found it necessary to live there; and Spinoza would hardly have been allowed to do his work in any other country.

Among other activities, Descartes avidly pursued his anatomical researches during these years, acquiring animal parts from local butchers for dissection. In 1635, while he was staying with a friend in Amsterdam, he fathered a child with a maid named Hélène. According to Jack Vrooman, this was "the only relationship in [Descartes'] life where by his own admission the sexual act played a significant role." Although he referred to the child, Francine, as his "niece," he seems to have been genuinely fond of her and to have provided for her and her mother. When the child died of a fever in 1640, he is said to have remarked that it was the greatest sorrow of his life. (Geneviève Rodis-Lewis describes the birth and death of his daughter as "the most intimate episode of Descartes' life.")

Beginning in 1639, the Netherlands became distinctly less hospitable. Descartes became the target of abuse from one Gisbert Voetius, a professor of theology at the University of Utrecht, who, as Gaukroger observes, "set out to destroy Descartes" in a campaign of insinuation and slander that was to last for more than five years. At one point, Descartes was in danger of being expelled from the city and having his books burned. So it is not perhaps surprising that when Queen Christina of Sweden invited Descartes to come to Stockholm under her protection he (after some hesitation) decided to accept. Descartes arrived in Sweden in October of 1649. At first, he had almost no duties. But in January—the most bitterly cold in many years—he began tutoring the Queen, whom Bertrand Russell aptly describes as "a passionate and learned lady who thought that, as a sovereign, she had the right to waste the time of great men." The tutorials commenced at 5:00 A.M. three days a week and lasted for some five hours. For Descartes, who was accustomed to sleep late and preferred working in bed, the regime was too much. After nursing a sick friend to health, he himself came down with pneumonia and died in February 1650.

THE DESCARTES who emerges in Gaukroger's and Rodis-Lewis's books is a somewhat knottier figure than the serene rationalist we know from Philosophy 101. The knots are of several varieties. Descartes tried desperately to stay out of theological controversy and craved the *imprimatur* of Church authority. When Galileo's work was condemned in 1633 for teaching the Copernican system, Descartes promptly suppressed his book *Le Monde*, which also depended on Copernicus: "if it is false," Descartes wrote in dismay to Mersenne, "so too are the entire foundations of my philosophy." Many have criticized his action as timorous, which perhaps it was; but it was also a witness to Descartes' humility about theological issues: "I wouldn't," he wrote to Mersenne, "want to publish a discourse which had a single word that the Church disapproved." Alas, theological controversy dogged him—not, it must be said, without reason—though his works were not placed on the Index until 1663.

If Descartes exhibited a remarkable reticence when it came to theological matters, he was not in other respects notable for his humility. In 1629, believing that Isaac Beeckman claimed credit for some of his theories about music, Descartes fired off a long, vituperative letter in which he broke off relations with his friend and former mentor, demanding that he return the *Compendium Musicae* and remarking (among much else) that he had learned as much from Beeckman as he had learned "from ants and worms." As Gaukroger notes, "it is just not possible to take Descartes' side in this dispute." Descartes wildly over-reacted to an innocent statement by Beeckman and, besides, there can be no doubt that Descartes *was* intellectually indebted to his early collaborator. Descartes was a philosophical and mathematical genius of the first water; but he shared with lesser men some unfortunate qualities, including a tendency to intellectual vanity that made it difficult for him to acknowledge the achievements of others. In a letter to Mersenne, he referred to the great mathematician Pierre de Fermat as "dung"; others who had criticized his work on geometry were dismissed as "two or three flies"; Thomas Hobbes was "extremely contemptible"; the letters of the mathematician Jean Beaugrand were only fit to be used as toilet paper; etc.

Gaukroger remarks dryly that "the simple fact is that Descartes did not like criticism." Obviously this is an understatement. What is remarkable, though, is the image we have of Descartes as a calm and diligent inquirer who cared for the truth above everything. The fact that he first published his greatest work, the *Meditations on First Philosophy*, complete with a set of objections by such eminences as Hobbes, Mersenne, Antoine Arnauld, and Pierre Gassendi, only reinforces this image. If the reality was at variance with the image it is partly because Descartes cultivated his image so assiduously.

In an often-quoted passage from the *Cogitationes Privatae* ("Private Thoughts"), a collection of fragments written around 1619 and known to us from a copy made by Leibniz, Descartes writes that

> just as comedians are counselled not to let shame appear on their foreheads, and so put on a mask (*personam induunt*): so likewise, now that I am about to mount the stage of the world, where I have so far been a spectator, I come forward in a mask (*larvatus prodeo*).

Many writers, above all Jacques Maritain, have made a great deal of this passage. It does not seem to have impressed Gaukroger particularly (he nowhere mentions Maritain). But it is I think at least curious that Descartes, the proverbial champion of clear and distinct ideas, should have set forth on his career with an admission of deliberate—what? Duplicity? Subterfuge? Artifice? And it is even more striking that he should have chosen the word *larvatus*, which can mean "masked," but which also means "bewitched." (*Persona* is the common Latin word for "mask.")

Descartes told one correspondent that his motto was *Bene vixit, bene qui latuit*: a tag from Ovid that can mean "He lived well who concealed well" or "He lived well who was private and unobtrusive." The more we know about

Descartes, the more both renderings seem appropriate. In this context, it is worth saying a word or two about Descartes' prose, certainly one of his most impressive achievements. Quite apart from the substance of his work, one of Descartes' chief attractions has always been his style. Together with Plato, Hume, Schopenhauer, and (a more florid example) Nietzsche, Descartes is one of the great philosophical stylists of all time. Especially in his more strictly philosophical books—above all the *Discourse on Method* and *Meditations on First Philosophy*—Descartes wrote with beguiling simplicity. The simplicity is beguiling because it is at least in part only the *appearance* of simplicity. His celebrated embrace of the "clear and distinct" as criteria for truth (or at least immunity from doubt) has a corollary in the elegantly supple lucidity of his prose. When first reading Descartes, one has the sensation of utter clarity and comprehension. It is only when looking back and re-reading that doubts and difficulties, like the influence of Descartes' "evil genius" in the *Meditations*, begin to undermine one's confidence.

At the beginning of his book, Gaukroger writes that "it is easily forgotten just how controversial, reviled, and celebrated a figure Descartes was, not just in his own lifetime, but for the next 150 years or so." In fact, the revilement continues even today. The great peculiarity is that although we inhabit a world that is inconceivable without the influence of Descartes, no philosopher is more regularly abused and excoriated. For many, the term "Cartesian" is these days little more than a handy negative epithet, an all-purpose term of abuse suggesting by turns sterile rationalism, a predatory attitude toward nature, and even nasty capitalist habits of acquisitiveness. Thus it is that one trendy academic historian warns in his latest work of "cultural studies" against "the Cartesian ethos of consumer culture," the "commodity fetishism [that] . . . underwrote a Cartesian vision of an isolated self in an inert world of objects," etc. It would be exceedingly polite, though not entirely inaccurate, to describe such uses of "Cartesian" as spasms of late Romantic irrationalism: more or less feeble protests against a world that seems unaccountably indifferent to our desires.

Not that there isn't a great deal to criticize in Descartes. Philosophers from Pascal (who in his *Pensées* dismissed Descartes as *"inutile et incertain"*) to Wittgenstein and beyond have found themselves vexed by what Descartes had to say about God, knowledge, the self, the physical world, and other matters. The number of "definitive" arguments mounted against dualism, the cogito, and the ideal of clear and distinct ideas has been legion. Nevertheless, Descartes remains: he is one of those intellectual giants who seem endlessly vulnerable but who are somehow ever unavoidable.

The point is that the ambivalence we feel about Descartes is a reflection of the ambivalence we feel about modernity. Despite the prattlings of contemporary academic "humanists," New Agers, and other intellectually handicapped persons, no one can in good faith utter a simple "no" to modernity. The affluent protestors who chat on their cell phones and jet around the world to demonstrate against "globalization" embody in their lives the very things they pretend to reject. Still, an unqualified "yes" to the modern world is also impossible. Descartes' dream of a philosophy that would render us the "masters and possessors of nature" has been all but realized. The question is whether we can really *inhabit* the world that we rule over with such thoroughness. Advances in genetic engineering, in nanotechnology, and other frontiers of science pose deep challenges to any traditional notion of humanity and moral order.

Paul Valéry summed up the problem in his brief sketch for an essay on Descartes. Like many moderns, Valéry found himself bewitched by the heroic solipsism of Descartes' formula, *cogito ergo sum*. Yet he knew that a corollary of that formula was a world in which "the word 'Knowledge' is increasingly denied to anything which cannot be translated into figures." Among other things, this meant that "the truth for modern man, which is exactly related to his freedom of action over nature, seems more and more to be in opposition to everything that our imagination and our feelings would like to be true." As Valéry understood, we owe our humanity not only to our ability to reason, but also to our status as creatures of feeling, imagination, and moral responsibility. In the end, the idea that we are the "masters and possessors of nature" is a risible illusion bred by overweening cleverness. For ultimately it is nature that masters and possesses us, a fact we deny to our intellectual peril and moral diminishment. What's left of Descartes? Just look around. Descartes is everywhere. Which is both the glory and the frightening challenge of modernity.

Schiller's "Education"

It is now about twenty years since the whole race of Germans began to "transcend." Should they ever wake up to this fact, they will look very odd to themselves.
—Johann Wolfgang von Goethe, 1826

It is still the question whether the philosophy of art has anything to say to the artist. [I myself] applied the metaphysic of art too directly to objects and handled it as a practical tool for which it is not quite suitable.
—Friedrich Schiller, 1798

Why does the Aesthetik *of every German philosopher seem to the artist like the abomination of desolation?*
—William James

I T IS a difficult problem to say why many of the simplest questions are the hardest to answer. Philosophy, of course, is littered with such difficult simplicities: What is truth? What is knowledge? Can virtue be taught? Is there such a thing as free will? What is the good life? Many people, including many philosophers, have dismissed such questions as illegitimate and unanswerable.

Unanswerable they may be, but the human heart can be counted on to dismiss those dismissals. Very few people actively devote themselves to pondering such simple imponderables. That is doubtless a good thing all around, not least for the business of everyday life. But even fewer people, I suspect, are entirely untroubled by such questions. That, too, is a good thing, not least because, as Socrates famously put it, the unexamined life is not worth living. Is that an overstatement? Perhaps. But if it errs, it does so in the right direction. What Socrates did not say—but what Plato's *Dialogues* may show in the dramas they enact—is that there is more than one way to lead an examined life. It may be hard to come up with a satisfactory answer to the question "What is knowledge?" But we all answer that question daily in a currency other than words.

It is the same in other departments of life. "What is justice?" is a question whose answer we *live* even if we cannot put it into adequate words. We know that virtue can be taught because it *is* taught, putative demonstrations of its impossibility notwithstanding.

Among other things, such reflections should inculcate a healthy scepticism—including scepticism about doctrinaire scepticism. Our cleverness, like our language, often fails to produce the unarguable answers we desire. Which doesn't mean that we stop asking, only that we typically find ourselves in that arguable realm where deeds come to the aid of dicta and felt truths illuminate the obscurities left over when reason has done its work. "*La coeur,*" as Pascal put it, "*a ses raisons que la raison ne connaît pas.*" And the heart's reasons have their own axioms and arguments, their palpable QEDs that are in their way as persuasive as Euclid's. Intelligence, that is to say, is more than intellection. Can it be purely fortuitous that *sapientia*—wisdom—has its root in *sapor*, taste: a faculty of feeling, intuition, sensibility? What deep truth does that etymology suggest?

Well, the question of taste can be counted on to generate

many of those simple questions we cannot definitively answer but also cannot help asking. Consider the question, inevitable when we ponder the operation of taste, of why we care so much about art. *That* we care is graven in the stones of our museums, theaters, and concert halls, embossed on the pages of novels and volumes of poetry, enshrined in the deference—financial, social, spiritual—that the institutions of art command in our society. But why? Art satisfies no practical need; it is not useful in the sense in which a law court or a hospital, a farm or a machinist's shop is useful. And yet we invest art and the institutions that represent it with enormous privilege and prestige. Why? Why is something apparently useless accorded such honor?

One reason, of course, is that utility is not our only criterion of value. We care about many things that are not in any normal sense useful. Indeed for many of the things we care about most the whole question of use seems peculiarly out of place, a kind of existential category mistake. But we still can ask: what is it about art, about aesthetic experience, that recommends itself so powerfully to our regard?

A lot of ink has been spilled trying to answer that question. The word "aesthetics" was not coined (and the discipline it names was not born) until the middle of the eighteenth century, but a fascination with beauty is perennial. From Plato on down, philosophers and artists—and philosopher-artists—have eulogized beauty as providing intimations of spiritual wholeness and lost unity.

This is one reason that, of all branches of philosophy, aesthetics tends to be the most oleaginous. Especially in times when traditional religious commitments are in retreat, many people look to art for spiritual dividends previously sought elsewhere. This burdens art, and intellectual talk about art, with intoxicating expectations. The expectations are consistently disappointed, but the intoxication remains. The result is the hothouse rhetoric of romanticism, full of infinite longings, sublime impatience, impetuous raids on an ever-retreating, capital-A Absolute.

One problem with this tendency to invest art with unanchored religious sentiment is that it makes it difficult to keep art's native satisfactions in focus. The difficulty is compounded because aesthetic delight involves a feeling of wholeness that is easy to mistake for religious exaltation. Art does offer balm for the spirit, but it is not a religious balm. Exactly what sort of balm is it? One of the most impassioned attempts to answer this question was made at the end of the eighteenth century by the German poet, playwright, and philosophical essayist Friedrich Schiller (1759–1805).

I hasten to add that Schiller did not entirely avoid the confusion of art and religious sentiment. He made an heroic effort to understand and explain why aesthetic experience on its own terms is important. But Erich Heller was right when he observed, in "In Two Minds About Schiller," that Schiller presented

> a striking instance of a European catastrophe of the spirit: the invasion and partial disruption of the aesthetic faculty by unemployed religious impulses. He is one of the most conspicuous and most impressive figures among the host of theologically displaced persons who found a precarious refuge in the emergency camp of Art.

It is a telling biographical detail that as a child Schiller liked to play-act at being a minister. He practiced giving sermons, bestowing benedictions and pronouncing anathemas as the occasion demanded. When it came time for school, he wanted passionately to go to a theological seminary. But his father, a low-level army officer in the employ of Duke Karl Eugen of Württemberg, was obliged by the duke to send the thirteen-year-old to his newly-established military school in Stuttgart. In his biography of Schiller— published in 1825—Thomas Carlyle noted that the six years Schiller spent there were "the most harassing and comfortless of his life." The duke's idea of education was extremely rigid. It was formed, Carlyle wrote, on the principle "not of cherishing and correcting nature, but rooting it out, and supplying its place with something better."

Schiller studied law and medicine, qualifying in 1780 to become a regimental doctor. But he also threw himself into poetry. His first poem was published in 1777 when he in his late teens. His first play, *Die Räuber* ("The Robbers"), was printed at Schiller's own expense in 1781 and was performed the following year in Mannheim. It was a sensation. A wild *Sturm und Drang* affair, *The Robbers* embodied all of Schiller's frustration at the narrow, regimented life he was forced to lead in the duke's employ. It tells the story of Karl Moor who, falsely accused of criminal activity by his younger brother, flees home and becomes the leader of a vicious band of robbers, his noble nature irreparably tainted by an uncaring society. Things end badly for everyone. Schiller's portrayal of blighted passion and an individual's doomed struggle with recalcitrant authority encapsulated the explosive, antinomian mood of the moment. Coleridge spoke for many when, reading the play in 1794, he wrote to Robert Southey, "My God! Southey! Who is this Schiller? This Convulser of the Heart?"

Duke Eugen, however, was not at all pleased by the spectacle of one of his minions making such a rebellious display. He insisted that Schiller attend to his medical duties and submit any poetry he contemplated publishing to him for approval. Forced to choose between a career with the duke and poetry, Schiller fled Württemberg and took up a post as resident playwright in Mannheim.

The succeeding years saw Schiller struggling to make a living. Indeed, struggle of various sorts was a leitmotif of Schiller's life: a fact of life that became an existential principle. Things tended not to come easily to him. He was undoubtedly a genius, but he lacked the effervescent facility that often attends the character of genius. His was a divided, introspective nature. In this he differed markedly from Goethe, whom he met in 1788 and cordially envied and, at first, disliked. Goethe returned the wariness, if not the envy. But in time, the two became friends, literary collaborators, and joint representatives of cultural earnestness—two species of romantic who had mutated into the maturity of classicism.

Schiller later enshrined the difference between Goethe and himself in his essay *On Naïve and Sentimental Poetry* (1795), one of his best known works. (Thomas Mann called it "the greatest of German essays.") In his view, he and Goethe between them divided the world. "Poets," he wrote,

> will either *be* nature, or they will *seek* lost nature. From this arises two entirely different modes of poetry which, between them, exhaust and divide the whole range of poetry.

Naïve poets—Homer was the great model and, in his own day, Goethe—were at one with nature and the world: their poetry was realistic, affirmative. Poets he called "sentimental"—by which Schiller meant self-reflective, not cloyingly emotional—were metaphysical latecomers. For them all poetry was a form of elegy: a rehearsal of loss, rupture, distance. Schiller's entire literary output—his critical essays as well as his poetry and drama—forms an illustration of what he meant by *sentimentalische*.

In 1789 Schiller went to Jena to become a professor of history: an appointment that gave him a position but meager financial support. He embarked on a popular history of the Thirty Years War and, in 1790, married Charlotte von Lengenfeld. Like many others, he watched with enthusiasm and then horror as the French Revolution unfolded and the Terror took hold. Although delicate, Schiller always drove himself mercilessly. In 1791, his health collapsed, apparently from pneumonia exacerbated by overwork. He never fully recovered. It is interesting to consider whether, had he enjoyed Goethe's robust health, he might have enjoyed Goethe's ease of temperament. Bodily vigor may not always yield what Schiller described as a "naïve" sensibility, but its lack certainly renders such simplicity difficult. Goethe once observed that "If a man is to write poetry, he must have a certain good-natured love for the Real." But a good-natured love for the real is much easier to come by when the real in its treats one good-naturedly.

When Schiller became ill, a ministering angel arrived in the form of a pension from two admirers of his work, Prince Friedrich Christian and Count Ernst von Schimmelmann, German Danes. Schiller used the freedom his new sinecure provided to throw himself into the study of Kant. The *Critique of Pure Reason* had appeared in 1781—by a nice coincidence, the same year that *The Robbers* was printed—followed by Kant's treatise on ethics, the *Critique of Practical Reason*, and, in 1790, the *Critique of Judgment*, his book on aesthetics and teleology. It was a fateful intellectual encounter, about the effects of which Schiller himself, like many of his commentators, came to regard with a deep ambivalence.

At the end of 1799, Schiller moved to Weimar. For the remaining five years of his life he was enormously productive. New plays followed in quick succession—*Maria Stuart, The Maid of Orleans, The Bride of Messina, William Tell*, and, at the end, the fragmentary *Demetrius*. In 1802, he received a patent of nobility, and could henceforth style himself von Schiller. By the time of his death, in 1805 at the age of forty-five, his literary reputation in Germany was second only to that of Goethe's. During his final illness, someone asked Schiller how he felt: "calmer and calmer" was the reply. It was a quietus he richly deserved.

In Germany, Schiller, like Goethe, is still a cultural institution, a living presence. In the English-speaking world he has receded to being little more than an occasion for academic lucubration. Many people know that he wrote the "Ode to Joy" that Beethoven set as the finale of his Ninth Symphony, but few have actually read his poems. Some of his plays—*The Robbers, Don Carlos*, the trilogy *Wallenstein* (for many readers, his masterpiece)—are occasionally read; every now and then one is performed; but far better known is the plot of his late play *William Tell* because it formed the literary basis for Rossini's opera. Philip Toynbee was not quite right when he remarked that "the English have never . . . been very much interested in Schiller. . . . We know that he *must* be a great writer, but we find it hard to respond to his fervent sublimities." At one time, the English responded heartily indeed to those fervent sublimities. Largely through the mediation of Coleridge, Schiller became an important source for English Romanticism. It has been shown, for example, that Wordsworth's famous definition of poetry as "emotion recollected in tranquillity" has its source, via Coleridge, in a phrase from Schiller.

Schiller was a strange mixture, half-poet, half-philosopher, total idealist, a sort of Germanic Shelley with less money and more fastidious morals. (Schiller once spoke of himself in a letter as an intellectual *Zwitterart,* a hermaphrodite, a remark that doubtless will form the basis of some Ph.D. thesis in "queer theory" before long.) Schiller described himself as an amateur when it came to philosophy. But it was part of his *sentimentalische* nature to crave for his poetry the imprimatur of philosophical authority. What effect this had on his art is a matter of contention. A common reaction is Erich Heller's: "Friedrich Schiller is the name of a poetical disaster in the history of German literature, a disaster, however, of great splendour." Schiller's addiction to the ideal opened up a gulf that no art could adequately fill.

At the same time, his meditations on the importance of art and the aesthetic dimension of experience are among the most evocative and influential ever penned. It is perhaps a dubious honor, but René Wellek was right that Schiller's writings about art "proved to be the fountainhead of all later German critical theory." Although the essay *On Naïve and Sentimental Poetry* is probably his most admired single piece, his short book *On the Aesthetic Education of Man* is undoubtedly his most influential critical work.† Its influence has been both broad and deep.

---

† The most readily available English translation of *Aesthetic Education* is the somewhat daunting scholarly edition by Elizabeth M. Wilkinson and L. A. Willoughby, published in 1967 by Oxford University Press under their Clarendon Press imprint. Wilkinson and Willoughby were nothing if not thorough. Their edition begins with an introduction of some one hundred and fifty pages, about half again as long as Schiller's text. They print their translation with Schiller's German on facing pages, and follow up with a seventy-page commentary, a thirty-page glossary, and four appendixes: one about the

Hegel's whole notion of dialectical progress owes an immense amount to Schiller's treatise. (It was Schiller, for example, who first used the fateful term *aufgehoben* in the paradoxical Hegelian sense of "simultaneously cancelled yet preserved.") And later thinkers, from Nietzsche and Karl Marx to Herbert Read, Georg Lukács, and Herbert Marcuse were in their various ways deeply indebted to the conception of aesthetic freedom that Schiller articulates in *Aesthetic Education*. Marx's fantasy about "unalienated labor" owes a great deal to Schiller's warning about man becoming "merely the imprint of his occupation," while, in *Eros and Civilization*, Marcuse explicitly invokes Schiller's book when he sets forth his extravagant scenario in which art "invokes a tabooed logic—the logic of gratification as against that of repression."

WOULD SCHILLER have liked serving as a prop for a radical reading of Freud? I doubt it, but intellectual influence exercises no control over its beneficiaries. Not that Schiller's influence has been confined to the Left (though it is perhaps most conspicuous there). On the contrary, his insistence on the irreducible nature of aesthetic experience, and his linking of aesthetic with moral freedom, and his

---

history and original publication of the book, one about previous translations, one devoted to schematic illustrations of Schiller's argument ("visual aids"), and the last "On the Impulse to Introduce Redundant Negatives Into Letter XXVI" (an impulse they bravely resist). The editors also provide a twelve-page bibliography and two indexes (names and key concepts). The Wilkinson-Willoughby edition is a monument to scholarly industry: erudite, informative, supererogatory. Anyone interested in *On the Aesthetic Education of Man*, will want to consult it. Most people wishing simply to read the book will be happy to find a copy of Reginald Snell's translation, published by Frederick Ungar in 1954, but now out of print.

celebration of ornament and the free play of the imagination have deeply impressed thinkers from the other side of the ideological spectrum.

SCHILLER PUBLISHED *On the Aesthetic Education of Man* in 1795, shortly before *On Naïve and Sentimental Poetry*. Both first appeared in installments in Schiller's short-lived magazine *Die Horen*. The book—an extended essay, really —is in the form of a series of letters addressed to Schiller's patron Friedrich Christian. Like Schiller himself, *Aesthetic Education* is an exotic hybrid: part philosophical reflection, part moral exhortation, part poetic effusion. Written during the Terror, as Schiller was revising his opinions about the French Revolution, it has a deliberate political dimension. (Schiller called the letters his "profession of political faith.") In part, Schiller hoped that the success of aesthetic education would help establish the freedom that political revolution had conspicuously failed to achieve.

The essay bears the stamp of many influences. From the art historian Johann Winckelmann came an idealized portrait of classical Greece as the embodiment of human and aesthetic perfection. From the philosopher Johann Fichte came some characteristic muddiness about the ideal man expressing itself in the state. From Rousseau came some back-to-nature comments about the dangers that civilization poses to spontaneity. From Goethe, Schiller fashioned his image of the ideal artist. ("You will find in these letters," he wrote to Goethe in 1794 when he was finishing the essay, "a portrait of yourself.") There are traces of Lord Shaftesbury's ideas about the universal nature of social feeling and his friend Johann Herder's ideas about art. But far and away the greatest intellectual influence on the book was the philosophy of Kant. *On the Aesthetic Education of Man* is at once a digest, an homage, and a response to Kant's theories about the nature of aesthetic experience and its relation to moral freedom.

"Tantalizing" is not a word most people associate with the work of Immanuel Kant. But the first half of the *Critique of Judgment*, which deals with the nature of aesthetic judgment, is full of tantalizing observations. Kant saw that the appeal of aesthetic experience was strikingly different from the appeal of sensory pleasure, on the one hand, and the satisfaction we take in the good, moral or practical, on the other. For one thing, with both sensory pleasure and the good, our satisfaction is inextricably bound up with *interest*, which is to say with the existence of whatever it is that is causing the pleasure. When we are hungry, a virtual dinner will not do: we want the meat and potatoes. It is the same with the good: a virtual morality is not moral. But things are different with aesthetic pleasure. There is something peculiarly disengaged about aesthetic pleasure. When it comes to our moral and sensory life, we are constantly reminded that we are creatures of lack: we are hungry and wish to eat, we see the good and know that we fall short. But when we judge something to be beautiful, Kant says, the pleasure we take in that judgment is ideally an "entirely disinterested satisfaction."

The great oddity about aesthetic judgment is that it provides satisfaction without the penalty exacted by desire. This accounts both for its power and for its limitation. The power comes from the feeling of wholeness and integrity that a disinterested satisfaction involves. Pleasure without desire is pleasure unburdened by lack. The limitation comes from the fact that, unburdened by lack, aesthetic pleasure is also unmoored from reality. Precisely because it is disinterested, there is something deeply subjective about aesthetic pleasure: what we enjoy is not an object but our state of mind. Kant spoke in this context of "the free play of the imagination and the understanding"—it is "free" because it is unconstrained by interest or desire.

It is a curious fact that in his reflections on the nature of aesthetic judgment Kant is only incidentally interested in art. The examples of "pure beauty" he provides are notoriously trivial: sea shells, wall paper, musical fantasies, architectural ornamentation. But Kant was not attempting to provide lessons in art appreciation. He was attempting to explain the mechanics of taste. It is not surprising that the *Critique of Judgment* became an important theoretical document for those interested in abstract art: on Kant's view, the purest beauty was also the most formal.

THERE IS, however, another side to Kant's discussion of beauty. This has to do with the moral dimension of aesthetic judgment. If the pleasure we take in the beautiful is subjective, Kant argued, it is nonetheless not subjective in the same way that sensory pleasure is subjective. You like your steak well-done, I like mine rare: that is a mere subjective preference. But when it comes to the beautiful, Kant observes, we expect broad agreement. And this is because we have faith that the operation of taste—that free play of the imagination and understanding—provides a common ground of judgment. We cannot *prove* that a given object is beautiful because the point at issue is not the object but the state of mind it occasions. Nevertheless, Kant says, "we woo the agreement of everyone else, because we have for it a ground that is common to all." Judgments about the beautiful are in one sense subjective, but in another sense they exhibit our common humanity. The feeling of freedom and wholeness that aesthetic experience imparts is thus not merely private but reminds us of our vocation as moral beings. In this context, Kant famously spoke of beauty as being "the symbol of morality" because in aesthetic pleasure "the mind is made conscious of a certain ennoblement and elevation." Thus it is that although taste is "the faculty of judging an object. . . . by an entirely disinterested satisfaction" it is also "at bottom a faculty for judging the sensible illustration of moral ideas."

It would be paltering with the truth to say that Kant's discussion in the *Critique of Judgment* is crystal clear. But it is certainly suggestive. It is rather like what he calls "aesthetical ideas," i.e., products of the imagination "which occasion much thought, but to which no definite concept is adequate." Schiller found Kant's discussion electrifying. In *On the Aesthetic Education of Man*, he endeavored to develop Kant's hints about the link between beauty and freedom, between aesthetic experience and moral fulfillment, into an educational program.

Schiller's basic idea is that, rightly understood, aesthetic experience is not a matter of merely private delectation but has a civilizing function as well. It is part of the human condition that we find ourselves torn between conflicting impulses, between reason and desire, duty and inclination, our purposes as individuals and as members of a community. There is much about the modern world, Schiller thought, that exacerbates those conflicts. The progress of science has yielded rich dividends for our understanding of the world, but it has also encouraged our analytical powers at the expense of our sensuous powers. The demands of specialization make it increasingly difficult to achieve a sense of wholeness in life. This is where the aesthetic comes in. By encouraging the "enlarged mode of thought" that Kant spoke of, aesthetic experience promises to heal these rifts and provide a vision of wholeness.

Schiller places much more emphasis on "the fine arts"—especially the "immortal examples" of classical art—than did Kant, who looked first of all to nature for examples of pure beauty. But like Kant, Schiller dilates on the curious duality of aesthetic experience. He noted that

> beauty gives no individual result whatever, either for the intellect or for the will; it realizes no individual purpose, either intellectual or moral; it discovers no individual truth, helps us perform no individual duty, and is, in a word, equally incapable of establishing the character and enlightening the mind.

For anyone who places an explicit moral burden on art, Schiller's view will be unacceptable. John Ruskin, for example, castigated this passage as "that gross and inconceivable falsehood."

Ruskin might have been somewhat mollified had he read on. For Schiller argues that although in one sense beauty yields nothing definite, in another sense "it is to be looked upon as a condition of the *highest reality*." The aesthetic alone, Schiller writes, "is a whole in itself." "Here alone, he wrote, "do we feel ourselves snatched outside time, and our humanity expresses itself with a purity and integrity as though it had not yet experienced any detriment from the influence of external forces." Of course that heady experience carries with it dangers of its own. If Schiller champions the humanizing power of aesthetic experience he also warns us against aestheticism: against using the "soul-captivating power" of beauty in the "interest of error and injustice." Precisely because aesthetic experience is disinterested experience, he notes, it involves "a dangerous tendency to neglect all reality entirely and to sacrifice truth and morality to an attractive façade."

Schiller's book is a very rich stew. As he acknowledges, when he waxes philosophical he often presents a path that is "not very exhilarating." Nor is it an entirely consistent path. On the one hand, Schiller speaks of the aesthetic as that which leads us from the life of sensuous appetite to the life of moral freedom. In this sense aesthetic education is a step on the road toward moral self-realization. On the other hand, he speaks of the aesthetic as a realm of experience that mediates between the moral and the physical, resolving the tension between them in a higher unity that is both physical and moral, sensuous and intellectual. In this sense, aesthetic education is an end in itself: an experience of freedom that relates "to the totality of our various functions without being a definite object for any single one of them."

Schiller does not really resolve this tension. Yet in one sense the tension underscores Schiller's point: that the aesthetic both points the way towards freedom and is itself an instance of freedom. These elements come together in his description of the aesthetic attitude as a playful attitude, an attitude that delights in appearance for its own sake. Schiller notes that "extreme stupidity and extreme intelligence have a certain affinity with each other, that both seek only the real and are wholly insensible to mere appearance." The serious things in life call for our commitment and intervention; beauty calls us to play. But this play is not frivolous. On the contrary, aesthetic play betokens "a real enlargement of humanity and a decisive step toward culture" because it affirms our humanity in its totality.

"What sort of phenomenon is it," Schiller asked, "that proclaims the approach of a savage to humanity? . . . [I]t is the same in all races who have escaped from the slavery of the animal state: a delight in *appearance*, a disposition toward *ornament* and *play*." The aesthetic simultaneously elevates the sensuous man and softens or cultivates the intellectual. "The reality of things is the work of nature, the appearance of things is the work of man, and a nature that delights in appearance is no longer taking pleasure in what it receives, but in what it does." By cultivating a "disinterested free appreciation of pure appearance"—of seeing and hearing for their own sakes—we not only distance ourselves from the pressures of everyday reality but also affirm ourselves as creatures of freedom: creatures who play.

As the critic Lesley Sharpe observed, Schiller's book on aesthetic education "can be regarded as the supreme statement of faith in the power of human creativity to heal and to restore to wholeness." It is a faith that history has sorely challenged. One thinks, for example, of those Nazi commandants who relaxed from their labors in the camps by listening to Haydn and Mozart. Or think of the preposterous spectacle afforded by contemporary culture, for which art is more often an excuse for pathology or political activism than aesthetic cultivation.

Nevertheless, the nobility of Schiller's vision remains. It challenges us to affirm ourselves in our totality, which means in our incapacity and weakness as well as our strength. Schiller was everywhere at pains to stress the limits as well as the advantages of the aesthetic. "Man shall *only play* with Beauty," he wrote, "and he shall play *only with Beauty*." If, as Schiller puts it, we are only fully human when we are playing, we are only truly playing when we understand the limits of aesthetic play. The ideal of the beautiful is "the most perfect possible equilibrium of reality and form." One of the chief lessons of aesthetic education is that this ideal must remain always only an ideal, something we approximate, never achieve. Another way of putting this is to say that for man, an inextricably finite creature, wholeness is always partial and beauty is always imperfect.

One of the ironies of Schiller's career is that he understood but refused to embrace this truth. Schiller was suspicious of idealism—well, of what he called false idealism. But there is a strong current of idealistic sentiment in his sensibility. Toward the end of 1795, he wrote to Wilhelm von Humboldt about his vision of the ideal. "Everything that is mortal is dissolved, nothing but light, nothing but freedom . . . no shadow, no barrier. . . . It makes me giddy to think of this task: . . . to compose a scene on Olympus. . . . I may do it one day when my mind is wholly free and cleansed from the pollution of the real world." Of course, that day will never come. That, indeed, was one of the main lessons of Schiller's letters on aesthetic education.

The Difficulty With Hegel

Philosophy need not trouble itself about ordinary ideas.
—G. W. F. Hegel, *Philosophy of Nature*

He described what he knew best or had heard most, and felt he had described the universe.
—George Santayana, on Hegel

Philosophers are hardly ever cynical manipulators of their readers' minds. They do not produce delusions in others, without first being subject to them themselves.
—David Stove, "Idealism: a Victorian Horror-story (Part One)"

HEGEL, Bertrand Russell observed, is "the hardest to understand of the great philosophers." Hegel would not have liked very much that Russell had to say about his philosophy in *A History of Western Philosophy* (1945). Russell's exposition is a classic in the library of philosophical demolition, much despised by Hegel's admirers for its vulgar insistence on common sense. (Best line: that Hegel's philosophy "illustrates an important truth, namely, that the worse your logic, the more interesting the consequences to which it gives rise.") But I am not at all sure that Hegel would have disagreed with Russell's comment about the difficulty of understanding him. He knew he was difficult. He was always going on about the "labor of the negative," the superficiality of mere common sense, and the long, "strenuous effort" that genuinely "scientific" (i.e., Hegelian) philosophy required. It is even said that on his deathbed Hegel declared that there was only one man who had understood him—and he had misunderstood him.

I first came across that *mot* in Søren Kierkegaard's *Concluding Unscientific Postscript* (1846), another anti-Hegelian salvo, quite different from Russell's. Neither Kierkegaard nor his editors supply a source for the observation, and Terry Pinkard, in *Hegel: A Biography* (Cambridge University Press, 2000) sniffily describes it as an "apocryphal story," "emblematic of the anti-Hegelian reaction that quickly set in" after the philosopher's death in 1831.

I was sorry to learn that. Like many people who have soldiered through a fair number of Hegel's books, I was both awed and depressed by their glittering opacity. With the possible exception of Heidegger, Hegel is far and away the most difficult "great philosopher" I have ever studied. (Kant is plenty difficult, but with Kant one feels that the difficulty has, so to speak, a bottom.) There was much that I did not understand in Hegel. I secretly suspected that no one—not even my teachers—*really* understood him, and it was nice to have that prejudice supported by words from the master's own lips.

Is it worth the effort? I mean, you spend a hundred hours poring over *The Phenomenology of Spirit* (1807)— widely considered to be Hegel's masterpiece—and what do you have to show for it?† The book is supposed to take

---

† I suspect that at least part of the success of Hegel's book was due to its title, which combines the edifying (*Geist*, spirit) with the recherché (phenomenology). What exactly is a *phenomenology* of

you from the naïve, "immediate" (*unmittelbar*, a favorite Hegelian term of contempt) position of "sense certainty" all the way to Absolute Knowledge, "or Spirit that knows itself as Spirit."

That sounds pretty good, especially when you are, say, eighteen and are busy soaking up ideas guaranteed to mystify and alarm your parents. But what do you suppose it means? Pinkard notes that at Jena in the early 1800s, "Hegel seemed to inspire two kinds of reaction: he was either highly admired and even idolized, or he was disparaged." In fact, Hegel's work has always inspired these opposite reactions, throughout his lifetime and afterwards. Pinkard, who teaches philosophy at Georgetown University and who has written several other books about Hegel, is firmly in the admirers' camp. I am not.

What Pinkard has given us with his book on Hegel is partly an intellectual biography, partly an outline of Hegel's work. Recognizing that some of his readers will be more interested in Hegel's life than in detailed discussions of his ideas (and vice versa), he has done his best to segregate the story of Hegel's life and intellectual formation from the book reports. He corrects some misconceptions. For example, I had always thought that Hegel died

---

spirit? The term "Phänomenologie" was coined by the eighteenth-century German scientist J. H. Lambert, who used it to mean the study of the illusory aspects of experience. As Pinkard points out, Hegel took the term from Kant, who with his distinction between "phenomena" (stuff we experience) and "noumena" (stuff we cannot experience), gave it a new twist. Just as biology is the "logos" or study of life ("bios"), so "phenomenology" is the logos or study of "appearances" (from the Greek *phenomena*, "things that appear"). Hegel's "phenomenology of spirit," then, attempts to describe the unfolding appearances of self-consciousness from its dawn to its full maturity.

of cholera when an epidemic of that disease swept through Berlin in 1831. Not so, says Pinkard. What Hegel really died of was "most likely . . . some kind of upper gastrointestinal disease." Good to know that. And like almost every sympathetic commentator on Hegel I have read, Pinkard sternly points out that the one thing everyone remembers about Hegel's philosophy—that it says reality develops according to a process of "thesis/antithesis/synthesis"—is actually nowhere to be found in Hegel's writings. It was in fact a shorthand devised by a "deservedly obscure" professor called Heinrich Moritz Chalybäus. The popularity—could it be the clarity?—of that formula seems to incense Hegelians. Pinkard argues that it "misrepresents the structure of Hegel's thought," though I have to say that readers who encounter Hegel's description of "the movement" in which thought "becomes estranged and then returns to itself from estrangement, and is only then presented in its actuality and truth" might be forgiven for making the same mistake.

Pinkard does an adequate job—not more than that, I'd say. He is clearly in command of the material, biographical as well as philosophical and historical; he has all the right quotations from Kant and Fichte, Hegel's primary philosophical inspirations; he provides astute summaries of contemporary events and controversies. Nevertheless his presentation is plodding and curiously repetitious. How many times, for example, do we need to be reminded that Hegel was excessively fond of wine—he had good taste in claret, which is something—and of playing cards? How often do we need to be told that he had the nickname "old man" when he was at school?

All this is part of Pinkard's effort to humanize Hegel. But he is also careful to preserve Hegel from seeming *too* human. In 1829, the composer Felix Mendelssohn (who had studied with Hegel) organized a performance of Bach's St. Matthew Passion in Berlin, an event that was instrumental in reviving Bach's reputation, then in eclipse. Hegel, who was in his late fifties at the time, attended the performance and a dinner party following. Therese Devrient, the wife of one of the soloists, arrived late and was squeezed into a seat between Mendelssohn and Hegel, whom she had not met. "He continually tried to talk me into drinking some more wine," Devrient complained later,

> and to fill my glass, which I declined. He unrelentingly gripped my furthermost lace sleeve "in order to protect it!," as he put it . . . In short, he so annoyed me with his gallantrics that I turned to Felix and asked: "Tell me who this dimwit beside me is." Felix held his handkerchief over his mouth and then whispered: "The dimwit there beside you is the famous philosopher, Hegel."

Recounting this story in *The Daily Telegraph*, the journalist Daniel Johnson comments: "Thus the Zeitgeist enjoyed a joke at the expense of its prophet, whose contribution to this genuinely world-historical event was to lower the tone from the sublime to the lecherous."

Pinkard duly reproduces this story, and notes that Hegel's "mannerisms vis-à-vis women" sometimes gave offense. "Mannerisms"? In Pinkard's account, the philosopher is a courtly old gent rather than a tipsy lecher. Hegel, Pinkard writes, "liked playing the role of a 'gentleman of the old order' and apparently was oblivious to just how his affectations were being received." Perhaps. Or maybe it was less a matter of Hegel's affectations than his unwanted attentions—an undialectical difference that even a non-philosopher may be expected to grasp. Pinkard also exhibits some unfortunate verbal tics. He is overly fond of the word "alienation," for example, a popular Hegelian-Marxoid epithet. When the young Hegel spends Wednesdays and Saturdays at the library instead of at home, it is a sign of the "alienation he felt as a teenager"—that sort of thing.

One problem for Pinkard is that Hegel's life was really not eventful enough to support a graceful biography of nearly eight hundred pages. Born in Stuttgart in 1770 (the same year as Beethoven, Wordsworth, and his friend Hölderlin), Hegel came of age in the period of high Romanticism. His philosophy, which everywhere betrays a hankering after the infinite, is very much an expression of Romantic longing, a fact that Pinkard both registers and manages to discount. In his early years, Hegel was a model student. But by the time he got to the theological institute at Tübingen in 1788 (where he roomed with Hölderlin and, beginning in 1790, with Schelling), Hegel had begun to chafe under the yoke of established authority and hidebound pedagogy. Bertrand Russell remarked that Hegel was attracted to mysticism when young and that his mature philosophy was "an intellectualizing of what had first appeared to him as mystic insight." If you look at Hegel's philosophy, that seems plausible, though Pinkard gives no evidence for "mystic insight" in the young Hegel. What is true, I think, is that in Hegel we see a theological student who became disenchanted with theology but could not see his way clear to dispensing with the aura of profundity that theology offered. The result was the attenuated theology of Hegelian idealism, in which the Absolute stands in for God.

HEGEL LIVED in tumultuous times. The French Revolution was one contemporary "world-historical" event that fired his imagination. The other was the career of Napoleon. Hegel was at Jena, teaching and finishing the *Phenomenol-*

ogy of Spirit, when Napoleon came through in 1806. (Though Pinkard points out that it is not true, as Hegel suggested in a letter, that the book was completed on the eve of the Battle of Jena.) Like many Romantics, Hegel worshipped power, and in Napoleon ("this extraordinary man, whom it is impossible not to admire") he saw power incarnate. When the emperor rode through town, Hegel wrote excitedly to a friend that he had seen "the world-soul . . . astride a horse."

But what did Hegel *do*? He was a private tutor, headmaster at a high school, briefly the editor of a provincial newspaper, and for most of his career a university professor: at Heidelberg from 1816 to 1818, and then at Berlin until his death. Although he became a great celebrity at Berlin, Hegel's lecturing style was not universally admired: students not susceptible to his spell, Pinkard tells us, complained that he began every third sentence with "therefore." One note of drama came in 1807 when Hegel fathered an illegitimate child, named Ludwig, with his landlady. Pinkard notes that after Hegel was married (in 1811) and had two other sons, he arranged for Ludwig to live with his family. It ended badly. Ludwig wished to study medicine, but Hegel refused to pay for his education. (In general, it seems that he treated Ludwig as a second-class citizen.) Ludwig broke with the family around 1826, commenting that "I always lived in fear but never in love of my parents." Pinkard deals fairly with the story of Ludwig in his text but, curiously, there is no sign of the child in the index, either in his own right or as an episode in Hegel's life. Under "Hegel, Georg Wilhelm Friedrich," we find entries for everything from "beer" to "napping on sofa," but nothing under "illegitimate child" or "Ludwig." A very Hegelian sense of priorities.

The tone and embonpoint of Pinkard's book suggest that

with Hegel we are dealing with a figure of the first importance. It is a common feeling, among academics. Another
commentator on Hegel, J. N. Findlay, spoke for many
when he said that Hegel was, "without doubt, the Aristotle
of our post-Renaissance world." (Findlay also said that
Hegel's personality was "characterized by an almost
English sobriety and good sense," a remark that surely
casts suspicion on *his* good sense.) For my own part, I
believe that when you finish working your way through
Hegel what you have are two things: some deep if scattered
insights about philosophy, art, and society, on the one
hand, and acquaintance with—often contamination by—
one of the most powerfully obfuscating philosophical
methodologies ever devised. (In fairness, I should add that
you also have at least one profound witticism. Reflecting
on the saying that "No man is a hero to his valet," Hegel
replied, "But not because the hero is not a hero, but because the valet is a valet.") I am perfectly happy to acknowledge that Hegel was a genius. But so what? That
doesn't mean he was right. It doesn't even mean that he
was intelligible. As the English essayist Walter Bagehot observed in another context, "In the faculty of writing nonsense, stupidity is no match for genius."

Hegel wrote a great deal of nonsense. He did not do it
on purpose. Arthur Schopenhauer, one of Hegel's bitterest
enemies, was right to complain about "the stupefying influence of Hegel's sham wisdom." (No one under the age
of forty, he thought, should read Hegel: the danger of intellectual corruption was too great.) But I believe that
Schopenhauer was wrong to attribute mystifying *motives*
to Hegel. He may have been, as Schopenhauer also said, a
"charlatan," but Hegel was a sincere charlatan. He said a
lot of loopy things: about knowledge, about nature, about
history. He believed them all.

Kierkegaard saw something essential about Hegel when he noted that Hegel and his philosophy "constitute an essay in the comical." Hegel, Kierkegaard said, was like a man who had built a palace but lived in the guard house. His elaborate "System" of philosophy promised to chart the necessary development not only of consciousness but also of world history and even of nature—indeed, for Hegel, there were no hard and fast distinctions to be drawn among these realms. On the first page of his preface, Pinkard plaintively asks how it is that Hegel "came to be so badly misunderstood." That is one question I think I can help him answer. Item: "A rational consideration of Nature," Hegel wrote in his *Philosophy of Nature*,

> must consider how Nature is in its own self this process of becoming Spirit, of sublating its otherness—and how the Idea is present in each grade or level of Nature itself: estranged from the Idea, Nature is only the corpse of the Understanding. Nature is, however, only implicitly the Idea, and Schelling therefore called her a petrified intelligence . . . ; but God does not remain petrified and dead; the very stones cry out and raise themselves to Spirit.

Which leaves us—where? Between a rock and a hard place, anyway. All but Hegel's most abject admirers are (at least secretly) embarrassed by his philosophy of nature. It takes a strong man to read, for example, that "the antithesis that has gone back into itself is the earth or the planet as such," etc., without blanching. A peek into that part of Hegel's oeuvre is the quickest way to highlight Kierkegaard's point: the discrepancy between pretension and achievement is like Falstaff's dishonesty: "gross as a mountain, open, palpable." The formidable difficulty of Hegel's writings might make it seem that one must be extensively trained in philosophy to answer him effectively. But this, Kierkegaard wrote, "is by no means the case. All that is needed is sound common sense, a fund of humor, and a little Greek ataraxy [tranquillity]." Of course, it is not without irony that those homely things—common sense, humor, and tranquillity—may be in even shorter supply these days than the sort of dialectical prowess that playing with Hegel's philosophy requires.

The real issue for Kierkegaard was the place of the individual in this grand chronicle purporting to recapitulate—nay, to *be*—Spirit's self-unfolding. (There is a worrisome ambiguity running through all of Hegel's work: does he believe that his philosophy is *reporting* on its subject matter—logic, world history, self-consciousness, whatever—or does he thinks his philosophy somehow *is* its subject matter?) The problem is that the individual seems to get lost in the process. Kierkegaard saw the unintended comedy of a system picturing the development of self-consciousness in which the self in any recognizable form is shuffled off rather early. Yes, Hegel constantly assures us that each "stage" or "moment" of development is simultaneously *cancelled* and yet *preserved* as Spirit progresses. This after all is the famous dialectical process whereby each level of development is said to contain its opposite and is *aufgehoben*.

There is, I am happy to say, no English equivalent for that participle. It is usually translated as "sublated."† What this Hegelian philosopher's stone means is that you can eat

† The word is the gift of a clever translator who remembered that *sublatum* was the perfect passive participle of the Latin verb *tollo*, which means both "to raise up" or "preserve" and "to take away," "remove," "destroy." A very Hegelian sort of word, *tollo*.

your contradiction and have it too. "The essence of each thing," Hegel wrote in his *Lectures on the History of Philosophy*, "lies in determination, in what is the opposite of itself." Let's think about that statement for a moment. If the essence of X is not-X, what then? Nothing good, of that much we can be sure. Is the essence of truth falsehood? Is the essence of goodness evil? A deconstructionist might argue that way in earnest, but no sane person would. The embarrassing fact is that Hegel's dialectic is a universal cognitive solvent. It licenses epistemological anarchy. It makes a hash of logic. And generalized to an attitude toward life and society, it can be made to underwrite any excess. The philosopher Leszek Kolakowski underscored the sober truth of the matter: "We must finally conclude that in the Hegelian system humanity becomes what it is, or achieves unity with itself, only by ceasing to be humanity."

So why read Hegel? For one thing, he has startling flashes of insight—about the nature of modernity, the relationship between the state and civil society, the self-enchantments of freedom. Hegel's encyclopedic brilliance makes for a thrilling intellectual adventure. Hegel really *is* deep. He is also muddy. His work, the philosopher Roger Scruton observed, is "like a beautiful oasis around a treacherous pool of nonsense, and nowhere beneath the foliage is the ground really firm." It may be worth visiting, but both the going and the getting back are treacherous. Many who make the journey never return.

A second reason to read Hegel has to do with that treacherousness. Just as doctors learn a lot about health by studying diseases, so we can learn a lot about philosophical health by studying Hegel. As Russell noted, Hegel "epitomized better than anyone a certain kind of philosophy." It wasn't, Russell thought, a good kind of philosophy—he believed that "almost all of Hegel's doctrines are false"—

but it vividly illustrated the mental consequences of looking at the world in the peculiar way that Hegel's philosophy teaches us to. Plutarch, we saw, occasionally dwelt upon defective characters in order to appreciate noble ones more fully. Similarly, Hegel's stupendous philosophical fantasia can serve as a salutary admonition about what happens if you begin by assuming that "The essence of each thing . . . lies . . . in what is the opposite of itself."

A third reason to read Hegel is his influence, which everybody—foe as well as friend—admits was enormous. "No philosopher since 1800," Walter Kaufmann wrote in his 1965 appreciation of Hegel, "has had more influence." That influence took several different directions, of which I will mention three. In the first place, Hegel's writings, especially the *Phenomenology* and the *Philosophy of Right* (1820), were a definitive influence on the philosophy of Karl Marx and, through him, on Lenin and Stalin and on Marxism in general. It is true that Marx devoted many pages to criticizing Hegel's philosophy. But he firmly embraced Hegel's view of history as a realm of ineluctable dialectical progress—progress, that is to say, which is *necessary*, i.e., inevitable, and which proceeds by continuous negation. As the philosopher Louis Dupré put it, Marx accepted the method of Hegel's philosophy while discarding its content. One often hears that Marx attempted to "stand Hegel on his head." What Marx actually said (in *Capital*) was that Hegel's idealism left his dialectic "standing on its head. It must be turned right side up again, if you would discover the rational kernel within the mystical shell."

Just how "rational" Marx's appropriation of Hegel turned out to be, we now know. The murderous legacy of Marxism cannot be laid at Hegel's door—except, perhaps, insofar as Hegel's philosophy unfits the mind for exercising serious criticism. (It is a nice detail that the Russian-born French philosopher and civil servant Alexandre Kojève, whose famous Paris seminar on the *Phenomenology* in the 1930s and 1940s made such a deep impression on figures from André Breton and Georges Bataille to Raymond Aron, Maurice Merleau-Ponty, and Jacques Lacan, should have turned out to be a KGB spy.) Marx never tired of excoriating Hegel for his "mystification." Quite right, too. But Marx took on board a particularly noxious piece of mystification when he swallowed Hegel's dialectic—an intellectual monstrosity that, as Santayana noted in *Egotism in German Philosophy*, presupposes the preposterous effort of "making things conform to words, not words to things."

Hegel's admirers hate that sort of criticism. It seems downright philistine to point out that the idea of one thing "containing" (or "positing," as Hegel liked to say) its opposite is really just a piece of verbal legerdemain. That is exactly the sort of thing your man in the street, someone who hadn't had the benefit of reading Hegel, would say. But then Hegel has always been especially popular among people whose entire livelihood is bound up with verbal legerdemain—I mean academic professors of philosophy. Whatever else can be said about Hegel, he is the professor's ideal philosopher. He has been extremely helpful in keeping the mills of academic industry grinding away. Not only does the inherent difficulty of his books guarantee a virtually endless stream of work—Hegel's philosophy cries out for academic commentary, the more the better—but also his view of the universe was calculated to be deeply gratifying to academic philosophers. After all, his philosophy puts them and their profession at the very apex of creation. Artists have an intuitive grasp of the Absolute, Hegel thought; in religion, one is "*implicitly* reconciled with the divine Being"; but it is only with philosophy that

Spirit achieves "the supreme freedom and assurance of its self-knowledge." This, Hegel tells us, "is not a presupposition of study; it is a *result* which happens to be known to myself because I already know the whole." Convenient, that, if you happen to be a professor of philosophy.

Finally, Hegel has been immensely influential on the development of post-Kantian idealism. What is idealism? It is the contention that thought makes or (better, because more portentous) "constitutes" reality. Pinkard speaks of Hegel's "supposedly 'idealist'" philosophy, but that is much too modest. Hegel's brand was the real McCoy. Idealism exercises a variety of attractions. For one thing, it is deeply flattering to its proponents, because it suggests that reality is in some obscure way dependent on them. (Hence Santayana's charge of "egotism," which he defined as "subjectivity in thought and willfulness in morals.") Idealism also, as the philosopher David Stove pointed out, offers a steady diet of religious consolation while simultaneously pretending to take it away. The basic procedure is quite simple. You begin be denying you are an idealist. As Stove observed in his essay "Idealism: a Victorian Horror-story (Part One),"

> In every idealist manual after Kant, the first lesson is the same: *kick Berkeley.* This is sure to start things off on the best possible footing, by engaging your readers' common sense on your side. This way, you cut off their retreat, and you can then torment them at your leisure, about how, although the universe is *of course* thought, it is not, indeed, *your* thought, or my thought, or even everybody's thought. It is objective, or public, or Absolute, Thought.

Hegel was a supreme master at this sort of thing. In the long preface to the *Phenomenology*, for example, he early on tells his readers that "philosophy must beware of the wish to be edifying." He castigates his immediate pre-cursors—Kant, Fichte, Schelling—for getting everything wrong (Schelling's idea of the Absolute, Hegel memorably said, was "cognition naïvely reduced to vacuity," a "night in which all cows are black"). Fortunately, Hegel himself has seen the light. We know this because he tells us so himself. "What I have set myself to do is to help bring philosophy closer to the form of Science, to the goal where it can lay aside the title '*love* of knowing' and be *actual* knowing."

Fair enough, you say. "Science," "*actual* knowing": that all sounds eminently worthwhile. Thank God Hegel is not some crazy Berkeleyan who thinks that "to be is to be per-ceived" or whatever. But exactly what does Hegel mean by "science," by "*actual* knowing"? Perhaps the following passages will clear things up. The first is from the preface to the *Phenomenology*, the second from its last chapter:

> The True is the whole. But the whole is nothing other than the essence consummating itself through its development. Of the Absolute it must be said that it is essentially a *result*, that only in the *end* is it what it truly is; and that precisely in this consists its nature, *viz.* to be actual, subject, the spontaneous becoming of itself. Though it may seem contradictory that the Absolute should be conceived essentially as a result, it needs little pondering to set this show of contradiction in its true light. The beginning, the principle, or the Absolute, as at first immediately enunciated, is only the universal.

> Spirit . . . has shown itself to us to be neither merely the withdrawing of self-consciousness into its pure inwardness, nor the mere submergence of self-consciousness into sub-stance, and the non-being of its difference; but Spirit is *this movement* of the Self which empties itself of itself and sinks itself into its substance, and also, as Subject, has gone out of

that substance into itself, making the substance into an object and a content at the same time as it cancels this difference between objectivity and content. . . . Spirit, therefore, having won the Notion, displays its existence and movement in this ether of its life and is *Science* (*Wissenschaft*).

"Science," eh? Just about every commentary in English about Hegel has a portentous paragraph or two advising readers that the German word *Wissenschaft* embraces so much more than the paltry English word "science." The implication is that *Wissenschaft* is something finer, deeper, more spiritual than mere "science." But Hegel's inflation of the word *Wissenschaft* reminds us that it can also be something much *less* than science. Among other things, it shows the extent to which Hegel's thought is imbued with the aroma of religiosity—religion so to speak "sublated" into the frightful patois of philosophical idealism. In the introduction to his *Lectures on the Philosophy of World History*, Hegel assures readers in one breath that of course "the universal spirit or world spirit is not the same thing as God. It is the rationality of spirit in its world existence. Its movement is that it makes itself what it is, i.e., what its concept is." We must be thankful for that clarification. But in the same work he tells us that philosophy has demonstrated that "Reason . . . is both substance and infinite power, in itself the infinite material of all natural and spiritual life as well as the *infinite form*, the actualization of itself as content. . . . the True, the Eternal, the Absolute Power and that it and nothing but it, its glory and majesty, manifests itself in the world." Amen.

Hegel is also an acknowledged expert at another maneuver, the art of the philosophical thunderclap, what Stove describes (in the second of his two essays on idealism) as "reasoning from a sudden and violent solecism."

Say or imply, for example, that in English "value" means the same as "individuality." You can be miles down the track of your argument before they get their breath back.

This method is not only physiologically but ethologically sound. Of course it should never be used *first*. You need first to earn the respect of your readers, by some good reasoning, penetrating observations, or the like: *then* apply the violent solecism. Tell them, for example, that when we say of something that it is a prime number, we mean that it was born out of wedlock. You *cannot* go wrong this way. Decent philosophers will be so disconcerted by this, that they will never do the one thing they should do: simply say, "That is NOT what 'prime number' means!" Instead, they will *always* begin . . . [by] casting about for an *excuse* for someone's saying what you said, or a half-excuse, or a one-eighth excuse; nor is there any danger that they will search in vain. And with this, not only is your philosophy of arithmetic launched, but you have already got other people working for you, free of charge, at its development.

Hegel is full of philosophical thunderclaps. It is difficult for most of us not to be discommoded when we read, in Hegel's *Science of Logic* (1812–1816), that "logic must certainly be said to be the supernatural element which permeates every relationship of man to nature." But when we get to his discussion of the syllogism and read that "not only is the syllogism rational, but *everything rational is a syllogism*," the only healthy response is panic.

It is probably unfair to pick on Hegel's *Logic*. The book really has very little to do with the discipline of the same name. Let us turn instead to one of the most profound and widely admired passages in Hegel, the celebrated "master/slave dialectic" in the *Phenomenology*. This section has made a deep impression on thinkers from Marx to Francis

Fukuyama. It describes the way that we come to recognize and deal with the fact of other people, other self-consciousnesses. According to Hegel, self-consciousness exists "only in being acknowledged." Like Rodney Dangerfield, it is not complete in itself but demands the respect, the recognition of the other. This, Hegel says, leads to a struggle for recognition, a contest that quickly escalates to a life-or-death struggle:

> They must engage in this struggle, for they must raise their certainty of being *for themselves* to truth, both in the case of the other and in their own case. And it is only through staking one's life that freedom is won; only thus is it proved that for self-consciousness, its essential being is not [just] being, not the *immediate* form in which it appears, not the submergence in the expanse of life, but rather that there is nothing present in it which could not be regarded as a vanishing moment, that it is only pure *being-for-self*. The individual who has not risked his life may well be recognized as a *person*, but he has not attained to the truth of this recognition as an independent self-consciousness. Similarly, just as each stakes his own life, so each must seek the other's death, for it values the other no more than itself.

Gee. Does this sound like anyone you know or have ever heard of—excluding, that is, current or potential guests of your local penal establishment or madhouse? I know, I know: that is a terribly vulgar question. After all, Hegel is not talking about you or me; he is talking about the necessary unfolding of self-consciousness as it struggles into a recognition of its own freedom on the pitiless stage of world history, etc. If you find *that* convincing, I submit, then you have the makings of a true Hegelian.

Of course, the master/slave dialectic is Hegel at his most

dialectically nimble. It might be better to start, as he does, with simple sense certainty. At the beginning of the *Phenomenology*, Hegel tries to unsettle some of our most basic ideas about what counts as knowledge.

> To the question: "What is Now?," let us answer, e.g., "Now is Night." In order to test the truth of this sense-certainty a simple experiment will suffice. We write down this truth. A truth cannot lose anything by being written down. . . . If *now, this noon*, we look again at the written truth we shall have to say that it has become stale.
>
> The Now that is Night is *preserved*, i.e., it is treated as what it professes to be, as something that *is*; but it proves itself to be, on the contrary, something that is *not*. . . . This self-preserving Now is, therefore, not immediate but mediated; for it is determined as a permanent and self-preserving Now *through* the fact that something else, *viz.*, Day and Night, is *not*.

What should we think of this argument? Badly, anyway. It threatens to destabilize the meaning of some perfectly good words by, so to speak, falsely existializing them. *Of course* "now" refers to one thing at noon and another at midnight; knowing that is part of knowing what "now" means. If at noontime someone said to Hegel, "George, bring me that book now," and he waited until night to do it because, after all, that was when he had inscribed the word "now" on a piece of paper, we wouldn't think him clever.

Hegel treats us to a parallel argument about "here."

> The *Here pointed out*, to which I hold fast, is similarly a *this* Here which, in fact, is *not* this Here, but a Before and Behind, an Above and Below, a Right and a Left. . . . The Here, which was supposed to have been pointed out,

vanishes in other Heres, but these likewise vanish. What is pointed out, held fast, and abides, is a *negative* This, which *is* negative only when the Heres are taken as they should be, but, in being so taken, they supersede themselves.

All of which means—what? That the word "here" refers to different things depending on what the user of the word intends? Is that news?

Hegel is one of two authors who makes it into the subtitle of this book. He has a lot to say about the "dialectic of sense certainty." But the other author in my subtitle, though briefer about the subject than Hegel, is not notably less illuminating. At the beginning of P. G. Wodehouse's story "The Crime Wave at Blandings," Lady Constance bursts into her brother's library to complain that their niece has become infatuated with an inappropriate young man. "Apparently," she moans, "they have been corresponding regularly, and now the man is here."

"Here?"
"Yes."
"Where?" asks Lord Emsworth, gazing in an interested manner about the room.

Well, by "here" Lady Constance meant "at the inn in the village," but it takes the boneheaded peer a moment to grasp that. Most readers of Wodehouse are not so slow on the uptake, hence the humor in Lord Emsworth's confusion. The crucial point is this: that part of learning language is learning the *limits* of language—grasping what it cannot tell us as well as what it can. How much philosophy operates by selectively ignoring this distinction?

Let me conclude with another literary illustration. On my desk when I wrote this essay was *Big and Little: A Book of*

Opposites by Richard Scarry, a very different sort of philosopher from Hegel. It recounts in vivid detail the exploits
of Hilda the hippo, Squeaky the mouse, and many other
admirable characters. Our son, *aetat.* two at the time, had
absorbed the difference between big and little, now and
then, here and there, without once positing the negative or
mediating the immediate. I asked him about what Hegel
said and he just laughed. Whom would you trust?

Almost everyone who reads very far into Hegel is struck
by his famous observation, in the preface to the *Philosophy
of Right*, that "The rational is the actual and the actual is
the rational." Hegel's sympathetic commentators keep telling us not to worry, that although it might seem more or
less equivalent to a cynical defense of the status quo
("Whatever is, is right"), really, in its *true determination*, it
doesn't mean that. But how can you tell? Hegel presents
his system as the very incarnation of freedom. But, as Russell noted, what Hegel describes is "a very superfine brand
of freedom. It does not mean that you will be able to keep
out of a concentration camp. It does not imply democracy,
or a free press." Why should it? If the "essence of each
thing lies . . . in what is the opposite of itself," then let's
face it, anything goes. In *The Science of Logic*, Hegel
remarks in passing on the advantages of German as a language for philosophy. "Some of its words," he observes,
"even possess the further peculiarity of having not only
different but opposite meanings so that one cannot fail to
recognize a speculative spirit of the language in them."
That "speculative spirit" is at the very center of Hegel's
philosophy. It implies a kind of verbal intoxication in
which reality is subordinated to unanchored cogitation. At
one point in the *Phenomenology*, Hegel defines "the True"
as "the Bacchanalian revel in which no member is not
drunk." He wasn't kidding.

Schopenhauer's Worlds

THOMAS MANN was in his early twenties—and in the middle of writing *Buddenbrooks*—when he first read Schopenhauer. The intoxicating effect of "drinking that metaphysical magic potion," he recalled years later, "can only be compared with the one which the first contact with love and sex produces in the young mind." For Mann, as for so many writers and artists of his generation, the discovery of Schopenhauer was nothing less than a revelation, a new way of looking at the world and one's place in it. From *Buddenbrooks* and *Death in Venice* to *The Magic Mountain* and *Doctor Faustus*, Mann's work exhibits the stamp and spirit of Schopenhauer's influence, and it is only natural that he named Schopenhauer, together with Nietzsche and Wagner, as one of "the three great Germans who were the shapers of my nature."

Nietzsche and Wagner paid similar homage to Schopenhauer. The young Nietzsche, in *Schopenhauer as Educator*, the third of his *Untimely Meditations*, wrote that "I am one of those readers of Schopenhauer who when they have read one page of him know for certain that they will go on to read all the pages and will heed every word he ever said." Though Nietzsche later repudiated Schopenhauer's romantic pessimism as "decadent," he never denied the formative impact that Schopenhauer had on his own thinking, and he continued throughout his career to extoll him as a model of intellectual independence and honesty. Many of Nietzsche's central philosophical ideas—his doctrine of the will to power, his distinction between the Apollonian and Dionysian—derive largely from Schopenhauer. And Wagner, in his autobiography, recalled the excitement of his first encounter with Schopenhauer's work: "Schopenhauer's book [*The World as Will and Representation*] was never completely out of my mind, and by the following summer I had studied it from cover to cover four times. It had a radical influence on my whole life."

By the turn of the century, such tributes to Schopenhauer's influence were commonplace, especially among artists and writers. Schopenhauer had become an inescapable cultural force, his philosophy epitomizing the mood—at once extravagantly febrile, even enervated, yet bursting with creativity—of *fin de siècle* Europe. Indeed, it may be said that Schopenhauer provided a systematic vocabulary for those distinctively modern feelings, perceptions, experiences that were to transform the artistic and intellectual life of the West from the 1870's to the end of the First World War.

Schopenhauer published the first edition of his major work, *The World as Will and Representation*, in 1818, but it was not until the 1850's, when he was in his sixties, that his work began to exercise any real influence. No doubt the widespread disillusionment that followed in the wake of the revolutions of 1848 helped pave the way for the triumph of his relentlessly disillusioning philosophy, particularly among the young. As one commentator noted, Schopenhauer's book is

bound to appeal to an adolescent who has lost his religious

faith and is looking for something to replace it. For while Schopenhauer recognizes "man's need for metaphysics," he insists that it is neither necessary nor possible for an intelligent person to believe in the literal truth of religious doctrines. To expect that, Schopenhauer says, would be like asking a giant to put on the shoes of a dwarf.

Schopenhauer's atheism and evolutionism, his insight into the unconscious and irrational dimension of human nature, his assertion of the primacy of sexuality, his apotheosis of art and aesthetic experience as a *compensation* for life: these were the features of Schopenhauer's thought that answered to the age's impatience with Enlightenment optimism and its naïve trust in reason and science, its faith in inevitable progress and the perfection of man.

Yet despite Schopenhauer's once colossal presence, his influence declined steadily through the Twenties and Thirties. By 1938 Mann could write in his essay on Schopenhauer that he was attempting "to evoke a figure little known to the present generation." And while there is no question of Schopenhauer's attaining anything like his former stature—the novel elements of his teaching have been too completely assimilated by conventional wisdom for that to happen—Bryan Magee convincingly argued in his study of Schopenhauer (Oxford University Press, 1983) that there are "unmistakable signs of a serious revival of interest." No doubt the renewed interest in *fin de siècle* culture—one thinks, for example, of popular studies like Carl Schorske's *Fin de Siècle Vienna* or Allan Janik and Stephen Toulmin's *Wittgenstein's Vienna*—is in part responsible for the revival of interest in Schopenhauer that Magee discerns. But it is also the case, as Magee argued, that the current disenchantment with positivism—as much in art and literary studies as in philosophy—has helped kindle a renaissance of interest in Schopenhauer not only as a cultural influence but also as a thinker in his own right.

It is appropriate that Schopenhauer, who despised the academy and academic philosophy, should find as a contemporary champion a decidedly non-academic man of letters. A Member of Parliament and author of books on Karl Popper, modern British philosophy, and Wagner, Magee sets out in *The Philosophy of Schopenhauer* to provide an introduction to Schopenhauer's thought and an overview of his influence. As such, he has succeeded in producing the most comprehensive work in English on Schopenhauer since Patrick Gardiner's *Schopenhauer* (1963). Magee not only outlines his philosophical system but also reminds us of how crucial an ingredient in *fin de siècle* cultural life Schopenhauer was. It is no exaggeration to say that many of the leading figures of that time—including Wittgenstein and Freud—cannot be understood without some appreciation of their debt to Schopenhauer.

MAGEE'S BOOK opens with a biographical sketch and then proceeds to review the philosophical tradition out of which Schopenhauer emerged. It offers a reasonably thorough exposition of his main philosophical writings, concentrating on *The World as Will and Representation*. Magee goes *seriatim* through each of the four parts of that book, treating in turn Schopenhauer's epistemology, his metaphysics, his theory of art, and his ethics. He concludes with some criticisms and a long series of appendices—they come to more than a third of the book—that investigate various extra-philosophical issues, such as Schopenhauer's relation to Buddhism, and detail Schopenhauer's profound influence on thinkers and artists from Nietzsche and Wagner to Tolstoy, Proust, Conrad, and Mann. The only significant omission here concerns Schopenhauer's considerable influence on the visual arts—one thinks of the patently Schopenhauerian pronouncements of the *Blaue Reiter* group, for example, or of the work of Gustav Klimt, or the writings of Giorgio de Chirico—which Magee has left out of his account.

Magee has thus assembled a great deal of material, and most students of Schopenhauer will find it a useful, if not especially original, synopsis of his philosophy as well as a handy compilation of facts about his life and influence. In many respects the biographical introduction and the appendices are the most valuable parts of the book. For example, Magee points out that the oft-noted similarity between Schopenhauer's philosophy and Buddhism is not—as is usually held—a result of Buddhism's *influence* on Schopenhauer. On the contrary, Schopenhauer had formulated the central tenets of his philosophy well before he became acquainted with Eastern texts. The important thing was that he arrived at such similar insights independently, for in his mind this argued for the fundamental truth of the ideas in question.

But while Magee displays an impressive command of Schopenhauer's *oeuvre,* the book is not without serious problems. The more strictly philosophical portions of his text—his discussion of Schopenhauer's philosophical precursors, his explication of transcendental idealism, even his understanding of Schopenhauer's doctrine of the will—are neither rigorous nor reliable. And there is the additional question of whether a secondary source, however competent, really provides the best introduction to Schopenhauer's philosophy. Schopenhauer himself wrote with such clarity and verve—his model is said to have been Hume— that his own works remain the best and most accessible entree to his thought. One may disagree with a lot that Schopenhauer has to say, but one is seldom at a loss to understand *what* he is saying, a claim that one would hesitate to make for many of his philosophical compatriots.

Schopenhauer is famous above all for his pessimism. As Magee shows, the philosopher's biography supplies ample support for this dimension of his thought. Schopenhauer's father died, apparently by his own hand, when Schopenhauer was in his teens. Young Arthur then joined the prosperous family firm as his father had wished, but he found it stifling and soon left to devote himself to learning. "Life is a wretched business," he remarked around this time, "I've decided to spend it trying to understand it." In 1813, Schopenhauer completed his doctoral dissertation and moved to Weimar, to live with his mother, a socially ambitious woman who had achieved considerable renown for her romantic novels. It was here, in Johanna Schopenhauer's fashionable *salon,* that the young Schopenhauer became friendly with Goethe and other literary and artistic figures. Unfortunately, relations between mother and son were at the best of times cool, and now they broke down completely. "She threw him out altogether in the spring of 1814," Magee writes, "and they never saw each other again during the remaining twenty-four years of her life."

After this debacle, Schopenhauer moved to Dresden, where he spent the next four years writing *The World as Will and Representation.* He published it with great expectations and was bitterly disappointed when it went virtually unnoticed. Then, after an extended stay in Italy, Schopenhauer moved to Berlin and made his single bid for a university teaching career. In a characteristically defiant gesture, he deliberately scheduled his lectures at the same time that Hegel—who was then at the pinnacle of fashion but whose philosophy Schopenhauer detested—had scheduled his. The consequence was that no one came and the class had to be cancelled. Yet Schopenhauer's amalgam of stubbornness, courage, and intellectual independence—together with the financial independence that he had inherited—enabled him to persevere with his philosophy in the face of almost total neglect. He continued to refine and elaborate his system, bringing out a second, greatly-expanded edition of *The World as Will and Representation* in 1844.

Important influences on Schopenhauer's thought include elements of Plato's philosophy and British empiricism, but his chief philosophical debt is to Kant, in his estimation "the most important phenomenon which has appeared in philosophy for two thousand years." All the same, Schopenhauer's deeply empirical cast of mind and curiosity about the natural world made him an oddity in the dominant strain of post-Kantian German philosophy. His "unmistakable, almost physical, rootedness in lived thought and experience," as Magee puts it, shows itself as much in the style of his philosophizing as in the substance of his teaching. It also remarkably prefigures the novelties —substantive as well as stylistic—usually attributed to American pragmatism. And given his lapidary prose style and Romantic pessimism, it is perhaps not surprising that Schopenhauer would come to exercise a more pervasive influence on the arts and, through Freud, on psychology than on philosophy. For the wellspring of Schopenhauer's influence lies not in any technical innovation in epistemology—which since Descartes has been the chief interest of most professional philosophers—but in his re-evaluation of the irrational and unconscious elements of man's nature, in his doctrine of the will.

Adapting Kant's distinction between phenomena and things-in-themselves, Schopenhauer divided the world into a realm of interconnected, knowable *representations* and an essentially unfathomable *will*. In his view, man is not primarily a *"rational* animal," "thinking substance," or

"person"—as the traditional epithets would have it—but an
animal, a creature of will. In a figure that strikingly anticipates the insights of Freudian psychology, Schopenhauer
compares the human mind to a body of water. Conscious
ideas are on the surface, but the depths consist of "the indistinct, the feelings, the after-sensation of perceptions and
intuitions and what is experienced in general, mingled with
the disposition of our own will that is the kernel of our
inner nature." Reason, the intellect, far from being a
"pilot" that guides man's will, is a mere servant of the will,
a technician that discovers ways to expedite the will's direc-
tives. "For consciousness," Schopenhauer insisted,

> is conditioned by the intellect, and the intellect is a mere
> accident of our being, for it is a function of the brain. The
> brain, together with the nerves and spinal cord attached to
> it, is a mere fruit, a product, in fact a parasite, of the rest of
> the organism, in so far as it is not directly geared to the
> organism's inner working, but serves the purpose of self-
> preservation by regulating its relations with the external
> world.

Schopenhauer thus inverts the traditional, rationalistic
image of man, inaugurating an intellectual revolution that
looks forward to Darwin (*On the Origin of Species* was
published in 1859) and modern evolutionary theory. As he
wrote in the second volume of *The World as Will and
Representation*,

> all philosophers before me, from the first to the last, place
> the true and real inner nature or kernel of man in the
> *knowing* consciousness. Accordingly, they have conceived
> and explained the I, or in the case of many of them its
> transcendent hypostasis called soul, as primarily and essen-

tially *knowing*, in fact *thinking*, and only in consequence of this, secondarily and derivatively, as *willing*. . . . My philosophy . . . puts man's real inner nature not in consciousness but in the will.

It is important to note that by "will" Schopenhauer did not mean primarily "free will." In Schopenhauer's view, our will speaks first of all with the immediacy of feelings, moods, desires—especially sexual desire—not in deliberate reasoning or conscious motives. And, as Magee rightly stresses, Schopenhauer sees human willing as merely one expression of the unfathomable procreant urge that animates all nature. If his reader were to reflect on the inexplicable urgings of his own will, writes Schopenhauer, he would recognize that

> the force that shoots and vegetates in the plant, indeed the force by which the crystal is formed, the force that turns the magnet to the North Pole, . . . and finally even gravitation, which acts so powerfully in all matter, pulling the stone to earth and the earth to the sun; all these he will recognize as different only in the phenomenon, but the same according to their inner nature. He will recognize them all as that which is immediately known to him so intimately and better than everything else, and where it appears most distinctly is called *will*.

Schopenhauer describes the will as "the thing-in-itself," the "inner content" or "essence" of the world. An endless and ultimately purposeless striving, the will shows itself as much in the pull of gravity or the germination and growth of plants as in man. In most of the will's manifestations, then, the question of "intentions" does not arise.

But Magee misses Schopenhauer's point when he suggests

that the term "force" or "energy" would have been preferable to the term "will." Schopenhauer insists on calling the fundamental animating principle of the world "will" (*Wille*) precisely because our understanding of the dynamic reality of nature is rooted in the immediate, intuitive grasp we have of our own dynamic reality as striving, wanting, lacking creatures, as creatures of will. Reading ourselves into nature, we extend the name of the reality we know best to the reality of the external world. "I therefore name the genus after its most important species," Schopenhauer explains, "the direct knowledge of which lies nearest to us, and leads to the indirect knowledge of all the others."

According to Schopenhauer, it is the body that, through mood, feeling, perception, individuates man and roots his experience in the dimension of the will. For we experience our body not only as "representation," as one object among others, but also as the locus of our needs and desires, as the theater of the will. And it is just this bodily relation to the will that accounts for the *weight* or *significance* that we attach to our experience. For if we were purely knowing creatures—"winged cherub[s] without a body," as Schopenhauer put it—then we would view the world completely disinterestedly, as a series of representations that had no real claim on us. Nothing would move or attract or frighten us. But as bodily, willing creatures, the world continually impinges on us. And since we never get to the bottom of the will, we never get to the bottom of experience. Reality, including our own reality, remains in this sense an inexhaustible mystery, ever capable of surprising us. "We often do not know what we desire or fear," Schopenhauer observes in another passage that reminds us of Freud:

For years we can have a desire without admitting it to ourselves or even letting it come to clear consciousness, because the intellect is not to know anything about it, since the good opinion we have of ourselves would inevitably suffer thereby. But if the wish is fulfilled, we get to know from our joy, not without a feeling of shame, that this is what we desired.

At the center of Schopenhauer's philosophy is the contention that man's bondage to the will is just that, a bondage. "*Willing,*" he writes, "springs from lack, from deficiency, and thus from suffering." And because we are essentially will, we are essentially needy, essentially lacking. Every apparent satisfaction gives way to boredom or fresh desire. "No attained object of willing can give a satisfaction that lasts and no longer declines," Schopenhauer muses,

> it is always like the alms thrown to the beggar, which reprieves him today so that his misery may be prolonged till tomorrow. Therefore, so long as our consciousness is filled by our will, so long as we are given up to the throng of desires with its constant hopes and fears, so long as we are the subject of willing, we never obtain lasting happiness or peace.

But the foundation of Schopenhauer's gloomy diagnosis of the human condition does not lie in his doctrine of the will alone. Rather, it lies in the combination of that doctrine with his insistence that the only true satisfaction is a satisfaction that "lasts and no longer declines," a satisfaction beyond the vagaries of time. Together, they are ultimate source of his pessimism and his view of human life as tragic. For while Schopenhauer rejects the traditional view that locates man's essential nature in reason, he continues to embrace the traditional Platonic-Christian identification of happiness with completeness, with a final release from all striving.

In his most accomplished chapter, "The Flower of Existence," Magee shows that Schopenhauer's high estimation of art and aesthetic experience follows directly from his view of man as a prisoner tormented by a relentless, insatiable will. In Schopenhauer's view, aesthetic experience offers not a *satisfaction* of willing, but a momentary release from the will's demands. Providing an oasis from time in time, aesthetic experience, he writes, "raises us out of the endless stream of willing, and snatches knowledge from the thralldom of the will . . . . for the moment we are delivered from the miserable pressure of the will. We celebrate the Sabbath of the penal servitude of willing; the wheel of Ixion stands still." Schopenhauer thus follows Kant in his understanding of aesthetic experience as essentially will-less, disinterested experience. Momentarily suspending the claims of desire or interest, aesthetic experience pleases by intimating a completeness denied to us as creatures inextricably submerged in time. Disinterested, we are exempt from the imperatives of desire and the will; we are, for the moment, free.

But the episodic nature of aesthetic experience renders it incapable of providing any lasting solution to the problem of the will. For Schopenhauer—and it is here that he is close to the teaching of Buddhism—genuine salvation lies only in the definitive renouncing of the will and the emancipation from the will's imperatives. Just how this is to be accomplished remains somewhat obscure. Schopenhauer claims that the renunciation of the will "does not proceed directly from the will, but from a changed form of knowledge." Yet such emancipatory insight does not come about through any effort on the part of the individual; it is not by an act of will that the will is overcome. Rather, Schopenhauer writes, it is something akin to "what the Christian mystics call the *effect of grace*."

WHAT SCHOPENHAUER proposes is less an emancipation *of* life than an emancipation *from* life. Yet the renunciation of the will he envisions has exerted such an irresistible fascination on so many artists, writers, and thinkers because it promises to relieve one of individuality, of the burden of having to be oneself. What aesthetic experience adumbrates the renunciation of the will fulfills: "we are, so to speak, rid of ourselves." Schopenhauer here gestures toward a wholeness that mere life, with its kaleidoscope of tasks, projects, and desires, can never achieve.

Of course, from any normal human perspective, the renunciation of the will is tantamount to annihilation. Schopenhauer acknowledges this. Indeed he insists upon it. "We freely acknowledge," he writes, "that what remains after the complete abolition of the will is, for all who are still full of the will, assuredly nothing. But also conversely, to those in whom the will has turned and denied itself, this very real world of ours with all its suns and galaxies, is— nothing." For Schopenhauer, meditation on the fact of death is the chief source of the philosophical attitude. "Undoubtedly," he writes, "it is the knowledge of death, and therewith the consideration of the suffering and misery of life, that give the strongest impulse to philosophical reflection and metaphysical explanations of the world." Properly understood, he believes, the fact of death leads to a devaluation of life. From *this* perspective, death appears as a form of redemption. Thus Mann's Thomas Buddenbrook, soon to confront his own demise, can stumble onto a volume of Schopenhauer, sit reading "for four hours, with growing absorption," and rhapsodize about death and the dissolution of individuality:

"What *was* Death? The answer came, not in poor, large-sounding words: he felt it within him, he possessed it. Death was a joy, so great, so deep that it could be dreamt of only in moments of revelation like the present. It was the return from an unspeakably painful wandering, the correction of a grave mistake, the loosening of chains, the opening of doors . . . . Individuality?—All, all that one is, can, and has, seems poor, grey, inadequate, wearisome.

Whatever one thinks of Schopenhauer's recommendations for redemption, they make it difficult to accept Magee's claim that his pessimism is "logically independent" of his philosophy. "Non-pessimism," he tells us, "is equally compatible with his philosophy. The traditional identification of him as a pessimist is largely irrelevant to a serious consideration of him as a philosopher." In fact, Magee here betrays a radical misunderstanding of Schopenhauer's philosophy. For according to Schopenhauer, we are *essentially* will; and since we crave a satisfaction beyond the unappeasable urgings of the will, we must deny our essence in order to achieve happiness. "Existence is certainly to be regarded as an error or mistake," he tells us, "to return from which is salvation." This is the unavoidable, deeply pessimistic, core of his teaching.

But though pessimism is inseparable from Schopenhauer's philosophical *Weltanschauung*, it is possible to credit his description of man as a creature of will without therefore subscribing to pessimism or indulging in romantic *Todesliebe*. For one thing, as Magee astutely notes, there is a "disparity between the content of what Schopenhauer said . . . and the way he said it. The content was so often negative—corrosive, sarcastic, derisive, pessimistic, sometimes almost despairing—yet the manner was always positive, indeed exhilarating." Schopenhauer's exhilarating—and often devastatingly witty—manner is one reason that his pessimism has been so attractive and influential—so, one might almost say, optimistic. For it is the *style* of Schopenhauer's pessimism that lets one understand how the young Nietzsche could endorse so pessimistic a thinker as one who exhibits "a cheerfulness that really cheers." In this respect, Schopenhauer's writing appeals to us perhaps more as art than as philosophy, affecting us, as Thomas Mann put it, "more through its passion than its wisdom."

Further, as Magee himself observes in his criticism of Schopenhauer's position, it is by no means clear that we should follow Schopenhauer in regarding the exercise of the will as something essentially negative. "We are indeed exhilarated by relief from pain or danger," Magee writes,

> but in the enjoyment of great art, or love, or friendship, there is something altogether more outgoing than this. These things involve us in a relationship with something or someone outside ourselves, a gratified extension of ourselves which is self-enhancing, and thus life-enhancing.

At bottom, though, we may also want to challenge Schopenhauer's identification of happiness with a "satisfaction that lasts and no longer declines." This in effect was what the mature Nietzsche did. In criticizing Schopenhauer's "Romanticism"—what he referred to in *Ecce Homo* as "the cadaverous perfume of Schopenhauer" —Nietzsche did not take issue with his description of man as a creature of will. For Nietzsche, too, man is will incarnate, always striving, never satisfied. But he regarded this as the challenge, not the tragedy, of human existence. The tragedy lay in man's tendency to deny himself as a creature of will, in his attempt to extricate himself from the finitude of the human condition.

Goethe, who managed to live the world-affirming philosophy that Nietzsche preached, summed it up in an admonitory couplet that he wrote for Schopenhauer when the young philosopher was leaving Weimar for Dresden in 1814:

Willst du dich des Lebens freuen,
So musst der Welt du Werth verleihen.

"If you want to delight in life, then you must grant value to the world." By making happiness incompatible with man's essence, Schopenhauer found himself deaf to Goethe's wisdom. "The world and life can afford us no true satisfaction," Schopenhauer insists, "and are therefore not worth our attachment to them." Saturated with what Nietzsche called the "rancor against time," Schopenhauer's philosophy, however fascinating, can only poison life, disparaging its real but always transitory pleasures for the dream of a will-less, timeless satisfaction that human life will never know.

What Did Kierkegaard Want?

Unfortunately, my life is far too subjunctive; would to God I had some indicative power.
—Journals, 1837

I sit and listen to the sounds in my inner being, the happy intimations of music, the deep, earnestness of the organ.
—Journals, 1843

He did not belong to reality, and yet he had much to do with it.
—Diary of the Seducer, 1843

WHAT AN IMPRESSION Kierkegaard makes when you first read him! Especially, I must add, if that first time happens to occur in adolescence. How electrifying, at that time of life, to encounter the statement "Subjectivity is truth." Perhaps you had suspected that all along. But to have it indited there in black and white in the middle of a 576-page book of philosophy called *Concluding Unscientific Postscript* is something else again. (Actually, the book is called *Concluding Unscientific Postscript to the Philosophical Fragments: A Mimic-Pathetic-Dialectic Composition, An Existential Contribution*, a deliberately parodic title that somehow makes the proposition that "Subjectivity is truth" even more impressive.)

In one way or another, the explosive idea that "subjectivity is truth" is the guiding theme in Kierkegaard's thought. In an early journal entry—written in 1835, eleven years before the *Concluding Unscientific Postscript* was published—the twenty-two-year-old Kierkegaard decided that

> What I really need is to get clear about *what I must do*, not what I must know, except insofar as knowledge must precede every act. . . . [T]he crucial thing is to find a truth which is truth *for me*, and to find *the idea for which I am willing to live and die.* Of what use would it be to me to discover a so-called objective truth, to work through the philosophical systems so that I could, if asked, make critical judgments about them, could point out the fallacies in each system; of what use would it be to me to be able to develop a theory of the state, . . . and constructing a world I did not live in but merely held up for others to see; of what use would it be to me to be able to formulate the meaning of Christianity . . . if it had no deeper meaning *for me and for my life?*

"Interpretive knowledge," he concludes, is all well and good but "*it must come alive in me* and *this* is what I now recognize as the most important of all."

This is potent stuff. "You shall know the truth," as the Gospel of St. John says, "and the truth shall set you free." We know what St. John had in mind. But how about Kierkegaard? In fact, he never really specified what he meant by "subjectivity is truth." Perhaps the closest he came was this "definition" in the *Concluding Unscientific Postscript*: "*An objective uncertainty held fast in the appropriation-process of the most passionate inwardness is the truth*, the highest attainable truth for an *existing* individual." How helpful is that? And more to the point, does it really describe *truth*?

Education is (or used to be) about getting *beyond* a private or subjective point of view and looking at things dispassionately, disinterestedly, objectively. And here comes a certified Great Thinker to tell you that what really counts is not dispassionateness but, on the contrary, *passion*. What our mediocre, bourgeois society needs, Kierkegaard says again and again, is more passion. In *The Present Age* (1846), he wrote that

> our age is essentially one of understanding and reflection, without passion, momentarily bursting into enthusiasm, and shrewdly relapsing into repose. . . . Nowadays not even a suicide kills himself in desperation. Before taking the step he deliberates so long and so carefully that he literally chokes with thought. It is even questionable whether he ought to be called a suicide, since it is really thought which takes his life. He does not die *with* deliberation but *from* deliberation.

How far is Kierkegaard willing to press the claims of passion against reason? Apparently all the way. "If you will understand me aright," he explains in *Either/Or* (1843), his first major work, "I should like to say that in making a choice it is not so much a question of choosing the right as of the energy, the earnestness, the pathos with which one chooses." Really?

Of course, that statement, like the statement "Subjectivity is truth"—like, indeed, many of Kierkegaard's most piquant observations—was delivered not by S. Kierkegaard himself, but by a pseudonym. Kierkegaard deployed a variety of pseudonyms as part of his program of "indirect communication." Seeking not so much to impart knowledge as to dispel illusion, Kierkegaard saw himself as a sort of spiritual therapist. The world around him, he thought, was both complacent and deluded. His aim was to unsettle the complacency by unmasking the delusion. But there was no point in trying to reason with people who thought they had the truth. One had to trick them into seeing their spiritual poverty by clever literary stratagems.

> A direct attack only strengthens a person in his illusion, and at the same time embitters him. There is nothing that requires such gentle handling as an illusion, if one wishes to dispel it. If anything prompts the prospective captive to set his will in opposition, all is lost. And this is precisely what a direct attack achieves.

Thus Kierkegaard set about trying to "deceive people into the truth," a goal that he strove to reach not directly, through reasoned argument, but indirectly, through the semi-fictional discourse of his pseudonyms.

Kierkegaard eventually acknowledged the authorship of his pseudonymous works, but early on he took considerable pains to cover his tracks. He dealt with his printer through a third party. And although he was working practically around the clock in the mid-1840s, he would drop into the theater every night for five or ten minutes at intermission to foster his reputation as an idler-about-town, too frivolous to write books. Part of the fun in reading Kierkegaard is seeing how his various personae play off and criticize one another. But the fact that something is said by one of Kierkegaard's pseudonyms rather than *in propria persona* does not mean we can discount it. Kierkegaard used pseudonyms not only to dissimulate about the essentials of his thought but also to express them. Pseudonymity, as one commentator has observed,

159

was in Kierkegaard's hands a means of exposure as well as of concealment. Most of the really radical statements uttered by Kierkegaard's pseudonyms—"subjectivity is truth," for example—represent ideas that Kierkegaard himself endorsed.

Or endorsed most of the time. Kierkegaard was a deliberately slippery thinker, fearless when it came to contradiction. If he regularly touted the claims of passion against the dictates of reason, he also cautioned against misinterpreting "all my talk about pathos and passion to mean that I intend to sanction every uncircumcised immediacy, every unshaven passion."

That is a welcome concession. It is difficult, however, to know what to make of it. Leave aside the embarrassing question of what the tonsorial arts have to do with "immediacy" or passion. (The New Testament speaks about the "circumcision of the heart": what do you suppose a "circumcised immediacy" would look like?) The plain truth is that Kierkegaard never bothered to specify the conditions under which he thought pathos and passion justified a particular decision.

In *Fear and Trembling* (1843), one of his most famous books, Kierkegaard asks whether there is such a thing as a "teleological suspension of the ethical." That is a polysyllabic way of asking whether certain individuals are exempt from the moral strictures that bind the rest of us. Kierkegaard clearly thought, or hoped, that there were such individuals, individuals whose exceptional nature or religious calling put them beyond the claims of ordinary ethical commandments. Indeed, it is pretty clear that he believed he was one such exceptional individual.

Kierkegaard enlists the biblical story of Abraham and Isaac to illustrate his point. In order to test Abraham's allegiance, God tells him to take Isaac, his only son, and offer him up as a sacrifice. This Abraham sets out to do. He is just about to deliver the fatal blow when an angel stays his hand. God spares Isaac at the last moment. But what about Abraham? "Either," Kierkegaard wrote, "Abraham was every minute a murderer, or we are confronted by a paradox which is higher than all mediation."

Kierkegaard never actually comes right out and says "Abraham was exempt from the moral law; it would have been okay for him to murder Isaac." But he raises that possibility in a tantalizing way. Indeed, *Fear and Trembling* is a literary and rhetorical *tour de force*. Whatever Kierkegaard's readers conclude about Abraham, they come away dazzled, entertaining the thought—half flattering, half frightening—that, being individuals themselves, perhaps they, too, deserve to be exceptions to the moral law.

Part of Kierkegaard's effort in *Fear and Trembling* is to remind us that important ethical choices can rarely be made by rational calculation alone. They almost always involve a non-rational element, what Kierkegaard famously called a "leap," even a leap "by virtue the absurd." If he overstated things, well, Kierkegaard specialized in a certain kind of overstatement. (He liked to refer to his work as a "corrective": going too far in one way because people had gone too far in the other.) In fact, what impresses one most about Kierkegaard is the pathos and passion he brought to his defense of pathos and passion. It was a performance designed to make the whole process of raising objections seem niggling and small-minded: we're talking about life here, not logical nicety! That, anyway, is how many people respond on a first reading.

Which is to say that Kierkegaard's reputation rests as much upon his style as upon the substance of his thought. He was an exceptionally prolix writer. (He would have had to be: he died at forty-two, yet managed to write some

thirty-five books—most of them between 1842 and 1850—
and fill twenty-two posthumously published volumes of
journals.) He was also an unusually exuberant writer, by
turns gripping, caustic, and sentimental. He could be extremely funny: "All men are bores," he wrote in "The
Rotation Method" (a key essay in *Either/Or*).

> Surely no one will prove himself so great a bore as to con-
> tradict me in this. . . . The gods were bored, and so they
> created man. Adam was bored because he was alone, and
> so Eve was created. Thus boredom entered the world, and
> increased in proportion to the increase of population.
> Adam was bored alone; then Adam and Eve were bored
> together; then Adam and Eve and Cain and Abel were
> bored *en famille*; then the population of the world in-
> creased, and the peoples were bored *en masse*. To divert
> themselves they conceived the idea of constructing a tower
> high enough to reach the heavens. This idea is itself as
> boring as the tower was high, and constitutes a terrible
> proof of how boredom gained the upper hand.

Kierkegaard was very astute on the subject of boredom.
He understood "the curious fact that those who do not
bore themselves usually bore others, while those who bore
themselves entertain others." He also understood that
boredom could be far more than a passing mood of name-
less dissatisfaction. In Kierkegaard's view, boredom is essentially a spiritual malaise, endemic wherever a purely
naturalistic conception of man holds sway. Hence he
defines boredom as "the daemonic side of pantheism." On
a good day, the pantheist sees a god in every rock and
celestial beacon: reality seems brimming with significance.
But boredom has the power to undercut that emotion of
repletion. It is the dark side of a life devoted to amuse-

ment, pleasure, diversion. What happens when amusement palls and pleasure fails to please? Boredom yawns before one, a paralyzing abyss. (Compare Tolstoy's definition of boredom as "the desire for desires.") "At its maximum," Kierkegaard notes elsewhere, boredom "is despair." It is part of Kierkegaard's task to show that boredom can only be defeated by moving beyond what he calls the "aesthetic" conception of life, a mode of life unleavened by moral or religious engagement.

Kierkegaard was especially good at puncturing intellectual pomposity. "Like Leporello," he wrote in his journal, "learned literary men keep a list, but the point is what they lack; while Don Juan seduces girls and enjoys himself— Leporello notes down the time, the place, and a description of the girl."

As we have seen, Kierkegaard reserved some of his best barbs for Hegel, the philosopher to whom he owed the most but whose pretensions to Absolute Knowledge (his confusion of "the logical with the existential") Kierkegaard found preposterous.

If Hegel had written the whole of his *Logic* and in the Preface disclosed the fact that it was only a thought-experiment (in which however at many points he had steered clear of many things), he would have been the greatest thinker who ever lived. As it is, he is merely comic.

Hegel, Kierkegaard wrote, was like a man who had built a palace (the great Hegelian System) but lived in the guard house (ordinary life with its slings and arrows).

Kierkegaard expended a lot of ink, especially in his journals but also in some published works, explaining what he had attempted to accomplish as a writer. (*The Point of View for My Work as an Author*, written in 1848 but published posthumously, is devoted to nothing else.) In the *Concluding Unscientific Postscript*, the pseudonymous Johannes Climacus (drawing heavily on one of Kierkegaard's own journal entries) recalls how he resolved to become an author one Sunday while strolling in the Fredericksberg Gardens in Copenhagen:

> I sat and smoked my cigar until I lapsed into thought. . . . "You are going on," I said to myself, "to become an old man, without being anything and without really undertaking to do anything. . . . [W]herever you look about you . . . you see the many benefactors of the age who know how to benefit mankind by making life easier and easier, some by railways, others by omnibuses and steamboats, others by the telegraph, others by easily apprehended compendiums and short recitals of everything worth knowing, and finally the true benefactors of the age who make spiritual existence in virtue of thought easier and easier, yet more and more significant. And what are you doing?" . . . [S]uddenly this thought flashed through my mind: "You must do something, but inasmuch as with your limited capacities it will be impossible to make anything easier than it has become, you must . . . undertake to make something harder." This notion pleased me immensely. . . . I conceived it as my task to create difficulties everywhere.

That sudden reversal, that ambition "to create difficulties everywhere," is vintage Kierkegaard. It also shows the extent to which Kierkegaard modelled his activities on one of his culture heroes, Socrates. (Not for nothing was Kierkegaard's M.A. thesis called *The Concept of Irony: With Constant Reference to Socrates*.) In *The Apology*, Socrates described himself as the gadfly of Athens. His task was to sting the consciences of his interlocutors, persuading them that their chief concern ought to be not for their bodies or possessions "but for the highest welfare of their souls." Like Socrates, Kierkegaard set about using humor, learning, satire, homiletics—the full arsenal of his rhetoric—to sting the consciences of his fellow denizens of Copenhagen.

In *Irrational Man* (1958), his book about existentialism, the philosopher William Barrett began a sympathetic essay on Kierkegaard with this passage from the *Journals*: "It was intelligence and nothing else that had to be opposed. Presumably that is why I, who had the job, was armed with an immense intelligence." Using intelligence to battle overweening intelligence: that was how Kierkegaard understood his task. From one point of view this represented a mortification of the intellect: no longer was Hegel's Absolute Knowledge the goal. No longer was reason humanity's trump card. But from another point of view Kierkegaard's intelligent opposition of intelligence can be seen as a perfection of the intellect. Kierkegaard clearly placed himself in the (heterodox) tradition of *credo quia absurdum*: "I believe because it is absurd." Is this excessively hard on reason? Probably. But if Kierkegaard was right that "paradox" is "the source of the thinker's passion" and the supreme paradox "is the attempt to discover something thought cannot think" (two large *if*s, admittedly), then his entire campaign can be understood as a vindication of the intellect in its highest vocation—in Kierkegaard's eyes, to serve the dictates of a faith beyond reason.

JUST AS SOCRATES gave up reading the scientific works of Anaxagoras because they told him nothing about the fundamental ethical reality of man, so Kierkegaard repudiated the rationalism of his culture, insisting that "the real subject is not the cognitive subject . . . [but] the ethically existing subject." In this sense, as Barrett notes, Kierke-

gaard's motivation was essentially religious, not philosophical. "He never aimed at being a philosopher and all
his philosophy was indeed incidental to his main purpose,
to show what it means to be a Christian."

Given Kierkegaard's emphasis on decision, passion, and
the individual, it is not surprising that his own formative
decisions—the determining passions of his life, his personal
contests to salvage individuality—should have stamped
themselves so thoroughly on his work. To an unusual extent, Kierkegaard's biography is implicated in his teaching.
It's a story that has been told many times. The first biography in English (1938) was by the indefatigable Walter
Lowrie, the pious gent who was smitten by Kierkegaard,
translated or helped translate many of his works, and introduced him to an English-speaking audience.

Since then Kierkegaard has developed from a cottage
industry into a huge academic enterprise. More biographies, translations galore, studies beyond number. In a review
of a selection from Kierkegaard's journals in 1966, John
Updike wondered whether "the United States needs still
more translations of Kierkegaard." But this was *avant le
déluge*. Within a few years, Princeton had published
English translations of most of his works. Then Howard
and Edna Hong came along and proceeded to retranslate
everything into academese, replete with notes—hundreds,
in some cases thousands of them—scholarly commentaries
and page references to the Danish edition. The seven fat
volumes of Kierkegaard's *Journals* are impressive and useful. But Kierkegaard's *Edifying Discourses* became the
barbarous *Upbuilding Discourses* (just in case anyone
missed the hint of "edifice" in "edification"), a book on
"Experimental Psychology" became a book about "Experimenting Psychology," etc. Curiously, the title *Philosophical Fragments* was retained, even though *Smuler*

means "scraps" or "crumbs," not "fragments." How Kierkegaard would have savored it all! "And when I am dead,"
he wrote in 1854, "how busy all the assistant professors
will be stripping me and mine, what competition to say the
same thing, if possible, in more beautiful language."

A recent contribution to this flood is Alastair Hannay's
biography (Cambridge University Press, 2001), a competent book by a veteran Kierkegaard scholar. Is it an advance on other biographies? Hannay has a surer grasp of
philosophy than many people who write about Kierkegaard, and he has beavered away to uncover some mi-
nutiae about the master's student days. There are no
revelations. Not that one expected any; the ground is too
well trod. Kierkegaard was a tortured and tumultuous
spirit, a fascinating "case." But outwardly, his life was uneventful. He never married, had no "career" in the ordinary sense, and never ventured further from his native
Copenhagen than Berlin, which he visited three times, once
for a few months to attend lectures by Friedrich Schelling
(he wasn't impressed), twice on holiday.

BORN IN 1813, Kierkegaard was the seventh and last child
of Michael and Ane (or Anne) Kierkegaard. Michael began
life as a peasant. He grew up in the desolate heath country of Jutland, in western Denmark. He was formally in
thrall to a local priest, whose land he worked. (Hence
the name "Kierkegaard"—pronounced "Keer-ke-gore"—
which means "churchyard" or "graveyard.") At twelve, he
was sent to Copenhagen to apprentice in the clothing trade
with his uncle. This was the break he needed. Smart, industrious, and lucky, he advanced quickly. At twenty-one,
he was officially released from serfdom. He went into
business on his own and, canny about money, made a
small fortune, enough to retire at the age of forty, leaving

his business in trust to a nephew. Michael's first wife died childless after two years of marriage. Ane, who had been a servant in their house, was promoted to wife sometime after she became pregnant by Michael. "In the premarriage settlement," Hannay notes, "Ane was denied the usual inheritance and became virtually Michael's employee, with a salary and a fixed annual housekeeping budget. There was no provision for her in the event of divorce, not even custody of the child."

Michael Kierkegaard was clearly a difficult man. As one commentator put it, he ran both his business and his family with an iron rod. He read widely, savored intellectual debate, and was afflicted by incurable religious melancholy. He never recovered from the fact that at the age of eight, cold and hungry while tending sheep one night on the Jutland heath, he cursed God for his fate. Walter Lowrie correctly remarked that Michael Kierkegaard's "profound melancholy impressed upon his religion a character of severity and gloom which was disastrous to his children." Hannay (who curiously never mentions Lowrie) says that although the Kierkegaard household was not "fundamentally unhappy" it was "certainly unhealthy" for a child. Kierkegaard agreed. "Humanly speaking," he wrote in a posthumously published work, he was "insanely" brought up.

Many of Kierkegaard's siblings died before he settled into adulthood. He was six when one brother died of a brain hemorrhage, nine when a sister died of nephritis. He was twenty when another brother died of consumption shortly after moving to America. His two remaining sisters died following childbirth in the early 1830s. By the time Michael Kierkegaard died, in 1838 at the age of eighty-two, there remained only Søren and his brother Peter to split the estate. Søren's share amounted to some 30,000 rixdalers, more than $400,000 by today's reckoning. It made him financially independent for the rest of his life—just. It is said that in October 1855, when Kierkegaard collapsed in the street and was taken to the hospital, it was after withdrawing the last of his capital from the bank. He died a few weeks later.

Although physically frail—he may have suffered from epilepsy—Kierkegaard was spiritually very much his father's son. He brooded. In the early 1830s, when he learned that his father had once cursed God and had had premarital relations with his mother, he was devastated. His first response seems to have been to embark on a period of mild dissipation. "May it not," he asked in his journal at this time, "be best to go through all the dissipations just to experience life?" A few years later, he wrote in his journal about a man who

> in an overwrought irresponsible state visits a prostitute. . . .
> Now he wants to get married. Then anxiety stirs. He is
> tortured day and night with the thought that he might pos-
> sibly be a father, that somewhere in the world there could
> be a created being who owed his life to him.

Whatever Kierkegaard did, it allowed him the luxury of guilt. Even "a whole life devoted to God," he wrote in his journal in 1839, would "hardly suffice to atone for my youthful excesses." Kierkegaard was no easier on his father than on himself. In what is perhaps the last journal entry he made, in September 1855, he wrote that he came into the world through a "crime" and "against God's will" and that his punishment was to have lived "bereft of all lust for life."

Isn't this carrying things a little too far? Yes. But Kierkegaard carried everything too far. In part, one suspects, it was for effect. In an early journal entry, he wrote about having been at a friend's where he was the life and soul of the party: "Everyone laughed and admired me—but I left, yes, that dash should be as long as the radii of the earth's orbit————and I wanted to shoot myself." As W. H. Auden noted in the first of his two essays on Kierkegaard, "occasionally . . . [he] carried on like a spiritual prima donna." Also, one might add, like an intellectual prima donna. Hans Lassen Martensen, a prominent philosopher-theologian in Copenhagen, was briefly Kierkegaard's tutor (and later a frequent intellectual target). "I recognized immediately," Martensen wrote, "that his was not an ordinary intellect but that he also had an irresistible urge to sophistry, to hair-splitting games, which showed itself at every opportunity and was often tiresome."

THE REAL QUESTION is whether Kierkegaard ever climbed off stage, out of the limelight. In 1837, when he was twenty-four, Kierkegaard met and soon fell in love with Regine Olsen, then fourteen. They were engaged in 1840. The very next day, Kierkegaard wrote in his journal in 1849, he saw that he had made a dreadful mistake. He tortured himself, and Regine, too, presumably, for over a year. Then he definitively broke the engagement, sending back her ring with this letter:

> In order not to put more often to the test a thing which after all must be done, and which being done will supply the needed strength—let it then be done. Above all, forget him who writes this, forgive a man who, though he may be capable of something, is not capable of making a girl happy.

Kierkegaard must have thought well of this note. He not

only inscribed a copy in his journal but also published it verbatim in his book *Stages on Life's Way* (1845).

In a letter to a friend, Kierkegaard wrote that "I do not turn her into poetry . . . I call myself to account." One wonders. Those are not mutually incompatible activities. Indeed, given Kierkegaard's insatiable appetite for self-scrutiny, not to say personal melodrama, one might say that he could find no more effective way of turning Regine into "poetry," into an occasion for reflection, than by "calling himself to account." I suspect she was right when she charged (as Kierkegaard reports): "So you have been playing a dreadful game with me." As Hannay comments, "far from escaping the thought of marriage, marriage was now something he could think rather than endure." And think it he did. Over the next several years, Kierkegaard proceeded to devote hundreds if not thousands of pages to showing how marriage is (as he put it in the second volume of *Either/Or*) "the most profound form of the revelation of life." He regularly declared that "If I had had faith I would have stayed with Regine," and then enumerated all the reasons it was impossible. Kierkegaard later said it was due to Regine, melancholy, and his money that he became a writer. That is probably true. Before the break with Regine, he had written only an academic thesis and a few pamphlets (including, in 1838, a critical essay about his slightly older contemporary, Hans Christian Andersen). Regine— the idea of Regine—made Kierkegaard into Kierkegaard. But where did that leave Regine?

Primarily, it left her as a figment of Kierkegaard's imagination. She was elevated from being a woman to the post of inaccessible muse. In *Repetition* (1843), Kierkegaard portrayed a young man who thinks he is in love, but really is only in love with the idea of being in love. The girl is merely "the occasion that awakened the poetic in him."

So it was with Kierkegaard himself. Just as Abraham had to sacrifice Isaac because of God's commandment, so he, Søren Aabye Kierkegaard, had to give up Regine—because of his "melancholy," because he was an exceptional, God-touched individual, maybe because he had visited a prostitute when he was twenty. Fortunately, Regine, after a bad patch, recovered herself, got engaged to someone with more red corpuscles than Kierkegaard, and was happily married. It seems pretty clear that Kierkegaard never really forgave her for that "betrayal."

WHAT WAS KIERKEGAARD'S most important contribution as a writer? There are numerous candidates for that prize. Some people would say his attack on the pretensions of Hegel's philosophy, others his affirmation of "inwardness" and subjectivity in religious life. He had many penetrating things to say about "the present age" that still resonate:

> A passionate tumultuous age will *overthrow everything, pull everything down*; but a revolutionary age, that is at the same time reflective and passionless, transforms that expression of strength into *a feat of dialectics: it leaves everything standing but cunningly empties it of significance.*

As a description of decadence, that is hard to beat. (Alas, Kierkegaard also said that "in the present age a rebellion is, of all things, the most unthinkable." That was in 1846. In 1848, revolutions inconveniently swept through France, Germany, Italy, Austria, and other parts of Europe.)

My own contender for Kierkegaard's greatest contribution is his analysis of the "aesthetic mode of existence"— the effort to distance oneself from reality by reflection. Probably the most famous section of *Either/Or* is the long "Diary of the Seducer" at the end of volume one. It portrays a man whose "life had been an attempt to realize the task of living poetically" by playing at love. In one sense, this is a familiar literary gambit. In *The Importance of Being Earnest*, for example, Algernon declares that he doesn't see "anything romantic in proposing" marriage.

> It is very romantic to be in love. But there is nothing romantic about a definite proposal. Why, one may be accepted. One usually is, I believe. Then the excitement is all over. The very essence of romance is uncertainty. If ever I get married, I'll certainly try to forget the fact.

But what Oscar Wilde offered as an entertaining fiction, Kierkegaard analyzed as a life project. At the center of that project is the effort to short-circuit reality by transforming it into the product of one's own imagination: experience, Kierkegaard wrote in "The Rotation Method," "is reduced to a sounding board for the soul's own music."

> The whole secret lies in arbitrariness. People usually think it is easy to be arbitrary, but it requires much study to succeed in being arbitrary so as not to lose oneself in it, but so as to derive satisfaction from it. One does not enjoy the immediate but something quite different which he arbitrarily imports into it. You go to see the middle of a play, you read the third part of a book. . . . By this means you insure yourself a very different kind of enjoyment from that which the author has been so kind as to plan for you. You enjoy something entirely accidental; you consider the whole of existence from this standpoint; let its reality be stranded thereon. . . . You transform something accidental into the absolute.

Kierkegaard was the supreme anatomist of the aesthetic

mode of life. He was also one of its most accomplished practitioners. Or perhaps I should say "victims." Kierkegaard was quite right to criticize Hegel's philosophy for being a gorgeous intellectual construct that included everything but the individual. The irony is that Kierkegaard succumbed to the same thing at one remove. In a frequently quoted passage from his journal, Kierkegaard wrote that "it is perfectly true, as philosophers say, that life must be understood backwards. But they forget the other proposition, that it must be lived forwards." Kierkegaard didn't forget the second proposition; he simply could not bring himself to heed it.

Kierkegaard was always going on about the "really existing individual." But his self-obsession, his addiction to the aesthetic mode of existence, prevented him from practicing what he preached. He lacked, as he noted in an early journal entry, "indicative power." From one point of view, the spectacle Kierkegaard presents is tragic; his really was a blighted, supremely unhappy life. From another perspective, the spectacle he presents is comic in precisely the sense that he says Hegel's philosophy is comic: the disproportion between theory and reality is absolute.

The well-known Nietzsche scholar Walter Kaufmann was on to something when he exclaimed "How strange Kierkegaard is when he speaks of himself, and how similar to Dostoevsky's underground man—in content, style, and sensibility!" Both were in love with their own suffering. Pride prevented them from stooping to accept happiness. In 1846, Kierkegaard invited the *Corsair*, a scurrilous satirical paper, to attack him. The editor, hitherto conspicuously friendly to Kierkegaard, obliged with a nine-month campaign of caricature and vilification. In short order, he turned the philosopher into a public laughingstock. Kierkegaard both savored and bemoaned the result. The idea, as Hannay notes, "was to begin a new chapter of self-induced torment with which, now that Regine had dropped into the background, to keep his mind and pen busy."

Kierkegaard was wont to see the chief difference between himself and Socrates as the difference between the pagan and the Christian worlds. There is that. But there is also the difference that Socrates set about his task with unfailing good humor while Kierkegaard was a model of anguish. Socrates spent his final hours in prison telling his friends to buck up. Kierkegaard wrote books with titles like *The Concept of Dread* and *The Sickness Unto Death* and spent his last months hectoring bishops in the established church of Denmark, telling them and their congregations that they were inadequate Christians. (The primate of Denmark, Kierkegaard wrote with unchristian ferocity, was "Christianly, quite plainly a criminal.") It is significant that there are about twice as many pages devoted to "suffering" in the English translation of Kierkegaard's *Journals* than to any other subject. Like the original Melancholy Dane, Kierkegaard accepted his task, but gloomily: "The time is out of joint. O cursèd spite/ That ever I was born to set it right."

KIERKEGAARD was a canny and provocative writer but ultimately a disappointing sage. Like many people who have delved into his work, W. H. Auden began with enthusiasm and ended disabused. In 1952, Auden wrote a vivid appreciation of Kierkegaard, not uncritical but plainly admiring. By 1968, in "A Knight of Doleful Countenance: Second Thoughts on Kierkegaard," Auden found his admiration decisively tempered:

> Like Pascal, Nietzsche, and Simone Weil, Kierkegaard is one of those writers whom it is very difficult to estimate

justly. When one reads them for the first time, one is
bowled over by their originality . . . and by the sharpness of
their insights. . . . But with successive readings one's doubts
grow, one begins to react against their overemphasis on one
aspect of the truth at the expense of all the others, and
one's first enthusiasm may all too easily turn to an equally
exaggerated aversion. Of all such writers, one might say
that one cannot imagine them as children. The more we
read them, the more we become aware that something has
gone badly wrong with their affective life; . . . it is not only
impossible to imagine one of them as a happy husband or
wife, it is impossible to imagine their having a single intimate friend to whom they could open their hearts.

There is, Auden went on to observe, something of the
Manichee about Kierkegaard: not intellectually but in
feeling, in sensibility. "Though he would never have . . .
asserted that matter was created by an Evil Spirit, one does
not feel in his writings the sense that, whatever sorrows
and sufferings a man may have to endure, it is nevertheless
a miraculous blessing to be alive." God made the world
and saw that it was good: that is an element of orthodox
teaching that is conspicuously downplayed in Kierkegaard's thought. Indeed, by the end of his life, in his attack
upon what he contemptuously called "Christendom,"
Kierkegaard veered perilously close to world-denying religious fanaticism. "To love God," he wrote in 1854, "is
impossible without hating what is human." A gentler—one
might say "more Christian"—form of Christianity teaches
that by loving what is human one does honor to God.

Kierkegaard insisted that (as he put in the title of one of
his *Edifying Discourses*) "purity of heart is to will one
thing." But is that really the case? Or would it be truer to
say that, being human with human weaknesses and human

frailty, the effort to "will *one* thing" cannot help but be a project of pride? Auden quotes this marvelous passage from Dietrich Bonhoeffer:

> We should love God eternally with our whole hearts, yet not so as to compromise or diminish our earthly affections, but as a kind of cantus firmus to which the other melodies of life provide the counterpoint. Earthly affection is one of these contrapuntal themes, a theme which enjoys autonomy of its own.

Kierkegaard was deaf to those other melodies—or, more accurately, he heard them but refused to acknowledge the pertinence of their charm.

Bonhoeffer provides one sort of antidote to Kierkegaard's unhealthy rigorism. Another is provided by St. Thomas Aquinas. Granting that too much self-love was a bad thing, Aquinas nevertheless affirmed that "well-ordered self-love, whereby man desires a fitting good for himself, is right and natural." Aquinas is also a better guide to the place of reason in life and faith. He understood that reason, a God-given blessing, did not oppose but complemented faith. Kierkegaard could not bring himself to embrace the fruits of "well-ordered self-love," largely, I believe, because he was too self-absorbed to permit the compromise with reality that enjoyment of those fruits requires. At the end of his life, Kierkegaard asked, "What do I want? Quite simply: I want honesty. . . . I am not Christian severity as opposed to Christian leniency. . . . I am . . . human honesty." But that declaration was disingenuous. What Kierkegaard wanted was not human honesty but inhuman mortification—one result, perhaps, of believing that subjectivity is truth.

George Santayana

Human infirmity in moderating and checking the emotions I
name bondage: for when a man is a prey to his emotions, he is
not his own master, but lies at the mercy of fortune: so much
so, that he is often compelled, while seeing that which is better
for him, to follow that which is worse.
—Spinoza, The Ethics

"Aplomb in the midst of irrational things"—that's my motto!
—Santayana to William Morton Fullerton, 1887

It is poverty's speech that seeks us out the most.
It is older than the oldest speech of Rome.
This is the tragic accent of the scene

And you—it is you that speak it, without speech,
The loftiest syllables among loftiest things,
The one invulnerable man among
Crude captains, . . .
—Wallace Stevens, "To an Old Philosopher in Rome"

WHEN John McCormick published *George Santayana:
A Biography* in 1987, he began the introduction by
registering his "bewilderment that so moving and powerful
a figure, justifiably famous in his own day, should have

been so unjustifiably neglected in ours." McCormick noted
with disgust that even *The Last Puritan* (1935)—Santayana's one novel and probably his most famous work—
had been "unavailable . . . for years."

McCormick's lament was understandable. There was a
time when Santayana's work was part of the normal furniture of educated discourse. Not only his autobiographical
novel, but also his poetry, essays, and wide-ranging philosophical writings were eagerly read and digested, flower-
ing in turn in the sentiments and opinions of several
generations of readers. At Harvard, Santayana's official
and unofficial students included Conrad Aiken, Robert
Frost, T. S. Eliot, Witter Bynner, Walter Lippmann, Wallace
Stevens, Scofield Thayer, Max Eastman, Van Wyck Brooks,
Felix Frankfurter, and James B. Conant, many of whom
(conspicuously excepting Eliot) registered their profound
debt to his teaching. Until yesterday, it seems, Santayana's
urbane influence was woven into the living tapestry of intellectual life. In our amnesiac day, Santayana's influence
seems to have been reduced to the literary equivalent of a
geometric point: a single epigram, to wit, "Those who
cannot remember the past are condemned to repeat it."
(Santayana is deliciously quotable, but his only other saying that has survived in wide currency is the admonition
that "Fanaticism consists in redoubling your effort when
you have forgotten your aim.")

The years following publication of McCormick's book
have partly redressed his bewilderment about Santayana's
neglect—but not without irony. In 1986, after *George
Santayana* was completed but before it was published, the
MIT Press brought out *Persons and Places: Fragments of
Autobiography*, the fat first volume of its Critical Edition
of *The Works of George Santayana*. Who knows when—or
indeed if—this monumental publishing project will be

completed. Sixteen years later half a dozen titles have appeared and there are many, many more to come.

Persons and Places was undeniably a good place to begin. Originally published in three volumes from 1944 to 1953 (the year after Santayana's death at eighty-eight), the book, like *The Last Puritan*, is among Santayana's most popular works. As its subtitle suggests, *Persons and Places* contains a good deal about Santayana's own life. It recounts his birth in Madrid in 1863 and early years in Avila with his father, his emigration, at eight, to Boston to live with his Scottish-born Catalan mother and her children by a previous marriage (to "a tall blond Puritan of aquiline features and perfect innocence of mind, George Sturgis of Boston"). Santayana takes the reader though his education at the Boston Public Latin School, Harvard, and in Germany, his relations with his family and peers, and his career as a professor of philosophy at Harvard. Although he was in many ways a retiring personality, Santayana seemed to know almost everyone worth knowing, and so *Persons and Places* also contains any number of vivid character sketches: of Bertrand Russell and his brother John Francis, of Lady Ottoline Morrell and Siegfried Sassoon, of Logan Pearsall Smith, Bernard Berenson, and Robert Bridges. Santayana's splendid accuracy as a judge of character may be gleaned from his description of Lytton Strachey, whom he met in 1915: "a limp cadaverous creature," "like a caricature of Christ": "*Obscene* was the character written all over him." That is Strachey to a "T."

Again like *The Last Puritan*, *Persons and Places* was a Book-of-the-Month Club selection, a fact that added greatly to its sales. And *Persons and Places* was a notable critical as well as popular success. Edmund Wilson, for example, searching for appropriate literary parallels, enthusiastically compared it to *The Education of Henry*

Adams, Yeats's memoirs, and finally to Proust's great novel. Moreover, *Persons and Places*, coming late in Santayana's career, had not made it into the previous collection of his works, the handsome Triton Edition published in fifteen volumes by Scribners from 1936 to 1940. All of which is to say that everyone interested in Santayana had reason to welcome the republication of *Persons and Places*.

The irony mentioned above enters when one considers the MIT edition in the light of McCormick's complaint about the neglect of Santayana's work. During his life and after, Santayana was sometimes criticized for overwriting. He commanded immense fluency and could be tempted into gorgeous elaborateness. ("To some people," he complained, "my whole philosophy seems to be but rhetoric or prose poetry.") Although trained as a philosopher, Santayana was an intensely literary man; occasionally, he descended into literariness. This was especially, although not exclusively, true in his poetry, most of which he wrote before 1900: often it listeth toward Georgian preciousness. Even in his philosophical works—the bulk of his output—Santayana tended to prefer nimble metaphor to patient exposition or argument. This preference is not, I hasten to add, necessarily a liability, even philosophically. As the philosopher David Stove observed, "some of the best philosophers never argue at all. . . . Santayana, for example. He simply tells you how he thinks the world is, and delicately makes fun of some other philosophers . . . who think there is more to the world, or less, than he does."

Besides, at his best—and he was often at or near his best—Santayana wrote with beguiling grace. Although he was a professor of philosophy for more than twenty years, he was never pedantic or willfully obscure. Even at his most technical (which was not all that technical)—in the five-volume *Life of Reason* (1905–1906), say, or *Scepticism and Animal Faith* (1923)—he is accessible to the educated general reader. His charm is irresistible. He begins *Scepticism and Animal Faith*, for example, with the admission that he comes bearing "one more system of philosophy."

> If the reader is tempted to smile, I can assure him that I smile with him, and that my system . . . differs widely in spirit and pretensions from what usually goes by that name. In the first place, *my system is not mine, nor new*. I am merely attempting to express for the reader the principles to which he appeals when he smiles.

Santayana is every bit as clever as any German metaphysician, only he is light-years less ponderous. It is important to stress that Santayana is accessible not merely stylistically—in the singing clarity of his prose—but also in terms of content. His philosophy dealt not with difficult abstractions but with matters of patent human exigency. "It was happiness or deliverance," he wrote in "A General Confession," an intellectual self-précis written in the 1930s, "that alone really concerned me. This alone was genuine philosophy: this alone was the life of reason."

Above all, Santayana wrote to be read. For many readers, he is most agreeable as an occasional essayist—in *Soliloquies in England* (1922), for example, which was written during and just after World War I when Santayana had installed himself in Great Britain. Ostensibly bagatelles on miscellaneous topics from "Atmosphere," "Cloud Castles," and "Dons" to "Death-Bed Manners" and "Skylarks," these fugitive pieces are full of pungent observation and sound judgment. Writing about "The British Character," at a moment when England was still mistress of an empire, he notes that "What governs the Englishman is his inner atmosphere, the weather in his soul."

Instinctively the Englishman is no missionary, no conqueror. He prefers the country to the town, and home to
foreign parts. He is rather glad and relieved if only natives
will remain natives and strangers strangers, and at a comfortable distance from himself. Yet outwardly he is most
hospitable and accepts almost anybody for the time being;
he travels and conquers without a settled design, because
he has the instinct of exploration. His adventures are all
external; they change him so little that he is not afraid of
them. He carries his English weather in his heart wherever
he goes, and it becomes a cool spot in the desert, and a
steady and sane oracle amongst all the deliriums of mankind. Never since the heroic days of Greece has the world
had such a sweet, just, boyish master. It will be a black day
for the human race when scientific blackguards, con-
spirators, churls, and fanatics manage to supplant him.

That is eloquently said, and the intervening decades have
underscored its accuracy.

Pleasure of a certain refined stamp was Santayana's
lodestar in life, and such pleasure was what he sought to
communicate through his writing. The beautifully produced Triton Edition (limited to some 950 sets) was the
perfect correlative of Santayana's style. It has no editorial
notes. But it makes up in readability what it lacks in critical apparatus. It is an edition to be read.

The MIT edition is meant to be . . . Well, let's see. *The
Letters of George Santayana: Book One, [1868]–1909* is
the first of a projected eight volumes of letters. Altogether,
those eight books will count as Volume V in the Critical
Edition of Santayana's works. Daniel Cory, who met Santayana in 1927 when he was twenty-two and who became
the aging philosopher's confidante, secretary, and literary
executor, brought out a selection of letters in 1955. That

volume includes some 300 letters; he added dozens more in a 1963 portrait of Santayana's later years. Santayana's letters—some of them, anyway—are certainly worth reading. Consider this 1937 missive to Cory about Ezra Pound:

> For Heaven's sake, dear Cory, do stop Ezra Pound from sending me his book. Tell him I have no sense for true poetry, admire (and wretchedly imitate) only the putrid Petrarch and the miserable Milton; that I don't care for books, have hardly any, and would immediately send off his precious volume to the Harvard Library or to some other cesspool of infamy. That is, if he made me a present of it. If he sent it only for me to look at and return, I would return it unopened; because I abhor all connection with important and distinguished people, and refuse to see absolutely anyone except some occasional stray student or genteel old lady from Boston.

Good stuff, no? The Critical Edition will run to some 3000 letters. Are they all indispensable? The first volume, which takes Santayana through schooldays to the threshold of fame at age forty-six, contains about 350 letters. Some, like those to William James, his teacher and then senior colleague at Harvard, shed light on his thought. Some, like those to the sexually ambidextrous William Morton Fullerton (the lover of Edith Wharton, among many others), are amusing and provide glimpses into Santayana's developing character. Not a few are like this one from 1906 to his beloved half-sister (and godmother) Susana:

> April 3.—It is delightful here in Montpellier. I think constantly of Avila & Greece. It is Spring at last.

How many such reports do we really need?

This volume of letters also features—in addition to the standard preface, acknowledgments, introduction, bibliography, index, and copious footnotes—some twenty pages of textual commentary, a long chronology of Santayana's life as well as a register of the dozens of addresses he occupied in the course of his many European and American travels. There are sixty pages of textual notes, which detail Santayana's every misspelling, crossing out, and insertion (e.g., "sharinge • ['e' *over* 'ing'].") There is a list of manuscript locations, letter recipients, and thus-far unlocated letters. There is even a Report of Line-End Hyphenation, which to my eye has an undeniable poetry: "good-looking" is followed by "anti-Hegelianism," which is followed by "ghost-and-faery-blind," etc.: a euphonious and edifying procession.

I wonder whether this is the sort of rescue from neglect that John McCormick had in mind? Such attention implies a certain flattery, of course. But then so does the process of embalming. It is not as if there are any grave difficulties about the texts that Santayana bequeathed to posterity. We are not dealing with a heap of damaged, barely legible papyrus or collations of scribal errors, after all. We are dealing with an eminently accessible twentieth-century writer whose texts are about as transparent and unproblematic as texts can be. It is interesting to speculate about what Santayana would have made of the Critical Edition of his work. His sense of humor, I suspect, and possibly his vanity, would have been gratified: Santayana always had a lively appreciation of the absurd. His sense of proportion would have been appalled.

Santayana enjoyed aspects of college life. He liked the semi-cloistered existence, the intellectual intimacy with burgeoning young minds, the easy proximity to handsome young faces. But he always loathed the academic industry.

Indeed, no sooner had he started teaching than he began plotting his escape. Being a teacher, he remarked in *Persons and Places*, was forced upon him by the necessity of earning a living, "but being a student was my vocation." He lived frugally, saved diligently, and was finally able to announce his departure in 1912, just shy of fifty, when his mother died leaving him a legacy of $10,000 (nearly $200,000 today). He left for Europe and never set foot in the United States again. (Santayana was not without affection for America, but he liked to say that his love for it, like his love for Spain, was "manifested . . . by living there as little as possible.")

Harvard, Santayana thought, had been ruined by people like Charles Eliot, the ambitious president from 1869–1909, who strove to transform Harvard College into a great modern university. Eliot and Santayana were like oil and water. Early in his teaching career, Santayana chanced to encounter the president; asked about the progress of his classes, Santayana explained that he had finished with Plato and was moving on to Aristotle. "No, no, Santayana," Eliot said, "what I mean by my enquiry is, *how many* students have enrolled for your lectures?"

It wasn't just a matter of administrative expansionism that bothered Santayana, though. The very discipline of academic philosophy rubbed him the wrong way. "That philosophers should be professors is an accident," he wrote, "and almost an anomaly. Free reflection about everything is a habit to be imitated, but not a subject to expound; and an original system, if the philosopher has one, is something dark, perilous, untested, and not ripe to be taught, nor is there much danger anyone will learn it." Looking back on his Harvard days in *Character and Opinion in the United States* (1920), he spoke of the new breed of philosophy professor who was "very professional in tone and conscious of his *Fach*," "open-minded, whole-hearted, appreciative," but also—deadly phrase—"toasted only on one side."

It is sometimes suggested that William James, though he died in 1910, had been instrumental in poisoning the atmosphere for Santayana at Harvard. This is emphatically not the case. Everyone quotes James's description of Santayana's early work as exhibiting a "perfection of rottenness" and "moribund Latinity." Few supply the context: "The great event in my life recently," James wrote to a colleague in 1900,

> has been the reading of Santayana's book [*Interpretations of Poetry and Religion*]. Although I absolutely reject the platonism of it, I have literally squealed with delight at the imperturbable perfection with which the position is laid down. . . . I now understand Santayana, the man. I never understood him before. But what a perfection of rottenness in a philosophy! I don't think I ever knew the anti-realistic view to be propounded with so impudently superior an air. It is refreshing to see a representative of moribund Latinity rise up and administer such reproof to us barbarians in the hour of our triumph.

James ends by asking that his letter be passed along to Santayana, adding: "He is certainly an *extraordinarily distingué* writer. Thank him for existing!"

Temperamentally, the two men were complete opposites—James bluff, hearty, the thorough New England pragmatist in manner as well as philosophical outlook: Santayana the super-refined, sonnet-writing, exquisitely disillusioned Catholic Spaniard. ("In renouncing everything else for the sake of English letters," Santayana remarked, "I might be said to have been guilty, quite unintentionally, of a little stratagem, as if I had set out to say plausibly in English as many un-English things as possible.") In many ways, Santayana was closer in spirit to William's brother Henry. They met only once, in England, toward the end of Henry's life. "In that one interview," Santayana recalled—sadly, I think—he "made me feel more at home and better understood than his brother William ever had done in the long years of our acquaintance. Henry was calm, he liked to see things as they are, and be free afterwards to imagine how they might have been." High praise from that apostle of clarity animated by subjunctive dispensation. Despite their differences, however, there was no contemporary to whom Santayana owed more, intellectually, than William James, whose "sense for the immediate," "for the unadulterated, unexplained, instant fact of experience" Santayana celebrated. The problem with Harvard was not William James but the increasing professional drift of the institution.

Although the Critical Edition of Santayana's works will probably help resuscitate the philosopher as a subject of academic scrutiny—we can expect, I believe, to see an uptick in dissertations on his work—there is a sense in which it is likely to extend rather than remedy the neglect he has suffered in recent decades. As John McCormick noted in his biography, Santayana "conveyed an attitude toward existence rather than a set of axioms, a totality of response rather than a geodetic survey of the world." That attitude, that totality of response, is not necessarily aided by excessive scholarly integument. Whatever one's final judgment about the value of Santayana's philosophy, he is certainly among the most approachable of writers. The Critical Edition assumes an amount of starch and formality that is almost comically at odds with the spirit of this genial and smilingly radical writer.

MANY PEOPLE who know Santayana only from anthologies are surprised to discover how thoroughly naturalistic a thinker he was. It somehow seems strange for a poet of his sometimes trembling fervency. But right from the start Santayana's primary philosophical inspirations were radical materialists like Democritus and Lucretius, Schopenhauer and Spinoza. (Spinoza, he said, "in several respects laid the foundation of my philosophy.") For Santayana, honest self-scrutiny presupposed materialism. "Those who are not materialists," he wrote, "cannot be good observers of themselves."

Santayana's naturalism assured his implacable hostility to supernaturalism, both the patent variety—his native Roman Catholicism, for example—as well as the covert versions populating many schools of philosophy: German idealism, say, in both its original and transplanted-to-England-and-America forms. (One of Santayana's most effective polemics is *Egotism in German Philosophy* [1916], which I quoted above in "The Difficulty with Hegel." Santayana's description of Hegel's dialectic as a futile attempt to make "things conform to words, not words to things" says everything one needs to know about that intellectual monstrosity.) In 1890, when he was in his late twenties, Santayana wrote to William James that "I doubt whether the earth supports a more genuine enemy of all that the Catholic Church *inwardly* stands for than I do," and he later noted that he had "never been what is called a practising Catholic." It was a position from which he never wavered. It is worth stressing this. Santayana spent the last twelve years of his life at the Blue Sisters' clinic in Rome. This has tempted some commentators to suggest that his atheism softened or even evaporated with age. But this was not the case. During his last illness, Santayana took pains to advise Daniel Cory that if he were unconscious and the sacrament of Extreme Unction were administered, no one should interpret that as a deathbed conversion. Santayana's attitude toward death is summed up with spare eloquence in these lines from "The Poet's Testament":

> I give back to the earth what the earth gave,
> All to the furrow, nothing to the grave.
> The candle's out, the spirit's vigil spent;
> Sight may not follow where the vision went.

Biology cannot hinder vision's flight, but it sets a definite limit to the life of sight.

If Santayana was a thoroughly naturalistic thinker, he came armed with a remarkable aesthetic sensibility and native appreciation of the imaginative resources that religion offered. Religions, he insisted, "are the great fairy-tales of the conscience." Nevertheless he also believed that religions are indispensable, not least because they nurture the emotion of piety, "Man's reverent attachment to the sources of his being and the steadying of his life by that attachment." Santayana was the enemy of religion considered as dogma, as a repository of moral commandments or "literal" truth. (Santayana had little time, probably too little time, for what he dismissed as "literal truth," "the horrid claim of ideals to literal truth." "My matured conclusion," he wrote, "is that no system is to be trusted, not even science in any literal or pictorial sense.") But he also saw in religion an irreplaceable friend of human yearning. Its disappearance, hailed by many as an emancipation, actually brought forth new forms of bondage. "The absence of a positive religion," Santayana wrote in the "General Confession," "was very far from liberating the spirit for higher flights: on the contrary, it opened the door to the pervasive tyranny of the world over the soul." When he looked around at the increasing secularization of the modern world, Santayana saw that the degradation of religion went hand-in-hand with the diminishment of culture. In "The Intellectual Temper of the Age" (1911), Santayana forlornly describes the dissolution of Christianity and the rise of "an emancipated, atheistic, international democracy."

> In vain do we deprecate it; it has possession of us already through our propensities, fashions, and language. Our very plutocrats and monarchs are at ease only when they are vulgar. Even prelates and missionaries are hardly sincere or conscious of an honest function, save as they devote themselves to social work.

It goes without saying that he did not regard this development as a sign of spiritual health.

Santayana seems to have had an ingrained suspicion of almost everything beginning with "pro": "professors," as we've seen, but also "prophets," "Protestantism," "protégés," and, above all, perhaps, "progress." "Those who speak most of progress," he wrote, "measure it by quantity and not by quality; how many people read and write, or how many people there are, or what is the annual value of their trade; whereas true progress would rather lie in reading or writing fewer and better things, and being fewer and better men, and enjoying life more." At a time when nearly everyone—conservative as well as liberal—has difficulty dissociating the ideas of "more" and "better," Santayana's unorthodox remarks are worth pondering.

There are many areas, in fact, where Santayana provides a welcome corrective. In his wry, understated manner, Santayana was a far more independent thinker than many who loudly proclaim their independence. He understood that tradition—that great storehouse of accumulated wisdom—was mankind's most lavish dower, to dispense with which was madness. "The life of reason," he wrote, "is our heritage and exists only through tradition. Now the misfortune of revolutionaries is that they are disinherited, and their folly is that they wish to be disinherited even more than they are." An accomplished craftsman in poetry and prose, Santayana well understood both the limits of technical skill and the bogus lure of inarticulateness masquerading as profundity. In *The Sense of Beauty* (1896), in a section called "Effects of Indeterminate Organization," Santayana admits that "the greatest mastery of technique" is not enough for success in art.

> When there is real profundity . . . there will accordingly be a felt inadequacy of expression, and an appeal to the observer to piece out our imperfections with his thoughts. But this should come only after the resources of a patient and well learned art have been exhausted; else what is felt as depth is really confusion and incompetence. . . . And a habitual indulgence in the inarticulate is a sure sign of the philosopher who has not learned to think, the poet who has not learned to write, the painter who has not learned to paint . . .
>
> Our age is given to this sort of self indulgence. . . . The crudity we are too distracted to refine, we accept as originality, and the vagueness we are too pretentious to make accurate, we pass off as sublimity. This is the secret of making great works on novel principles, and of writing hard books easily.

Santayana had a horror of intellectual and artistic sloppiness worthy of his classical education. He regarded ex-

perimentation in the arts—in human affairs generally—
with suspicion and everywhere preferred the familiar to the
exotic, the traditional to the avant-garde.†

Santayana's loftiness was also evident in his political
opinions. The philosopher Frederick Olafson noted that
there exists in Santayana's thinking "a pervasive animus
against democracy and liberalism." This is true. About
democracy in general, Santayana harbored the distaste of
someone committed to an aristocracy of talent. Like
Shakespeare's Ulysses (in *Troilus and Cressida*), he stressed
the virtues of class distinction: "Take but degree away, un-
tune that string, / and hark what discord follows." His affection for America, though genuine, was tempered by a
patronizing astonishment at its optimistic faith in the
benevolence of equality and the marketplace of ideas.

> Hitherto America has been the land of universal good-will,
> confidence in life, inexperience of poisons. Until yesterday
> it believed itself immune from the hereditary plagues of
> mankind. It could not credit the danger of being suffocated
> or infected by any sinister principle. The more errors and
> passions were thrown into the melting-pot, the more cer-
> tainly would they neutralize one another and would truth
> come to the top. Every system was met with a frank gaze.
> "Come on," people seem to say to it, "show us what you
> are good for. We accept no claims; we ask for no creden-

---

† It is not surprising that Santayana was impatient with abstract or
non-objective art. "Living arts," he wrote in *Reason in Art*, "exist
only while the well-known, much-loved things imperatively demand
to be copied, so that their reproduction has some honest non-aes-
thetic interest for mankind. Although subject-matter is often said to
be indifferent to art, and an artist, when his art is secondary, may
think of technique only, nothing is really so poor and melancholy as
art that is interested only in itself and not in its subject."

tials; we just give you a chance. Plato, the Pope, and Mrs. Eddy shall have one vote each."

Santayana was never less than provocative. But about some political matters, he was naïve if not obtuse. In a letter of 1920, for example, he wrote to a former Harvard colleague that "I think to be born under Bolshevism would not be worse than to be born in Boston." (Moscow, where Stalins speak only to Lenins, and the Lenins speak only to Marx?) Santayana never really came to terms with the enormity of Communism, or indeed of Nazism. Nor did he ever overcome the reflexive anti-Semitism he absorbed from the parochial Catholicism of his youth. But in many other respects, Santayana's traditionalist temperament and passion for individual liberty made him an astute social critic. He was especially penetrating about the contradictions of liberalism. In "The Intellectual Temper of the Age," he noted that

> Liberalism had been supposed to advocate liberty; but what the advanced parties that still call themselves liberal now advocate is control, control over property, trade, wages, hours of work, meat and drink, amusements, and in a truly advanced country like France control over education and religion; and it is only on the subject of marriage . . . that liberalism is growing more and more liberal.

In an important essay called "The Irony of Liberalism," Santayana dilates on the element of social presumption that stands behind the liberal's habit of coercion:

> No man . . . can really or ultimately desire anything but what the best people desire. This is the principle of the higher snobbery; and in fact, all earnest liberals are higher

snobs. If you refuse to move in the prescribed direction, you are not simply different, you are arrested and perverse. The savage must not remain a savage, nor the nun a nun, and China must not keep its wall. If the animals remain animals it is somehow through a failure of the will in them, and very sad. Classic liberty, though only a name for stubborn independence, and obedience to one's own nature, was too free, in one way, for the modern liberal.

Liberalism in the modern sense is deeply hostile not only to tradition—tradition is by definition an impediment to "progress"—but also to "the wilder instincts of man": "the love of foraging, of hunting, of fighting, of plotting, of carousing, or of doing penance." (The inclusion of penance is a characteristic Santayana touch.) The perfect liberal society, extolling freedom in theory, is actually one that excludes initiative.

The homogenizing imperative of liberalism has a psychological correlative in abstract moralism. Santayana memorably captures this in a vignette in *Persons and Places.* Under the rubric "A lesson in morals," he recalls an episode after lunch one day when he was a young boy. A single piece of cake remained on a plate. He asked his mother whether he might have it. "No," she said. "It is for the little birds."

> Though it was by no means a fixed habit of hers, she opened the window and spread the crumbs out for the sparrows. She did not care for sparrows, she never watched them or tried to tame them; and that day, having performed her act of zoological benevolence, she closed the window at once, and went upstairs to sit as usual in her own room. . . . I am sure that in her silence she felt that she had given me a lesson in justice and in universal love. She

had kept the cake from her son and given it to the sparrows. She was a liberal in politics.

One is tempted to add, after the fashion of his beloved Spinoza, Q.E.D.

Santayana was a curious hybrid. In one way, he was every bit as radical a thinker as Schopenhauer (whom he greatly admired) or Nietzsche (whom he did not). Ultimately, though, he was the cheerful, affirmative figure that Nietzsche pretended to be but wasn't. (No one, I think, ever accused Schopenhauer of being cheerful.) What Santayana described as his "scepticism" ran very deep indeed. "The truth is a terrible thing," he has the vicar of Iffley say in *The Last Puritan.* "It is much darker, much sadder, much more ignoble, much more inhuman and ironical than most of us are willing to admit, or even able to suspect." That is just the sort of thing one might expect to find in Nietzsche ("Truth is ugly," he declared in *The Will to Power*). But where Nietzsche engaged in unending histrionics ("God is dead," Zarathustra, the Übermensch), Santayana behaved like a gentleman. Nietzsche described himself as "the Antichrist," said he was "dynamite," and presumed to instruct us about "how to philosophize with a hammer." Santayana was much calmer. He sought no detonations. He wished to smash no idols. He came much closer, in fact, to being the disabused spiritual aristocrat that Nietzsche admired but sweated too much to resemble. "Criticism," Santayana said, "must first be invited to do its worst." But only for the indelicate, he thought, did thoroughgoing criticism lead to nihilism or madness. Out of scepticism came faith, but it was an *animal* faith, modest, grateful, thoroughly materialistic: disillusioned but also at peace.

There were two interrelated sources of Santayana's calm.

One was his aestheticism. Santayana strove to regard the entire world as a thing of beauty, which is to say a source of pleasure. (In *The Sense of Beauty* he defined beauty as "pleasure objectified": inadequate as a definition, no doubt, but useful as a barometer of temperament.) "I can draw no distinction," he wrote in a mature summing-up, "—save for academic programmes—between moral and aesthetic values: beauty being a good, is a moral good; and the practice and enjoyment of art, like all practice and all enjoyment, fall within the sphere of morals—at least if by morals we understand moral economy and not moral superstition." Santayana attempted to provide a philosophical justification for this thoroughgoing aestheticism with what he called his doctrine of "essences." How do we know that what we believe is true is true? what we find beautiful is in fact beautiful? Are we not everywhere besieged by error and illusion? Yes, but Santayana proposes

> to entertain the illusion without succumbing to it, accepting it openly as an illusion, and forbidding it to claim any sort of being but that which it obviously has; and then . . . it will not deceive me. What will remain of this non-deceptive illusion will then be a truth, and a truth the being of which requires no explanation, since it is utterly impossible that it should be otherwise.

How convincing is this? Not very. The fact that we embrace an illusion as an illusion does not automatically grant it the patent of truth. But it is worth noting that Santayana's criterion of trustworthiness is a quality often accorded to aesthetic and religious experience, namely the conviction that contingency, if but momentarily, had been defeated. It is also worth noting that it is not an attitude peculiar to Santayana. Wallace Stevens, for example, advocated something similar when he wrote that "The final belief is to believe in a fiction, which you know to be a fiction, there being nothing else. The exquisite truth is to know that it is a fiction and you believe in it willingly."

There are many problems with Santayana's (and with Stevens's) aestheticism. The chief problem is its subjectivity. By locating the criterion of morality and truth in a species of pleasurable sensation, Santayana in effect denies them any public measure. This means that—I won't call it the validity, but the attractiveness of Santayana's ideal depends largely on the quality of the individual espousing it. In the delicate hands of a Santayana this doctrine might provide a workable philosophy of life. Not everyone has the sensibility, the discipline, the restraint to make "all practice and all enjoyment fall within the sphere of morals."

The relation between enjoyment and restraint brings us to the other source of Santayana's calm, his Epicureanism. Colloquially, "epicurean" is often used to mean "devoted to sensuous pleasure." In fact, though, Epicureanism is a deeply ascetic philosophy. It is devoted to pleasure, but pleasure understood as the absence of pain. The goal is *ataraxia*: privative tranquillity: at peace because *not* disturbed by emotional tumult. Not so much happiness as invulnerability. In *The Last Puritan* (a model for which was Walter Pater's *Marius the Epicurean*), Santayana has his alter-ego Oliver Alden remark that "I have the Epicurean contentment, which is not far removed from asceticism." Santayana early on learned to regard the world as a threat that could be best countered by holding it at bay. The phrase "a detached observer" recurs frequently in his writings. It names not simply an intellectual ideal but an emotional imperative. "The moral pageantry of this world," Santayana wrote, "is calculated wonderfully to strengthen and refine the philosophy of abstention suggested to Epicurus by the flux of material things and by the illusions of vulgar passions."

Which passions were not vulgar? Those that did not collude to involve us emotionally—the dispassionate passions of observation, retrospection, and amused noninvolvement. In the 1890s, one of Santayana's colleagues at Harvard noted that "Santayana impressed us as an onlooker in the world more than a sharer in its struggle." It was an impression that Santayana was careful to cultivate. He was enormously generous—often anonymously—with money: Bertrand Russell, for example, was the recipient of thousands of pounds, and Santayana even offered to help Ezra Pound. The financial generosity came along with a definite emotional chilliness, or at least reserve. Daniel Cory reports that in 1931 when he told Santayana about the death of his old friend Frank Russell, the philosopher "reacted not at all." Taken aback, Cory asked: "Mr. Santayana, if I dropped dead in front of you at this moment, would you be emotionally moved at all?" To which Santayana replied: "You should not ask me personal questions." Noting Cory's dismay, Santayana added that he had known Russell "long ago," etc., but the impression of glacial *noli me tangere* persisted. In his recollection of a visit to Santayana in 1945 (in *Europe Without Baedeker*), Edmund Wilson describes the old philosopher as "perhaps the most international—or, better, the most super-national—personality I had ever met": decorous, gently ironical, amiably distant. "I had mentioned in our conversation having recently met two persons of whom he had once seen a good deal, and had been struck by his total failure to show even a conventional interest in how they were or what they were doing."

Santayana's distance from involvement was a leitmotif of his character. By disposition, he was homosexual, though it is not clear that he was ever sexually involved with anyone. Reflecting on a meeting he had with A. E. Housman, Santayana mused to Cory that "I think I must have been that way in my Harvard days—although I was unconscious of it at the time." McCormick regarded that as deliberately coy, but supplied no evidence to gainsay it. After some adolescent turmoil, Santayana came to regard sex the way he regarded emotional entanglements generally: as temptations to be avoided. "Carnal pleasures," he wrote, "are but welcome pains, [they] draw the spirit inwards into primal darkness and indistinction." Perhaps it was fortunate that Santayana was, or made himself, unsusceptible to such pleasures. "Love has never made me long unhappy, nor sexual impulse uncomfortable," he wrote in a letter of 1924. Burdens, responsibilities, emotional ties: these sutures of ordinary life are among the chief evils in the Epicurean's lexicon. Disturbing tranquility, they remind us of our essential poverty, our lack of self-sufficiency. But of course such entanglements are also our most reliable sources of joy. I suspect that this is something that Santayana understood, even if he refrained from indulging it. "It takes patience to appreciate domestic bliss," he wrote in *The Life of Reason*; "volatile spirits prefer unhappiness." Santayana did not at all prefer unhappiness. He was the opposite of a volatile spirit. But he was also reluctant to wager on a bliss burdened with the imperfections of the domestic. In a letter of 1924, Oliver Wendell Holmes, Jr., put his finger on something essential about Santayana. "In a general way," Holmes wrote, "his thinking more than that of other philosophers coincides with mine. But he has a patronizing tone—as of one who saw through himself but didn't expect others to." Such is the fate of those who aspire to be "The one invulnerable man among / Crude captains."

Wittgenstein:
The Philosophical Porcupine

Philosophy is a battle against the bewitchments of our intelligence by means of language.
—Ludwig Wittgenstein, *Philosophical Investigations*

THE PHILOSOPHER Ludwig Josef Johann Wittgenstein was born in Vienna in April 1889, the youngest of eight children. While the house of Wittgenstein had been prominent in Austria since the beginning of the nineteenth century, it was Ludwig's father, Karl, an engineer, who moved it from prominence to great riches with his brilliant manipulations of the steel industry and canny investments. When he died, in 1913, *The Times* of London eulogized him as "The Carnegie of Austria."

Although the Wittgensteins were of Jewish ancestry a fact that Ludwig would later take considerable pains to conceal—they had been Protestant for two generations. His mother, Leopoldine, was Roman Catholic, and, like his brothers and sisters, Ludwig was baptized Catholic. After a youthful period of intense hostility to Christianity, Wittgenstein became an equally fervent, if unorthodox, proponent: "Christianity," he declared in 1914, "is indeed the only *sure* way to happiness." As Roy Monk concluded in *Wittgenstein: The Duty of Genius* (Free Press, 1990)—the

most accomplished biography of the philosopher in English
—"In a way that is centrally important but difficult to
define, he had lived a devoutly religious life." Bertrand
Russell went so far as to call Wittgenstein "a complete
mystic" ("mystic" being a term of derision for Russell).
Nevertheless, Wittgenstein was not a church-goer and
seems to have had little sympathy with what has come to
be called "organized religion." His brand of Christianity
was inspired less by the Catholic Church than by Tolstoy's
Gospel in Brief, which he picked up in 1914 while serving
in the Austrian army. "The book captivated him," Monk
noted. "It became for him a kind of talisman: he carried it
wherever he went, and read it so often that he came to
know passages of it by heart. He became known to his
comrades as 'the man with the gospels.' "

In many respects, the Wittgensteins were the very embodiment of Viennese *haut bourgeois* sensibility and patri-
cian splendor. In his 1988 biography of the philosopher's
early years, the Wittgenstein scholar Brian McGuinness
even employs the adjective *wittgensteinisch* to describe that
compact of concentration, largesse, and nervous self-absorption that seemed to define the family. Although he later
affected a spartan simplicity that bordered on the comical,
Ludwig grew up in an atmosphere of *noblesse oblige*. In the
opening decades of the century, the Wittgensteins, as
McGuinness noted, "belonged to a spacious world with
time as well as energy enough, and above all to a culture not
yet fragmented and specialized, so that the music they
made, or the pictures they painted, at home differed in degree perhaps but not in kind from the highest achievements
of their age." Ludwig's sister Margaret had her portrait
painted by Gustav Klimt, and (equally impressive) Karl
Wittgenstein was often a target of Karl Kraus's barbs in the
satirical periodical *Die Fackel* ("The Torch").

It was music, especially, that united the family. F. R. Leavis recalls that Wittgenstein once told him that there were seven grand pianos in his childhood home. (A figure that Monk considered "of doubtful truth, there being only three or four grand pianos" at the family's principal Viennese establishment.) Clara Schumann had taught Karl Wittgenstein's sisters to play the piano, Brahms was a good family friend, and Leopoldine—who according to McGuinness brought to her household "a moral earnestness and selflessness which it is proper to call extreme"—is said to have been an exceptionally accomplished pianist. Ludwig himself, with characteristic idiosyncrasy, took up the clarinet instead of the piano, and could reputedly whistle with prodigious accuracy, reproducing whole concertos or (a favorite pastime) whistling the melody of Schubert's songs while a friend accompanied him on the piano.

Young Ludwig was educated at home by private tutors until the age of fourteen, when he was sent to secondary school in Linz (the same school that was attended by Adolf Hitler). He was apparently an indifferent student, though he learned French well and mastered English. Upon graduating from school in 1906, he decided, *faute de mieux,* to follow in his father's footsteps and embark on a career in engineering. After spending two unhappy years in Berlin studying mechanical engineering and acronautics, he went to England to continue his engineering studies at Manchester University. He is said to have done important work in aeronautics at Manchester, and it was around this time that he became interested in the foundations of mathematics and logic, the subjects that would lead him to Cambridge University to study philosophy with Bertrand Russell in 1911.

Despite his favored upbringing, however, Ludwig was visited by much unhappiness and personal tragedy. Three of his four brothers committed suicide, and his fourth brother, Paul, a pianist, lost his right arm fighting in the Great War. (Paul Wittgenstein nonetheless went on to have a distinguished career as a pianist, performing works he commissioned for the left hand.) Ludwig himself was of a melancholy, tortured disposition and, at least as a young adult, often brooded about committing suicide.

As befitted his station, he displayed an open-handed generosity toward his cultural enthusiasms, arranging, for example, for a large anonymous gift to Austrian artists and writers that aided Adolf Loos, Georg Trakl, Rainer Maria Rilke, and Oskar Kokoschka, among others. Sometimes his benefactions were more extravagant than effective, as when he donated one million crowns to the state during the Great War for the purchase of a 30 cm caliber mortar. Wittgenstein performed with conspicuous bravery during the war. According to one citation, "his exceptionally courageous behaviour, calmness, sang-froid, and heroism won the total admiration of the troops." Given Wittgenstein's passion for philosophy, it seems somehow appropriate that his first job was manning a searchlight on a ship at night. Later, at his request, he was posted to the Russian front, where he was given the extremely dangerous job of manning an observation post. "Perhaps," he wrote in his diary on the eve of a battle, "the nearness of death will bring me the light of life. May God enlighten me." As Monk observed,

> Wittgenstein had entered the war hoping it would change him, and this it had. He had undergone four years of active service and a year of incarceration; he had faced death, experienced a religious awakening, taken responsibility for the lives of others, and endured long periods of close confinement with the sort of people he would not previously have shared a railway carriage with. All this had made him

a different person—had given him a new identity. In a sense, he was not returning to anything in 1919: everything had changed.

As the many stories about Wittgenstein's eccentricities suggest—they have been a staple of academic folklore for decades—he was the epitome, almost the caricature, of angst-ridden genius. Toward the end of the war, he was captured, along with many other Austrian troops, by the Italians and was made a POW for nearly a year. In August 1919 he was released and, in order to accelerate his personal transformation, Wittgenstein decided to disburden himself of his wealth—all of it. He distributed his assets among his siblings so as not, he said, to corrupt the poor. In making the arrangements, he took particular care that there be no possibility that he could ever lay claim to any of the funds. "So," the notary who executed the empowering document observed, "you want to commit financial suicide." After the *Tractatus* was published Wittgenstein abandoned philosophy. He spent six years teaching school children in a succession of small villages in the Austrian mountains, worked as a hotel porter and as a gardener in a monastery, and in 1935 made a pilgrimage to Leningrad and Moscow, where he toyed with the idea of becoming a manual laborer or taking up a teaching post. Finally, he returned to Cambridge and to philosophy, eventually succeeding to G. E. Moore's chair in 1939.

Bertrand Russell remarked that Wittgenstein was "perhaps the most perfect example I have known of genius as traditionally conceived, passionate, profound, intense, and dominating." Initially, at least, it was less Wittgenstein's work than his appearance as a "genius as traditionally conceived" (along, no doubt, with his fortune and solemn, introverted good looks) that captivated Cambridge academic society and won Wittgenstein the wary devotion of everyone from G. E. Moore and Russell to John Maynard Keynes and the Bloomsbury set. For although Wittgenstein's writings are reasonably voluminous, he published very little during his lifetime. In addition to the *Tractatus Logico-Philosophicus*—a book of some twenty-thousand-words—he published one brief review of a textbook on logic, an article in the *Proceedings of the Aristotelian Society*, and an elementary language handbook for school children. His other most influential book, the *Philosophical Investigations*, a loosely connected series of remarks (Wittgenstein called it an "album") dealing with various aspects of language and logic, appeared posthumously in 1953 (Wittgenstein died in 1951, just after his sixty-second birthday, of cancer. "Tell them I've had a wonderful life" were his last words). There followed numerous volumes of notes, lectures, and miscellaneous reflections, some of them running to five hundred pages.

Because of the myths that have grown up around Wittgenstein, his eccentricities have been amply noted, repeated, elaborated, and sometimes simply invented. Often multiple versions of the same story appear. Russell, whose passions included an extremely well-developed taste for gossip, often improved his anecdotes about Wittgenstein as he recounted the same incidents in sundry letters and reminiscences. He transforms, for example, what was apparently a shy and even touching appeal by Wittgenstein for guidance and assurance about his philosophical abilities into a typical case of *wittgensteinisch* eccentricity:

> WITTGENSTEIN: Will you tell me whether I am a complete idiot or not?
> RUSSELL: My dear fellow, I don't know. Why are you asking me?

WITTGENSTEIN: Because, if I am a complete idiot, I shall become an aeronaut; but, if not, I shall become a philosopher.

One of the main privileges—but also, of course, one of the signal liabilities—of getting to know Wittgenstein was enduring the benefit of his critical acumen. The penetration and fundamental nature of his criticism could sometimes be paralyzing. After digesting Wittgenstein's comments on his work on the theory of knowledge, Russell—not generally a man lacking in self-confidence—confided to his mistress Lady Ottoline Morrell that "I saw that he was right and I saw that I could not hope ever again to do fundamental work in philosophy." Nor did Wittgenstein confine his criticism to the realm of ideas. He was endlessly analysing his relations with others, rehearsing his and their faults, nursing real or imagined slights, "pulling up feelings by the roots," as Russell put it, "trying to get the exact truth of what one feels towards him." In 1936, Monk reports, Wittgenstein decided to settle his emotional accounts with all his friends. He prepared a confession "describing the times in his life when he had been weak and dishonest," and then visited each person in turn to deliver the bad news.

WITTGENSTEIN'S DECISION to go to Cambridge to study with Russell seems to have been made on the spur of the moment. The great German mathematician Gottlob Frege, whom Wittgenstein visited in 1911, is credited with having advised him to study with Russell, who was seventeen years Wittgenstein's senior and then at the peak of his philosophical powers. After they became acquainted, Wittgenstein would typically come to Russell's rooms to talk at 4:00 or 5:00 in the afternoon, stay until Russell left for dinner, and then come back in the evening for several more hours of discussion and argument.

Like almost everyone who encountered Wittgenstein, Russell, too, would soon come under the spell of his brilliance. Within a year or so he would find himself dutifully taking down the reflections on logic that Wittgenstein dictated as he paced the room nervously, just as G. E. Moore would later find himself enlisted as Wittgenstein's amanuensis. But Wittgenstein's captivating effect on Russell was not immediate. Russell's well-known letters to Lady Ottoline at the time provide something of a chronicle of his developing acquaintance with the young philosopher. They show that, in the beginning at least, exasperation competed heartily with admiration in Russell's feelings about his peculiar new student.

19 OCTOBER: My German friend threatens to be an infliction.

25 OCTOBER: My German, who seems to be rather good, was very argumentative.

1 NOVEMBER: My German was very argumentative and tiresome. He wouldn't admit that it was certain that there was not a rhinoceros in the room.

2 NOVEMBER: My German engineer, I think, is a fool. He thinks nothing empirical is knowable—I asked him to admit that there was not a rhinoceros in the room, but he wouldn't.

As their acquaintance deepened into friendship—and before, as so often happened with Wittgenstein's friendships, it disintegrated into the formality of botched intimacy—Russell found himself one of Wittgenstein's prime spiritual confidants. The role cannot have been an unalloyed blessing. "On arrival," Russell reports, "he would announce that when he left my rooms he would commit suicide. So, in spite of getting sleepy, I did not like to turn him out. On one such evening after an hour or two of dead silence, I said to him, 'Wittgenstein, are you thinking about logic or your sins?' 'Both,' he said, and then reverted to silence."

Wittgenstein's impatience led him to rebel against methodical argumentation in favor of an extremely compressed, epigrammatic style of writing. This became most finely honed in Wittgenstein's later obiter dicta, in which, for example, we discover him observing that "a good picture should have the effect of a box on the ear." But already in 1912 we find Russell informing a correspondent that "I told him he ought not simply *state* what he thinks true but give arguments for it, but he said arguments spoil its beauty, and that he would feel as if he was dirtying a flower with muddy hands."

Framing *arguments*, as both the *Tractatus* and the *Philosophical Investigations* show, was not what Wittgenstein thought philosophy was all about. Both books *contain* arguments; but their main points are made by observation, not demonstration. What Wittgenstein sought were not deliberate arguments proving this or that proposition but *insights*. As McGuinness noted, "the particular excellence of his mind was his capacity for concentration." He was incessantly looking for *das erlosende Wort*—the formulation that would solve a particular logical problem but also "the saving word," the sudden inspiration that would install order and harmony amidst the chaos of his thoughts and feelings. For Wittgenstein the conundrums of logic were not abstracted from the perplexities of everyday life and feeling but were the purest, most concentrated expression of them. Wittgenstein experienced life as a kind of prison; his chief aim, as he put in a famous phrase from the

Investigations, was to show "the fly the way out of the fly bottle." Philosophy was not an abstract enterprise but an existential imperative. "Conversion in its various senses," McGuinness wrote, "is what he wanted in both logic and in life. *The* fundamental problem in logic had to be solved and he had to become a new person."

Nowhere is this connection more evident than in the *Tractatus*. It is an exceedingly odd work, in form as well as content. Wittgenstein organized the book—which comprises a series of brief remarks interspersed with logical formulae—into a series of seven propositions, each of which (except proposition 7, which stands alone and concludes the book) is followed by a series of numbered comments. The format—proposition 1 followed by comments 1.1, 1.11, and so on—gives the book a formidably technical aura. To what extent this *appearance* of logical structure is supported by the actual flow of the argument has been a matter of dispute since the book appeared.

Its logical structure notwithstanding, the *Tractatus* is almost universally considered a landmark of twentieth-century philosophy. Russell agreed to write an introduction for the book (an introduction that is generally conceded to have misrepresented Wittgenstein's thought), and when Wittgenstein later submitted it to be considered as a dissertation, G. E. Moore is famously said to have reported: "It is my personal opinion that Mr. Wittgenstein's thesis is a work of genius; but, be that as it may, it is certainly well up to the standard required for the Cambridge degree of Doctor of Philosophy." (Wittgenstein was less enthusiastic in his assessment of his benefactor: "Moore? He shows you how far a man can go who has absolutely no intelligence.") The German title—*Logisch-Philosophische Abhandlung*—literally means "Logical-Philosophical Treatise." Verbally, it recalls Spinoza's *Theologico-Political*

Treatise, though it is unlikely that Wittgenstein had encountered the work, still less likely that he named his own work with Spinoza's book in mind. It was Moore who proposed the now famous Latin title, and as is so often case in these matters, the idiosyncratic yet peculiarly catchy title has contributed greatly to the book's mystique. So successful has the title been that the book is often known by its Latin title (typically shortened to the *Tractatus*) even among Germans.

Already the first few propositions give one a good sense of the enigmatic character of the book.

1   The world is all that is the case.
1.1   The world is the totality of facts [*Tatsachen*], not things [*Dinge*].
1.11   The world is determined by the facts, and by their being *all* the facts.
1.12   For the totality of facts determines what is the case, and also whatever is not the case.
1.13   The facts in logical space are the world.

It is only in context of the work as a whole that these "oracular" statements (to adopt A. J. Ayer's appropriate characterization) begin to make sense. Wittgenstein's first task in the *Tractatus* is to establish once and for all the limits of language, to separate what can be expressed in language and what must forever elude linguistic expression. "The whole sense of the book," Wittgenstein wrote in his preface, "might be summed up in the following words: what can be said at all can be said clearly, and what we cannot talk about we must pass over in silence." This anticipates the famous concluding line of the book, proposition 7, where Wittgenstein's exacting prose teeters into poetry: "*Wovon man nicht sprechen kann, daruber muss man schweigen"*—"What we cannot speak about we must pass over in silence."

WHEN WE HEAR that a philosopher has distinguished rigorously between what can and cannot be expressed in language, our first impulse is probably to concentrate on the expressible. After all, we are likely to reason, if something cannot be put into words, it is probably not worth much attention. But our first impulse was not at all Wittgenstein's impulse. On the contrary, it is clear that Wittgenstein attached immense importance to the *in*expressible. Writing about the manuscript of the *Tractatus* to a prospective publisher, he insisted that "the point of the book is ethical."

> My work consists of two parts: the one presented here plus all that I have *not* written. And it is precisely the second part that is the important one. My book draws limits to the sphere of the ethical from the inside as it were, and I am convinced that it is the ONLY *rigorous* way of drawing those limits. In short, I believe that where *many* others today are just *gassing*, I have managed in my book to put everything firmly in place by being silent about it.

As a sales pitch, this statement has drawbacks. Few publishers can be expected to rejoice at the prospect of acquiring only the first, inessential part, of a two-part work. So it is not surprising that Wittgenstein had considerable difficulty finding a publisher. Completed toward the end of World War I, the *Tractatus* was not published until 1921, and then only in an obscure German periodical. (An English translation, which corrected many errors in the German printing, appeared in 1922.)

Wittgenstein's ambition to "put everything firmly in

place by being silent about it" is the underlying goal of the *Tractatus*. But because of Wittgenstein's reputation as the paterfamilias of Anglo-American linguistic philosophy, it is important to stress that his fundamental aim in the *Tractatus* was more *ethical* than logical or linguistic. In fact, Wittgenstein would have rejected the distinction: getting clear about the logical point was for him an ethical imperative. This is the burden of Wittgenstein's remark that "Philosophy is not a body of doctrine but an activity" (4.112)—specifically, an activity that can clarify our thoughts and thus lead us out of the illusions generated by language. In his book on Wittgenstein, A. J. Ayer compared Wittgenstein's efforts with those of Kant in *The Critique of Pure Reason*. Kant attempted to limit the claims of reason in order to make room for faith, not to advance the cause of skepticism; just so, Wittgenstein undertook to mark off the limits of the sayable primarily in order to preserve the integrity of the unsayable. That both were hailed as prophets of anti-metaphysical scepticism is an irony of intellectual history.

"There are, indeed," Wittgenstein wrote toward the end of the *Tractatus*, "things that cannot be put into words. They *make themselves manifest*. They are what is mystical" (6.522). Despite Wittgenstein's identification of "things that cannot be put into words" as the "mystical" —for him, a term of commendation—it is perhaps not surprising that the dominant analytic tradition of philosophy has interpreted Wittgenstein to mean that what cannot be put into words is nonsense: not so much the "mystical" as the "mystifying." "For an answer which cannot be expressed the question too cannot be expressed," Wittgenstein wrote in proposition 6.5. "*The riddle* does not exist." Wittgenstein's procedure was similar to that employed by Heinrich Hertz in his classic *Principles of Mechanics*

(1894), an important early influence on Wittgenstein's thought. Instead of asking what the thorny idea of "force" means in Newtonian physics, Hertz's suggests that we attempt to restate the problem omitting reference to the idea of force. "When these painful contradictions are removed," Hertz wrote, "the question as to the nature of force will not have been answered; but our minds, no longer vexed, will cease to ask illegitimate questions." It is easy to see how such statements could be taken as aid and comfort for the tradition of modern language philosophy, one of whose chief abusive epithets was the word "metaphysical."

Many things invited an anti-metaphysical interpretation of the *Tractatus*: the introduction by Russell, the formidably technical nature of the middle passages of the book, its adoption as a kind of catechism by the Vienna Circle positivists—all this made it easy to overlook the fact that the last sections of the book, the culmination of Wittgenstein's argument, were in fact deeply opposed to the anti-metaphysical tendency of positivism. Rudolf Carnap, perhaps the most distinguished member of the Vienna Circle, recalled that he first thought of Wittgenstein as a kindred spirit and advocate of positivism. Personal acquaintance taught him otherwise. "His point of view," Carnap wrote,

> and his attitude toward people and problems, even theoretical problems, were much more similar to those of a creative artist than to those of scientist; one might almost say, similar to those of a religious prophet or a seer. When he started to formulate his view on some specific philosophical problem, we often felt an internal struggle that occurred in him at that very moment, a struggle by which he tried to penetrate from darkness to light under an intense and

painful strain, which was even visible on his most expressive face. When finally, sometimes after a prolonged and arduous effort, his answer came forth, his statement stood before us like a newly created piece of art or a divine revelation. Not that he asserted his views dogmatically. . . . But the impression he made on us was as if insight came to him as through a divine inspiration, so that we could not help feeling that any sober rational comment or analysis of it would be a profanation.

Stephen Toulmin expands on Carnap's observation in *Wittgenstein's Vienna* (1973), his splendid intellectual history of the period:

Far from being a positivist, . . . Wittgenstein had meant the *Tractatus* to be interpreted in exactly the opposite sense. Where the Vienna positivists had equated the "important" with the "verifiable" and dismissed all unverifiable propositions as "unimportant *because* unsayable," the concluding section of the *Tractatus* had insisted—though to deaf cars—that *the unsayable alone has genuine value*. . . . Wittgenstein's silence in the face of the "unutterable" was not a mocking silence like that of the positivists, but rather a respectful one. Having decided that "value-neutral" facts alone can be expressed in regular proposition form, he exhorted his readers to turn their eyes away from factual propositions to the things of true value—which cannot be *gesagt* [stated] but only *gezeigt* [shown].

Toulmin is right, though in this context one cannot help remarking the irony that a book that put such stock in clarity of expression should invite such radically different interpretations.

It is also worth noting that one of the chief effects of

Wittgenstein's philosophy as expressed in the *Tractatus* is to render philosophy obsolete. Because (as Wittgenstein puts it in proposition 6.41) "the sense of the world must lie outside the world," philosophy as traditionally conceived—what is sometimes called "first-order" philosophy—is held to be impossible. Instead of attempting to discuss and to illuminate fundamental epistemological, moral, and aesthetic problems, philosophy, according to Wittgenstein's teaching here, must content itself with demonstrating its own pointlessness. In the penultimate proposition, 6.54, Wittgenstein candidly admits that

> My propositions serve as elucidations in the following way: anyone who understands me eventually recognizes them as nonsensical, when he has used them—as steps—to climb up beyond them. (He must, so to speak, throw away the ladder after he has climbed up it.)
>
> He must transcend these propositions, and then he will see the world aright.

It is in this sense that Wittgenstein could claim, in his preface to the *Tractatus*, that he considered "the *truth* of the thoughts" he had set forth to be "unassailable and definitive," yet then go on to point out "how little is achieved when these problems are solved."

In other words, in Wittgenstein's view, philosophy—and by extension rational discourse generally—is helpless when confronted with anything that really *matters*. Since "propositions can express nothing that is higher" (6.42), and since philosophy must limit itself to what can be expressed in propositions, philosophy turns out to have a purely negative function. It relieves one of the burden of having to think about pseudo-problems—which prominently include the classic pantheon of philosophical problems. ("Philosophical problems arise," he wrote in the *Philosophical Investigations* "when language *goes on holiday.*") Philosophy is the ladder one ascends to clarify one's thinking sufficiently to dispense with philosophy.

WITTGENSTEIN'S PHILOSOPHY changed radically in the years following publication of the *Tractatus.* Perhaps the most important change was his abandoning the hope to provide a complete account of *the* logical structure of language; instead of attempting to construct an ideal language in which all true propositions can be clearly expressed, he turned his attention to the rich variety of ordinary language. In a talk to the Moral Sciences Club at Cambridge in 1930, Wittgenstein recalled that

> I used at one time to say that, in order to get clear how a sentence is used, it was a good idea to ask oneself the question: "How would one try to verify such an assertion?" But that's just one way among others of getting clear about the use of a word or sentence. For example, another question which it is often very useful to ask oneself is: "How is the word learned?" "How would one set about teaching a child to use this word?" But some people have turned this suggestion about asking for the verification into a dogma as if I'd been advancing a theory about meaning.

As Wittgenstein put it in a telling paragraph near the beginning of the *Philosophical Investigations,*

> It is interesting to compare the multiplicity of the tools in language and of the ways they are used . . . with what logicians have said about the structure of language.
>   (Including the author of the *Tractatus Logico-Philosophicus.*)

("There are," he wrote to a friend, *very, very* many statements in the book with which I now disagree!")

WHATEVER THE DIFFERENCES between the outlook of the *Tractatus* and that of Wittgenstein's later philosophy, however, one thing that remained constant was the view that philosophy was a kind of disease that must be "cured" or otherwise overcome. "The real discovery," Wittgenstein writes in the *Investigations*,

> is the one that makes me capable of stopping doing philosophy when I want to.—The one that gives philosophy peace, so that it is no longer tormented by questions which bring *itself* in question.—Instead, we now demonstrate a method, by examples; and the series of examples can be broken off.—Problems are solved (difficulties eliminated), not a *single* problem. . . . "But then we will never come to the end of our job!" Of course not, because it has no end.

As McGuinness sums it up at the end of his book, "Philosophy requires logic and logic shows that there can be no philosophy, yet the fact that there can be none turns out to be the greatest liberation."

Early and late, Wittgenstein's philosophy contains coruscating insights and arguments of great subtlety and originality. But what Roy Monk says about the *Philosophical Investigations* is true of his philosophy as a whole:

> Other great philosophical works . . . can be read with interest and entertainment by [anyone interested in what the philosopher said]. . . . But if *Philosophical Investigations* is read in this spirit it will very quickly become boring, and a chore to read, not because it is intellectually difficult, but because it will be practically impossible to gather what

Wittgenstein is "saying." For, in truth, he is not *saying* anything; he is presenting a technique for the unravelling of confusions. Unless they are *your* confusions, the book will be of very little interest.

Monk may overstate the case; there are portions of the *Philosophical Investigations*—the elaboration of the idea of the language game, for example, and Wittgenstein's arguments against solipsism—that are of general philosophical interest. But he is right to stress the deeply personal character of Wittgenstein's philosophical enterprise.

The primary passions of Wittgenstein's life are to be found in his struggles with *himself*. It is significant that he judged Augustine's *Confessions* to be possibly "the most serious book ever written." The essential thing to grasp about Wittgenstein's character is his peculiar combination of tenacity and touchiness. Both are evident in all aspects of his life: intellectual, social, emotional. Craving affection, he nonetheless could not bear prolonged intimacy. He fell in love several times—generally with young men, but also with Marguerite Respinger, a Swiss girl he met at Cambridge and whom he contemplated marrying.

But Wittgenstein's emotional life was always edged with anguish. His passion was tempered by an unfathomable reserve, a certain coldness and unbridgeable self-absorption that made him unresponsive to the feelings, one might even say the reality, of others. One friend of mine commented in exasperation that Wittgenstein displayed all the symptoms of "high-functioning autism": "His behavior could pass in a Cambridge full of men with disturbed childhoods like Russell as 'eccentric,' but really it was worse than that." As Monk observes, "the philosophical solipsism to which he had at one time been attracted, and against which much of his later work is addressed, . . . has

LIVES OF THE MIND

its parallel in the emotional solipsism in which his romantic attachments were conducted."† This is the point of
Wittgenstein's fondness for Schopenhauer's parable of the
porcupines, to which McGuinness frequently adverts:
Crowding together for warmth on a winter's day, a group
of porcupines are pricked by one another's quills; so they
move back and forth until they find a middle distance—a
place mid-way between isolation and intimacy—that they
can comfortably support.

Understandably, Wittgenstein's extreme fastidiousness,
ruthless honesty, and readiness to take offense at the
slightest demurral made him a most demanding friend. His
letters are full both of protestations of affection and of
detailed explanations about why he must terminate relations with his correspondent. As McGuinness observes,
"though he often asked, in a material sense, very little, he
demanded that his individuality should be recognized. Exception must be made for it, rules must be circumvented.

---

† In *Wittgenstein* (1973), William Warren Bartley III portentously con-
fides that in addition to engaging in the usual sorts of biographical
research he went "to homosexual bars in Vienna and London in
search of those who knew Wittgenstein in another way; and I was
successful." He also claims that as a young man Wittgenstein was
"given to bouts of extravagant and almost uncontrollable promis-
cuity" that would take him out to the streets in search of anonymous
homosexual encounters. Since Bartley presents no evidence for these
claims, the reader is left to accept them on faith—or to reject them,
as most commentators on Wittgenstein have done. (McGuinness
peremptorily dismisses them as "gratuitous"; Monk devotes an appendix to undermining Bartley's sensationalistic claims.) Like Otto
Weininger, whose notorious *Sex and Character* (1903) made a deep
impression on him, Wittgenstein tended to distinguish sharply between sex and love. "Sexual arousal," Monk noted, "both homo-
and heterosexual, troubled him enormously. He seemed to regard it
as incompatible with the sort of person he wanted to be."

The world must be remade to fit his gifts. It was the only way he could make use of them."

But despite Wittgenstein's sometimes forbidding language and the assimilation of his thought to the ranks of academic linguistic philosophy, he was at bottom an exceedingly *un*academic character. Norman Malcolm and others report that he habitually tried to persuade students to give up their plans to teach philosophy because, as Malcolm put it, "He believed that a normal human being could not be a university teacher and also an honest and serious person." It is in fact a curious irony that this man who detested the academy and was convinced that being a professor of philosophy was "a kind of living death" should have spawned one of the busiest academic industries of our time. Wittgenstein's position on professional philosophy is perhaps best summed up in a letter he wrote in 1944: "what is the use of philosophy if all that it does for you is to enable you to talk with some plausibility about some abstruse questions of logic, etc., & if it does not improve your thinking about the important questions of everyday life." It remains an open question whether Wittgenstein's *philosophy* really helps to improve one's thinking about "the important questions of everyday life." But there can be little doubt that he saw his life as a struggle to bring philosophy back to the "important questions"—even if it turned out that philosophy itself had to be sacrificed as a result of that encounter.

Bertrand Russell:
Apostle of Disillusionment

When Mr. Apollinax visited the United States
His laughter tinkled among the teacups.
I thought of Fragilion, that shy figure among the birch-trees,
And of Priapus in the shrubbery
Gaping at the lady in the swing.
—T. S. Eliot, "Mr. Apollinax"

Thee will find out in time that I have a great love of professing
vile sentiments, I don't know why, unless it springs from long
efforts to avoid priggery.
—Bertrand Russell to Alys Pearsall Smith, 1894

I T MUST HAVE BEEN extraordinary, being Bertrand Russell. Born in an isolated spot near Trelleck, Wales, in 1872 when Victoria still had twenty-nine years to reign, he lived on in robust health until 1970. He lived, in other words, from the zenith of the British Empire through its gradual dismemberment and dissolution. A young adult when the Boer War broke out in 1899, he was a vigorous nonagenarian when the Vietnam War was being prosecuted in earnest. In his lifetime he saw the extension of the franchise to women, two world wars, the appearance of electric lights, telephones, movies, the automobile, the airplane, computers, and manned space travel, not to mention antibiotics and open-heart surgery. His first wife knew and corresponded with Walt Whitman; his fourth and last, whom he married when he was seventy-nine, helped him campaign for nuclear disarmament. (George Santayana, who greatly—and anonymously—helped Russell financially in the late 1930s, described him as "a leading mathematician, philosopher, militant pacifist, wit, and martyr, but unfortunately addicted to marrying and divorcing not wisely but too often.")

Of course, unusual longevity was hardly the only conspicuous thing about Bertrand Arthur William Russell. There was also his illustrious Whig family, his prodigious intellectual gifts and achievements, and his inveterate campaigning for all manner of progressive causes, from female suffrage, pacifism, and birth control to world government and humanistic atheism.

Political activism was practically part of the Russell birthright. A seventeenth-century ancestor, Lord William Russell, was executed in 1683 for his part in the Rye House Plot, an attempt to assassinate Charles II and his brother, the future James II. Bertrand's grandfather, whom Victoria made an earl in 1861, introduced the first Reform Bill in 1832 and was twice elected Prime Minister. His father, John, Viscount Amberley, was Lord Russell's eldest son. Two children survived to maturity: Frank, who was born in 1865, and Bertrand, their third and last child. John Stuart Mill, a close friend of the family, agreed to be Bertrand's secular "godfather" (though his death in 1873 relieved him from the duty of discharging that obligation).

Amberley was less successful but no less liberal than his father in politics, and he and his wife, Kate, made themselves notorious as freethinkers in religious and moral matters. There was, for example, the question of Kate's relationship with one of young Frank's tutors, Douglas Spalding, who by the 1870s was in an advanced stage of consumption. As Bertrand recalled in the first volume of his *Autobiography* (1967), "my father and mother decided that although [Spalding] ought to remain childless on account of his tuberculosis, it was unfair to expect him to remain celibate. My mother therefore allowed him to live with her, though I know of no evidence that she derived any pleasure from doing so."

Amberley and Kate fully intended to impart their emancipated views to their children. But Bertrand's emergence as a full-fledged freethinker was to be postponed by his parents' untimely deaths. Kate (along with her young daughter, Rachel) died in 1874 from consumption; Amberley, devastated by the loss, followed two years later from a combination of bronchitis and (it was said) inconsolable grief. He had directed that his children be brought up by Spalding and Bertrand's second "godfather," Thomas Cobden-Sanderson, another of Kate's admirers and a confirmed atheist. But revelation of Spalding's relationship with Kate led Lord and Lady Russell to contest these provisions. The result was that Frank continued his schooling at Winchester while Bertrand was promptly packed off to his grandparents' house in London, a grace-and-favor residence called Pembroke Lodge in Richmond Park.

Less than three years later, in 1878, Lord Russell died, aged eighty-six. He left young Bertrand in the care of his wife, who was twenty-three years his junior. Of Scotch Presbyterian stock, Lady Russell was a woman of high Whiggish principles. She hoped that her favorite grandson would one day take his place as a great liberal politician like his grandfather. Known as "Deadly Nightshade" by some of her husband's colleagues, she also exhibited a severe and unbending moral fervor. Duty ruled her life. She early on gave Bertrand a Bible with her favorite verses copied onto the fly-leaf. Among them was the injunction "Thou shalt not follow a multitude to do evil": it pleased the mature Bertrand Russell to believe that he had always striven to follow this commandment faithfully. Nor did creature comforts hold much appeal for the dowager Countess. "She disliked wine, abhorred tobacco, and was always on the verge of becoming a vegetarian," Russell recalled years later. "Her life was austere. She ate only the plainest food, breakfasted at eight, and until she reached the age of eighty, never sat in a comfortable chair until after tea." Emotional austerity, too, was part of the regimen: "It was obvious," he concluded, "that she never came anywhere near knowing what it feels like to be in love."

Unlike Frank, Bertrand continued to be educated at home by a series of tutors until he went up to Trinity College, Cambridge, in 1890. But "Granny" Russell was far and away the predominating influence on his early life: coddling yet stern, solicitous, exacting, indefatigable, ubiquitous. "She demanded that everything be viewed through a mist of Victorian sentiment," he noted. By his early teens, Bertrand had abandoned belief in God—a result, he said, of reading Mill's *Autobiography*. The misty sentiment that his grandmother required became increasingly difficult to abide: "Indeed, after the age of fourteen I found living at home only endurable at the cost of complete silence about everything that interested me."

It is not surprising that Bertrand Russell should later have complained of enduring a lonely and isolated childhood. "In adolescence," he recalled in *The Conquest of Happiness* (1930), "I hated life and was constantly on the verge of suicide, from which, however, I was restrained by the desire to know more mathematics." Lady Russell's unremitting attentions were a prescription for inducing introversion and loneliness. They were also a foolproof prescription for provoking rebellion. And rebellion, though delayed, did come in due course. Yet what is perhaps most remarkable is not the course of Russell's rebellion: that indeed was rather a predictable diet of apocalyptic atheism, cranky political activism, and insatiable philandering. More telling is the extent to which he remained faithful to his grandmother's sentimentalizing imperatives. The gospels that he preached were founded on different precepts, to be sure, but the mists of reformist, often utopian, moralism still wafted about in great profusion. T. S. Eliot was quite right when he noted, in a review of Russell's pamphlet *Why I Am Not a Christian* (1927), that "Just as Mr. Russell's Radicalism in politics is merely a variety of Whiggery, so his Non-Christianity is merely a variety of Low Church sentiment."

The complex story of Russell's life has already been told in several versions. There are, first of all, the multitude of fragmentary sketches that exist in letters, diaries, memoirs, poems, and novels by his wide and distinguished circle of friends and acquaintances. Eliot, Beatrice Webb, Virginia and Leonard Woolf, John Maynard Keynes, H. G. Wells, Santayana, A. J. Ayer, among others, as well as several of Russell's lovers and at least one of his wives have made notable contributions to the compendious stock of Russelliana. Then there are Russell's own memoirs and autobiographical writings, culminating in his three-volume retrospective, *The Autobiography of Bertrand Russell* (1967–1969), a patchwork of new and old writing that includes a generous selection of correspondence. There is also *The Life of Bertrand Russell* (1975), Ronald Clark's long and judicious biography, as well as more partisan efforts such as *Bertrand Russell: The Passionate Skeptic* (1957) by the philosopher's friend Alan Wood, and Alan

Ryan's *Bertrand Russell: A Political Life* (1988). More recent contributions to the store are biographies by Caroline Moorehead (1993) and Ray Monk (two volumes, 1996 and 2001).

Still, although the news about Bertrand Russell has scarcely been under-reported, Nicholas Griffin's two volumes of letters (1992 and 2001) do round out the picture of the mathematician-turned-philosopher-turned-political-activist. Russell's letters provide a richer and more detailed—if not necessarily more edifying—portrait of Russell's character, obsessions, and eccentricities than has hitherto been available. Russell's *Autobiography* resembles Rousseau's *Confessions* in its claim to present a portrait of *un homme dans toute la vérité de la nature*. But—again like the *Confessions*—it is determinedly calculated about exactly what counts as "all the truth of nature." Some warts pass muster and are bravely declared, others are discreetly concealed. Griffin's anthologies portray a more hesitant and bedeviled figure than Russell dramatized in his *Autobiography*. Moreover, the abundant commentary and notes with which Griffin accompanies the letters, confidently drawing on a wide range of material from writings by Russell and his correspondents, assures that the volumes succeed in their ambition of furnishing readers with a fresh "epistolary biography" of its subject.

Griffin, who teaches philosophy at McMaster University, Ontario—home of the gargantuan Russell archives—has assembled just over 600 letters in these two volumes. One is reminded how important letters once were, not only as a form of literary expression but also as a fundamental means of communication. In a time before telephones and automobiles (and before the deterioration of postal service), the habit of writing was cultivated by the educated classes as surely as any other social grace. Entire relation-

227

ships were conducted on paper in a way that would be difficult to credit today. (Of course, we have e-mail now, but one wonders, even if it is backed up, how much of that will remain for future generations to sift through.) The total number of letters by Russell in the archives, Griffin estimates, is currently between forty and fifty thousand, and is growing steadily as new correspondence is discovered.

With so many letters to choose from, there is inevitably something arbitrary about any selection of five or six hundred. Griffin readily concedes that he could have put together several other representative volumes with virtually no duplication. As it is, only a handful of letters printed here have been published in full before. In volume one, the only one is a famous dispatch from 1902 to the great German mathematician Gottlob Frege (1848–1925), written just as the second volume of his pathbreaking *Grundgesetze der Arithmetik* (first volume, 1893) was going to press. Russell's letter politely outlines a fundamental logical paradox in Frege's work, thus delivering a shattering blow to his entire philosophy of mathematics. At that time, Frege was still an obscure figure. Russell's letter confronted him with the unraveling of his life's work, yet he replied with a grace and intellectual integrity that are nothing short of exemplary. Granting Russell's point, Frege poignantly admitted that it had "shaken the basis on which I intended to build arithmetic" and that it "is all the more serious since . . . not only the foundations of my arithmetic, but also the sole possible foundations of arithmetic, seem to vanish." Frege's response, Russell noted some sixty years later, "was almost superhuman, a telling indication of that of which men are capable if their dedication is to creative work and knowledge instead of cruder efforts to dominate and be known."

Griffin begins his first volume with a few childhood

missives to relatives and ends with a handful of stunned notes written at the beginning of August 1914 just as World War I was breaking out. He shows us Russell in his college days at Trinity, his teaching there and membership in the famous *conversazione* society, the Apostles (so called because membership was limited to a dozen). He follows Russell through his long courtship of his first wife, Alys Pearsall Smith, whom he met when he was seventeen and married in December 1894. Along the way, we witness Russell's intellectual coming-of-age, his move from the chummy idealism of British Hegelianism to an absorption in the chaster, more rigorous tenets of mathematical logic. The volume concludes with some seventy letters (out of more than one thousand) to the celebrated society hostess Lady Ottoline Morrell (1873–1938), with whom Russell had a tempestuous and exceedingly wordy affair beginning in 1911. Lady Ottoline is gradually replaced in the second volume by Colette O'Niel, the stage name of Lady Constance Malleson (the wife of the actor Miles Malleson), who was thirty-five years Russell's junior. Russell had a long and ultimately unhappy affair with O'Niel; some eight-hundred letters from Russell to her survive.

The gossip quotient is high in both volumes of letters, but the first volume is intellectually the most substantial. It covers the period during which Russell did his most important philosophical work. Of the twelve books that he published between 1896 and 1914 (he published seventy-one altogether), at least three helped to change the tenor of modern analytic philosophy: *The Principles of Mathematics* (1903), *Philosophical Essays* (1910), and the three-volume magnum opus, *Principia Mathematica* (1910–1913), on which Russell collaborated for almost a decade with his former tutor, the philosopher Alfred North Whitehead (1861–1947). A projected fourth volume was never completed. These books, concerned as they are with the precise machinery of implication, deduction, class membership, and other basic logical concepts, are formidably technical. Russell's overall ambition, he wrote at the end of *The Principles of Mathematics*, was to demonstrate "that all pure mathematics deals exclusively with concepts definable in terms of a very small number of logical concepts, and that all its propositions are deducible from a very small number of fundamental logical principles." Russell did not succeed, but it is not surprising that the fruit of his effort to reduce mathematics to logic, the *Principia*, is filled with page after page of abstruse logical notation that is inaccessible to all but a few specialists.

It was also during this period that Russell made his first efforts as a philosophical popularizer. *The Problems of Philosophy*, a brief introduction to the subject that he referred to in several letters as his "shilling shocker," was published in 1912. Like almost everything that he published for non-specialists, *The Problems of Philosophy* is written with exceptional clarity and verve. (As T. S. Eliot noted, "Mr. Russell can write extremely well, and usually does write well, except when carried away by emotion.") Organized by topic ("Appearance and Reality," "How *A Priori* Knowledge Is Possible," "Truth and Falsehood," "The Limits of Philosophical Knowledge," etc.), it is still occasionally used in the classroom. Russell's attempts to win a larger readership for his philosophical writings (and to increase his earnings) culminated in 1945 when he published *A History of Western Philosophy*, a quirky but encyclopedic survey based on lectures that he had delivered at the Barnes Foundation in Philadelphia. Engagingly written, the book became an instant bestseller on both sides of the Atlantic, and its success did much to win Russell the Nobel Prize for Literature in 1950.

Russell's most famous pupil was undoubtedly Ludwig Wittgenstein, who, as we saw in the last chapter, had come to Cambridge to study philosophy with Russell in 1911 after abandoning a career in engineering. Wittgenstein makes poignant appearances in Russell's letters. Describing one of his first encounters with "my German," Russell reports that he "came back with me after my lecture and argued till dinner-time—obstinate and perverse, but I think not stupid." Indeed. It was not long before pupil and teacher were arguing as peers. "I think he has *genius*," Russell noted in a later letter. "In discussion with him I put out *all* my force and only just equalled his. With all my other pupils I should squash them flat if I did so." Within a few years, Russell was acting as an amanuensis, scribbling down thoughts that the twenty-four-year-old Wittgenstein, who found writing preternaturally difficult, dictated as he nervously paced back and forth in his tutor's rooms. "W. makes me feel it is worthwhile I should exist," Russell explained, "because no one else could understand him or make the world understand him." By 1914, Wittgenstein's ruthless dissection of inconsistencies in Russell's philosophy had a paralyzing effect. "Wittgenstein persuaded me that what wanted doing in logic was too difficult for me," Russell admitted in the second volume of his *Autobiography*. "So there was no really vital satisfaction of my philosophical impulse in that work, and philosophy lost its hold on me." In essence, Russell found that Wittgenstein had done for him what he had done for Frege a dozen years before.

Philosophical matters are sometimes broached in these letters—Russell's correspondents included G. E. Moore, Gilbert Murray, Whitehead, and sundry other professional colleagues—but for the most part their focus is adamantly personal. Without Griffin's copious commentary, readers unfamiliar with the outline of Russell's biography would often be lost. Griffin titles his first volume "The Private Years," but in some ways Russell's thirst for the stage of public life was already well advanced by the 1910s. He began dabbling in politics at an early age and was always susceptible to "causes." When the suffragettes came along, he was naturally a vocal champion (though he took exception to the violent tactics some of them employed). And already in 1907 he stood for Parliament (the first of three failed attempts). But it was really only with the advent of World War I that Russell emerged as a visible moral crusader and self-appointed public conscience. (His public position was enhanced in 1931 when his brother died *sine prole* and he succeeded to the earldom.) By the 1940s and 1950s we have not Russell the philosopher but Russell the preening activist: the guiding spirit of the Pugwash Conference, the Bertrand Russell Peace Foundation, and an International War Crimes Tribunal assembled to charge the United States with atrocities in Vietnam.

Taken *en bloc*, Russell's letters exhibit the process by which a fiercely shy, slightly morbid aristocrat blossomed into a brilliant, though tortured, enigma. About Russell's brilliance, there can be little question. Whitehead—himself a formidable intellect—concluded that his former pupil had the best analytic mind of any philosopher in history, "including Aristotle." And Leonard Woolf, reflecting on the impression that Russell made in the 1890s, conceded that he had "the quickest mind of anyone I have ever known; like the greatest of chess players he sees in a flash six moves ahead of the ordinary player and one move ahead of all the other Grand Masters. However serious he may be," Woolf continued, "his conversation scintillates with wit and a kind of puckish humour flickers through his thought."

As Woolf's observation suggests, Russell's brilliance was not confined to technical philosophical matters. He was immensely well read and delighted in the banter of Oxbridge repartee. "I am looking forward very much to getting back to Cambridge," he wrote to Alys in 1893, "and being able to say what I think and not to mean what I say: two things which at home are impossible. Cambridge is one of the few places where one can talk unlimited nonsense and generalities without anyone pulling one up or confronting one with them when one says just the opposite the next day." Given his taste for what Algernon Moncrieff might have called piffle, it is curious how often the words "prig" and "priggish" crop up in connection with Russell. He often accuses himself of priggishness; others, especially those closest to him, not infrequently concur. Sometimes it is in jest, or half in jest. As Russell recalls in his *Autobiography*, in 1891 he became a member in good standing of the Order of Prigs, a fanciful group established by Alys's older brother, Logan Pearsall Smith, the displaced American dandy and aphorist. Among the maxims and rules promulgated by Logan were injunctions to "Deny yourself in inconspicuous ways and don't speak of your economies" and "Abstain entirely from all intoxicating liquors, except for purposes of health."

Less obviously in jest was the priggishness that often surfaced in Russell's relationship with Alys. It was a difficult courtship all around. Five years Russell's senior, Alys was a neurasthenic feminist reformer whose main interests were female suffrage and the temperance movement. (For her sake, Russell became a teetotaler for many years.) She came from a wealthy and unusual American Quaker family living in England. In addition to Logan, there was her sister Mary, the eldest Smith child, who ran off with and eventually married Bernard Berenson, the great art connoisseur and doyen of I Tatti. The Quaker background accounts for the archaic *thees*, *thous*, and *thines* that dot Russell's correspondence with Alys beginning in 1894: touching in its way, perhaps, but finally a bit cloying. Alys deserves recognition as one of the few people in Russell's circle who could compete with him in self-righteousness. Typical was the proposal she made when they were engaged that they turn their house into a kind of hotel for the homeless. She also professed grave anxiety about sex—a more perfect caricature of the repressed Victorian lady would be hard to find—believing it an unpleasant and wholly regrettable requirement of continuing the race. Nervous discussion of the dreaded topic filled their correspondence for a time. A wretched, solicitous Russell did his best to reassure her, writing that "as to frequency, I am sure it ought not to be great."

Among other obstacles that the young couple faced was the adamant opposition of Lady Russell, who regarded Alys as a socially unsuitable parvenue (not to mention that she was an American) with improper designs on her grandson. When simple pleading failed to convince Russell to break off the engagement, she hired a doctor to certify that because of insanity on both sides of the family they should not have children. (This was not, alas, a groundless concern: Russell's son John, by his second wife, was in and out of mental institutions and two of his grandchildren were schizophrenics.) Russell's first response to this news was to suggest that they have children by other people, a prospect, Griffin reports, that Alys "hotly rejected." They decided at first to marry and not have children, discovering in the end that they couldn't, a contingency that intervened in their disagreement about whether or not to bring up their children as Christians. (The desire for progeny grew on Russell. He later had three children, two with his second wife, Dora Black, one with his third, Patricia Spence, known familiarly as "Peter.") What turned out to be an even more telling problem was Alys's worry that she was not intelligent enough for Russell. In retrospect, the reassurances he offered during their courtship bear the grim mark of habitual condescension. "Of course one doesn't imagine thee would do any brilliant original thinking," he wrote a month before they were married, "but thee might form part of the indispensable intelligent audience."

Despite this inauspicious litany, Bertie and Alys were reasonably happy for four or five years. As late as November 1901 he could rhapsodize that "since last winter I have known that life without thee would not be possible." Nevertheless, this was a period of great emotional tumult for Russell. There was, first of all, the quasi-mystical experience he had after hearing Gilbert Murray read part of his new translation of Euripides' *Hippolytus*. Returning to the Whiteheads' after the reading, he and Alys found Evelyn Whitehead, Alfred's wife, in the midst of a painful angina attack. As Russell recalls in his *Autobiography*,

> Suddenly the ground seemed to give way beneath me, and I found myself in quite another region. Within five minutes I went through some such reflections as the following: the loneliness of the human soul is unendurable; nothing can penetrate it except the highest intensity of that sort of love that the religious teachers have preached; whatever does not spring from this motive is harmful, or at best useless; it follows that war is wrong, that a public school education is abominable, that the use of force is to be deprecated, and that in human relations one should penetrate to the core of loneliness in each person and speak to that. . . . At the end of those five minutes, I had become a completely different person. For a time, a sort of mystic illumination possessed

me. . . . Having been an imperialist, I became . . . pro-Boer
and a pacifist.

No doubt this was the shattering, transformative experience that Russell presents it as. But it is also a splendid
example of the higher priggishness at work: "It follows
that . . ." What? That a public school education is
abominable? This is the logic of the proselytizer, not the
philosopher.

Some commentators have suggested that such passages
indicate a profound religious sensibility lurking beneath
Russell's probing empirical armor. In fact, Russell's entire
outlook was programmatically anti-religious. In "Has
Religion Made Useful Contributions to Civilization?"
(1930), for example, he begins by noting that he regards
religion as "a disease born of fear and as a source of
untold misery to the human race." But this sophomoric
conviction did not prevent him from exploiting an aes-
theticized mysticism for his own ends. Within a year of his
"mystic illumination," Russell discovered that life without
Alys, if not yet possible, was certainly desirable. I believe it
was the literary critic Harold Bloom who once remarked
that falling out of love is one of the great experiences of
life. Be that as it may, something of the sort seems to have
happened to Russell in 1902. He puts it thus in his *Autobiography*: "I went out bicycling one afternoon, and suddenly, as I was riding along a country road, I realized that I
no longer loved Alys. I had no idea until this moment that
my love for her was even lessening." In a canceled passage
that Ronald Clark reproduces in his biography, Russell
immediately added that "I now believe that it is not in my
nature to remain physically fond of any woman for more
than seven or eight years. As I view it now, this was the
basis of the matter and the rest was humbug."

Humbug or not, he and Alys continued to live together in brittle solitude even after he confessed that his love was dead. Logic, as Griffin observes, became Russell's "opiate." In an extraordinary feat of concentration, he threw himself into work on the *Principia,* struggling over it nine or ten hours a day for almost a decade. Although he claimed to have been celibate for the entire period, there was at least one emotional entanglement. Ronald Clark suggests that "the evidence, though circumstantial, is considerable" that Russell fell in love with Evelyn Whitehead around this time. If true, nothing came of it, and a lingering despondency settled over both Russell and Alys. In one of his most famous essays, "A Free Man's Worship" (1903), the depth of Russell's despondency shows itself in a credo of cosmological pessimism:

> That man is the product of causes which had no prevision of the end they were achieving; that his origin, his growth, his hopes and fears, his loves and his beliefs, are but the outcome of accidental collocations of atoms; that no fire, no heroism, no intensity of thought and feeling, can preserve an individual life beyond the grave; that all the labors of the ages, all the devotion, all the inspiration, all the noonday brightness of human genius, are destined to extinction in the vast depth of the solar system, and that the whole temple of man's achievement must inevitably be buried beneath the debris of a universe in ruins—all these things, if not quite beyond dispute, are yet so nearly certain that no philosophy which rejects them can hope to stand. Only within the scaffolding of these truths, only on the firm foundation of unyielding despair can the soul's habitation henceforth be safely built.

Russell presents all this as the necessary result of dispas-

sionate reflection. It is clear, at any rate, that it is a coefficient of his unshakable bleakness. In 1905, he wrote to one
correspondent that "of course if one could wholly kill the
desire for happiness, many things would cease to be tiring,
and one's power of work would be greatly increased. But
though I have laboured hard to produce this result, I have
not yet succeeded." Hence his cultivation of frivolity: when
everything real is full of pain, he lamented, "there is an
increasing temptation to live on the surface." Evelyn
Waugh aptly characterized this phase of Russell's bluster-
ing nihilism in a 1928 review of *Skeptical Essays*: "he is
able without a tremor," Waugh wrote, "to look into the
common and unfathomable abysses of pessimism and turn
aside with the judicial comment, 'Yes, I think it is probable
that we should all fall in.'"

Alys did not cast things in the grandiose terms that her
husband favored. But her gloominess was perhaps even less
pliable. In 1907, she developed a lump in her breast. Upon
discovering that it was not malignant, she confided to her
diary that

> Now my blissful hope of six months is destroyed—even the
> chance of death. I do so long to leave Bertie free to live
> with a woman who . . . does not bore him desperately and
> get on his nerves as I do. . . . Little duties keep me going
> from day to day. But they don't satisfy the awful craving
> hunger for Bertie's love. . . . If only I could die—it's such a
> simple solution.

Russell eventually shook off his depression. Alys seems
to have lived on with hers until the end. In the third
volume of his *Autobiography*, Russell reproduces a handful of letters he received from Alys in 1950, a year before
her death. Having divorced in 1921 so that Russell could

marry Dora Black, they had been completely out of touch for thirty years. He concludes by reprinting a pathetic passage from Alys's own memoirs. "Bertie was an ideal companion," Alys wrote, but "I was never clever enough for him, and perhaps he was too sophisticated for me. . . . Unfortunately, I was neither wise enough nor courageous enough to prevent this one disaster from shattering my capacity for happiness and my zest for life." Somehow, Bertie's insight that "in human relations one should penetrate to the core of loneliness in each person and speak to that" did not apply to Alys.

A PUBLIC RUPTURE with Alys did not come until 1911 when Russell began his affair with Ottoline Morrell. For several years, Ottoline was Russell's most important confidante, though he was never her only romantic interest. In the end, their relationship seems to have foundered on the question of sex. In fact, Ottoline typically seemed more interested in collecting admirers (Augustus John and Roger Fry were among her suitors) than sleeping with them. But for the newly awakened Russell, her sexual aloofness was frustrating. "In the spiritual region you do most fully satisfy me," he wrote in 1912. "But my lower nature sometimes yearns after the simple happiness I used to have at first." "Loving you," he wrote later, "is like loving a red-hot poker."

One solution was taking other lovers. In the spring of 1914, Russell came to the United States to teach at Harvard for a semester. He described Cambridge, Massachusetts, as "a soul-destroying atmosphere," Harvard as a "*ghastly*" place full of "*awful* people." It was during this stint at Harvard that Russell first met T. S. Eliot, inspiring the early poem "Mr. Apollinax." It was also during this trip that Russell commenced a sporadic affair with Helen

Dudley, a girl he met in Chicago. He promptly reported the incident to Ottoline. "I do not want you to think that this will make the very *smallest* difference in my feeling towards you," he wrote, "beyond removing the irritation of unsatisfied instinct." Besides, he continued, Helen was "not good looking—her mouth, and still more her nose, very ugly." Calculated or not, Russell's confession led to a brief recrudescence of his sexual relations with Ottoline.

Like many academic commentators on Russell, Griffin holds Russell in very high esteem. He does not, like A. J. Ayer, conclude with the exclamation that Russell was "a great and good man." But a conviction of Russell's essential high-mindedness is presupposed throughout his notes and commentary. In truth, though, Russell emerges as a deeply ambivalent—not to say discreditable—figure in these pages. He was charming, witty, and unfailingly generous with money. But if his brilliance and generosity are undeniable, so too are his moral high-handedness, his gloomy self-righteousness, his priggishness—what in his *Autobiography* he grandly called his "unbearable pity for the suffering of mankind." How much mankind has had to suffer at the hands of those who pity it! Combined with his inveterate zeal for reform, Russell's deployment of pity consistently nurtured a wide variety of utopian schemes. In a letter to Alys about socialism and "the woman question," for example, he writes:

> Thee might observe incidentally that if the state paid for child-bearing it might and ought to require a medical certificate that the parents were such as to give a reasonable result of a healthy child—this would afford a very good inducement to some sort of care for the race, and gradually as public opinion became educated by the law, it might react on the law and make that more stringent, until one

got to some state of things in which there would be a little genuine care for the race, instead of the present haphazard higgledy-piggledy ways.

Nor was Russell's utopianism confined to eugenics and family planning. In *Political Ideals* (1917), he suggests that with intelligent use of modern technology mankind could shortly "abolish all abject poverty, quite half the illness in the world, the whole economic slavery which binds down nine-tenths of our population: we could fill the world with beauty and joy, and secure the reign of universal peace." Whatever fondness Russell had felt for Aldous Huxley faded after Huxley portrayed him as the unpleasant Mr. Scogan in *Crome Yellow*. But many of Russell's pronouncements on social engineering might have come from one of Huxley's grim dystopian novels. Think, for example, of Russell's confident prediction in "What I Believe" (1925) that physiology and psychology would soon enable us "to produce far more the type of human beings that we admire. Intelligence, artistic capacity, benevolence—all these things could be increased by science. There seems scarcely any limit to what *could* be done in the way of producing a good world if only men would use science wisely."

Russell's glee about the beneficence of science paled noticeably with the advent of nuclear weapons. But his appetite for alarming international scenarios was left undiminished. Although he attempted to deny it later, shortly after World War II he several times advocated that the United States initiate a "preventive war" against the Soviet Union. "A *casus belli*," he explained, "would not be difficult to find." (Griffin reproduces a famous letter of 1948 to Walter Marseille, a professor at Berkeley, which warned that "If Russia overruns Western Europe, the destruction will be such as no subsequent re-conquest can undo.") In the mid-Fifties, however, Russell did an about-face and began agitating vociferously for disarmament. Ever since a trip to the Soviet Union in 1920, he had been a staunch anti-Communist. (Lenin's Russia, he observed, was "a close tyrannical bureaucracy, with a spy system more elaborate and terrible than the Tsar's.") But now an uncontrollable anti-Americanism took precedence: America, not the Soviet Union, became the emblem of political iniquity. In 1961, he delivered himself of a particularly violent burst of moral hysteria. "We used to think Hitler was wicked when he wanted to kill all the Jews," he said in a speech. "But Kennedy and Macmillan not only want to kill all the Jews but all the rest of us too. They're much more wicked than Hitler. . . . They are the wickedest people that ever lived in the history of man."

In part, Russell's political buffoonery stemmed from what the British historian Maurice Cowling identified as the attempt to generalize "the intelligentsia's values to the whole of life." If only the world would listen to him, the great logician and philosopher, peace, prosperity, and universal happiness would be promptly forthcoming. Alas, Russell never seemed to realize that the kind of consistency he could demand of a philosophical argument was unattainable—indeed, it was repugnant and destructive—in a world populated by human beings. It is significant that Russell had great difficulty remembering faces: he resorted to memorizing verbal descriptions of people, even friends, in order to recognize them. John Maynard Keynes summed it up neatly when, reminiscing about the intellectual climate of Cambridge before the First World War, he noted that "Bertie in particular sustained simultaneously a pair of opinions ludicrously incompatible. He held that in fact human affairs were carried on after a most irrational fashion, but that the remedy was quite simple and easy, since all we had to do was to carry them on rationally." The emotional, the human havoc wrought by Russell's unremitting Whiggish progressivism was registered by his daughter Kate in a book about her father: "Reason, progress, unselfishness, a wide historical perspective, expansiveness, generosity, enlightened self-interest. I had heard it all my life and it filled me with despair."

In a diary entry from 1902, Beatrice Webb correctly noted that

> Bertrand Russell's nature is pathetic in its subtle absoluteness: faith in an absolute logic, absolute ethic, absolute beauty, and all of the most refined and rarified type. His abstract and revolutionary methods of thought and the uncompromising way in which he applies these frightens me for his future and the future of those who love him or whom he loves. Compromise, mitigation, mixed motive, phases of health of body and mind, qualified statements, uncertain feelings, all seem unknown to him.

It is easy to conclude, with Webb, that Russell's ruling characteristic was an overweening desire for certainty. In a postscript to the third volume of his *Autobiography*, for example, he wrote that "I wanted certainty in the kind of way in which people want religious faith." And certainty, indeed, was part of the mesmerizing appeal that mathematics held for him. "The world of mathematics," he wrote in 1901, "is really a beautiful world; it has nothing to do with life and death and human sordidness, but is eternal, cold and passionless." And yet, as one reflects on Russell's philosophical career, it appears that behind this thirst for certainty there lurked an even deeper craving for disillusionment. Thus it is that in one of his first letters to

Ottoline he described himself as "a sort of logic machine warranted to destroy every ideal that is not very robust." The truth is that Russell regarded the very prospect of certainty as a challenge or affront. His quest for certainty was undertaken chiefly to establish its impossibility, not to secure it. This is one reason that Russell was so dismissive of religious faith: here he was confronted with a realm of experience that refused to submit itself absolutely to his scrutiny and dissection.

The union of Russell's desire for certainty and passion for disillusionment may also help to explain the curious air of unreality that attends so much of his thought. Whether the subject is logic, religion, society, or morals, Russell's approach is likely to impress one first of all by its cleverness and then by its artificiality. In a discussion of Russell's philosophy of Logical Atomism, the attempt "to construct the universe out of sense data," Santayana commented that, although it seems coolly realistic, Russell's theory is really "marvellously like empirical idealism. It has the same 'nothing but' quality: it is a substitution of means for ends and an analysis of knowledge for the object of it." *The substitution of an analysis of knowledge for the object of knowledge*: perhaps this is what T. S. Eliot had in mind when he said that Russell's "lucidity is often that of a mirror rather than that of clear water."

And this brings us to what a pragmatist might call the "cash value" of Russell's philosophy. The *Principia Mathematica* is indisputably a monument of twentieth-century thought. It will, as the British philosopher Roger Scruton remarked, "be remembered as long as civilisation lasts." But it is an inaccessible monument. Russell himself once conjectured that only six people had read it all the way through. In this context, it is noteworthy that Russell regarded his solution to an abstruse logical paradox about class membership as his single greatest contribution to philosophy. Supposing he was right about this: what should we make of it? Logical paradoxes have accompanied philosophical inquiry at least since the time of Zeno. But only someone addicted to epistemological arrogance would elevate them to the center of the philosophical enterprise or conclude that they demonstrate the futility of reason. The operation of reason generates paradoxes as surely as the sun casts shadows. In neither case are we justified in concluding that patches of darkness mean that nothing is illuminated.

In a review of Griffin's first volume of letters, a prominent academic philosopher proudly noted that Russell did much to foster the "professionalization" of philosophy. This is undoubtedly true. Not only modern logical notation, but also the entire image of philosophy as a kind of intellectual janitorial service in which propositions must be tidied up or discarded owes a tremendous amount to Russell's example. It is less clear, however, that the professionalization of philosophy has been a blessing—except, perhaps, for professors of philosophy. Modern analytic philosophy has tended to assume, with Russell, that "all fundamental work in philosophy is logical." But is this in fact the case? What about the ethical dimension of philosophy, the notion that philosophy is fundamentally about the "love of wisdom"? What about the idea that the chief impetus for philosophy is the question, How should I live my life? At the end of the *Republic*, Plato has Socrates say that the aim of philosophy is to enable us "to distinguish the life that is good from that which is bad, and always and everywhere to choose the best that the conditions allow." Socrates was not talking about logic. It was Russell's mistake, and philosophy's misfortune, to suppose otherwise.

Who Was David Stove?

For two hundred years we had sawed and sawed and sawed at
the branch we were sitting on. And in the end, much more
suddenly than anyone had foreseen, our efforts were rewarded,
and down we came. But unfortunately there had been a little
mistake. The thing at the bottom was not a bed of roses after all,
it was a cesspool full of barbed wire.
—George Orwell, 1940

Defects of empirical knowledge have less to do with the ways we
go wrong in philosophy than defects of character do: such things
as the simple inability to shut up; determination to be thought
deep; hunger for power; fear, especially the fear of an indifferent
universe.
—David Stove, "What is Wrong with Our Thoughts?"

I DISCOVERED the work of the Australian philosopher
David Stove (1927–1994) through a series of lucky acci-
dents. In the summer of 1996, I was rummaging through a
pile of books at my office that were destined for the used
bookstore when I chanced upon a copy of *The Killing of*
History by the Australian historian Keith Windschuttle.
This was the first bit of luck. Windschuttle's book turned
out to be a masterpiece of scholarly polemic, a devastating

anatomy of what has gone wrong in the teaching and writing of history. Windschuttle makes good on the promise of his dramatic subtitle and explains, in riveting detail, "How a Discipline Is Being Murdered by Literary Critics and Social Theorists." One of my chief debts to this book was discovering the work of David Stove. In a section of *The Killing of History* devoted to criticizing the vogue for relativism and irrationalism in the philosophy of science, Windschuttle relies heavily on some arguments that Stove put forward in his book *Popper and After: Four Modern Irrationalists.*[†]

Impressed by the snippets that Windschuttle quoted, I sought out a copy of the book. It was a revelation. With a combination of dazzling philosophical acumen and scarifying wit, Stove does for irrationalism in Karl Popper's philosophy of science (and that of such illustrious heirs as Thomas Kuhn and Paul Feyerabend) what the Romans did for Carthage in the Third Punic War: he assaults and destroys it utterly. It had been a long time since I had read a book of philosophy that was so entertaining and illuminating. An Australian friend to whom I mentioned my enthusiasm recommended *Darwinian Fairytales* (Ashgate, 1995), Stove's posthumously published attack on certain aspects of Darwinian theory, especially as applied to human beings.

Although it is dangerous to admit this—Darwinians, both lay and professional, are an extraordinarily prickly

---

† Published in 1982 by Pergamon Press. This edition is long out of print. A new edition, with a foreword by Keith Windschuttle and an afterword by James Franklin, was published in paperback under the title *Anything Goes: Origins of the Cult of Scientific Irrationalism* (Macleay Press, 1998) and then again as *Scientific Irrationalism: Origins of a Postmodern Cult* (Transaction, 2001). I refer to this book as *Anything Goes.*

lot when it comes to criticism—I found *Darwinian Fairy-tales* every bit as compelling as Stove's work on irrationalism in the philosophy of science. It is an invigorating blend of analytic lucidity, mordant humor, and an amount of common sense too great to be called "common." Once I started it, I could hardly put it down. But who, I wondered, was David Stove? How had this connoisseur of the use and abuse of intelligence escaped me all these years?

A few inquiries revealed that Stove's work had a kind of underground following. *Anything Goes*, especially, enjoys a high reputation among a small but fervent group of admirers. And *The Plato Cult*, seven essays attacking a variety of philosophical "wrong turns"—especially philosophical idealism—made something of a stir when it appeared in 1991. There are some signs that Stove's work is beginning to excite some of the interest it deserves.† But during his lifetime David Stove never achieved much public recognition, not outside Australia anyway. There were many reasons for this. Partly, I believe, it was due to such pedestrian details as the unsexy titles he chose for his books. For example, *Popper and After: Four Modern Irrationalists* does little to set the pulse racing. (The new title, *Anything Goes*, is much better, for it explicitly evokes the Jazz-Age philosophy that the book attacks with such gusto.) There was some irony in Stove's drab titles, for one needs only to open his books to see them sparkle. He was at once one of the funniest and most rigorous philosophical essayists going; reading him, one admirer wrote, is

---

† Publication of *Against the Idols of the Age* (Transaction, 1999), my anthology of Stove's writings, is one such sign; another is Alan Sokal's and Jean Bricmont's *Fashionable Nonsense: Postmodern Intellectuals' Abuse of Science* (Picador, 1998), which draws on Stove's arguments in *Anything Goes*.

"like watching Fred Astaire dance." But you would never know it from Stove's titles. Then, too, most of the books Stove published during his lifetime are absurdly expensive and hard to find: *The Rationality of Induction* (1986), for example, is a book of some 225 pages and sells for $113.95. It is a brilliant book, but you won't find it at Barnes & Noble.

No doubt Stove's anonymity was also partly a matter of design. Intellectually, he seems to have been the opposite of clubbable. He belonged to no school or party; his first allegiance was to the best argument, whoever propounded it. This was not a prescription for popular success. And then there was the matter of Stove's social and political opinions. They were by and large conservative opinions: they flew in the face of just about every intellectual cliché going, from relativism and irrationalism to doctrinaire Darwinism to the whole smorgasbord of established liberal orthodoxy about (e.g.) art, race, sex, nationalism, J. S. Mill, tobacco, education, and foreign policy.

Stove spent most of his career teaching philosophy at the University of Sydney. Disgusted by the mephitic winds of political correctness wafting through the Australian universities—winds, I regret to say, that originated largely on American campuses—he retired early, at the age of sixty, in 1988. He then devoted himself to writing and a variety of decorous private passions: music before Mozart, tending his rural property in New South Wales—and smoking. It saddens me to report that he died by his own hand in 1994 after a debilitating bout of cancer of the esophagus. He was sixty-six.

Obituaries by friends and colleagues all drew a similar picture. One described Stove as the Jonathan Swift of contemporary philosophy; another noted that, like David Hume (the philosopher he admired most), Stove delighted in finding objections—even, it should be said, to Hume's philosophy. Who else would have organized a competition to discover "the worst argument in the world"? The winning submission, Stove explained, would be distinguished not only by its intrinsic awfulness but also by its degree of acceptance among philosophers and the extent to which it had escaped criticism. In the event, Stove decided to give the palm to the family of arguments that he had contributed to the competition himself—arguments that will be horribly familiar to anyone who has studied philosophy:

> We can know things only:
> • as they are related to us
> • under our forms of perception and understanding
> • in so far as they fall under our conceptual schemes
> • etc.,
>
> So,
>
> We cannot know things as they are in themselves.

One reason that such arguments have mesmerized so many intellectuals is the prevalence of what Stove calls "cognitive Calvinism." "Calvinists," he observes, "believe in the total depravity of human nature: if an impulse is one of ours, it is bad, *because* it is one of ours. The argument,"

> Our knowledge is our knowledge,
>
> So,
>
> It is not knowledge of real things,

could seem valid only to someone who felt that any knowledge *we* have could not be the real thing, *because* we have it.

Stove wickedly dubs this family of arguments "the Gem." A Gem operates by leaping from a tautological premise to some interesting conclusion in the real world—from, say, the proposition that "All a man's interests are interests of his," which no one can deny, to "All our actions are self-interested," which is a calumny on the human race. Some Gems are popular chiefly among fatalists—a perennial favorite, Stove points out, is the argument from "Whatever will be, will be" to "All human effort is ineffectual." Some, like the one about knowledge, thrive mostly in the rarefied atmosphere of the philosopher's study.

Stove's criticisms of the Gem and cognitive Calvinism occur in two long essays attacking idealism. But it is important to note that the arguments he attacks are by no means propounded only by idealists. Indeed, in one version or another, such reasoning, as Stove points out, "is common to all the main varieties of cognophobe who now make up the staff of the faculties of arts in Western universities; and none of these is idealistic, even by implication."

> The cultural-relativist, for example, inveighs bitterly against our science-based, Europe-centered, white-male cultural perspective. She says that it is not only injurious but cognitively limiting. Injurious it may be; or again it may not. But why does she believe that it is cognitively limiting? Why, for no reason in the world, except this one: that it is *ours*. Everyone really understands, too, that this *is* the only reason. But since this reason is also generally accepted as a sufficient one, no other is felt to be needed.

Stove provides similar observations about Marxist cognophobes and the many followers of Thomas Kuhn; readers will easily be able to extend the list.

It is not quite true that Stove was a "purely negative

thinker," as he once said of himself. But he was at his best on the attack; he was, in fact, one of those writers from whom even praise was a kind of challenge. In his introduction to the posthumously published *Cricket versus Republicanism* (Quakers Hill Press, 1995), Stove's literary executor, the mathematician James Franklin, gives a clue to his friend's sensibility in a (partial) summary of his dislikes. "The list of what he attacked," Franklin wrote,

> was a long one, and included, but was certainly not limited to, Arts Faculties, big books, contraception, Darwinism, the Enlightenment, feminism, Freud, the idea of progress, leftish views of all kinds, Marx, . . . metaphysics, modern architecture and art, philosophical idealism, Popper, religion, semiotics, Stravinsky and Sweden. . . . Also, anything beginning with "soc" (even Socrates got a serve or two).

Of course, any crank could subscribe to such a list. The "Stove trick," as Franklin observes, "was to be against things for reasons one would not have thought of oneself." I will only add that Stove's reasons, more often than not, were as compelling as they were fresh. It may be easy to dislike some of Stove's views; it is generally much more difficult to dismiss them.

There are essentially three parts to Stove's *oeuvre*. Most of his technical philosophical work was related to the so-called problem of induction—to the problem, that is to say, of how we can reason convincingly from the observed to the unobserved. He wrote two books on this subject, *Probability and Hume's Inductive Scepticism* (1973) and the aforementioned *Rationality of Induction*. The second part of Stove's work, building on this abiding concern for what counts as a good argument, consists of his full-scale assaults on scientific irrationalism (*Anything Goes*), philosophical idealism (some essays in *The Plato Cult*), and certain central aspects of Darwinism (*Darwinian Fairytales*). This is Stove at his best and most deadly. He had the rare ability to cast familiar subjects in a new and inescapable light: always revelatory if not always flattering. Stove reports that T. H. Huxley, after he first read *The Origin of Species*, exclaimed, "How extremely stupid not to have thought of that!" One regularly has a similar experience reading Stove.

Finally, David Stove was an occasional essayist of considerable charm and polemical snap. Writing for such magazines as *The American Scholar* (when it was still worth reading) and *Commentary* in the United States, *Encounter* in England, and *Quadrant* in Australia, he expatiated on everything from English cottage gardens and the virtues of cricket (a game, he says, that "requires gentlemanliness, and teaches it") to feminism, racial antagonism, and John Stuart Mill. In *On Liberty*, Mill argued that we ought to welcome moral innovators (whose efforts Mill called "experiments in living") because all improvements in human life have come about as the result of some innovator. Of course, it works the other way, too: "someone first had to make a new departure for any change for the *worse* ever to have taken place." This is perfectly obvious, and is reason enough to regard innovators with suspicion, though you won't find it acknowledged in Mill. The question is, Stove asks, "How did an argument so easily answered ever impose itself upon intelligent people?" He answers: "Easily. It was simply a matter of ensuring . . . *a one-sided diet of examples.* Mention no past innovators except those who were innovators-for-the-better. . . . Never mention Lenin or Pol Pot, Marx or Hegel, Robespierre or the Marquis de Sade."

Stove is hilarious and devastating on Mill, as he is on the early birth-control proselytizers Margaret Sanger and Marie

Stopes. Their many disciples should be sure to read "O Pioneers! . . ." to discover how repulsive these benefactresses of humanity were in life. When Stopes's second husband lost nearly all his money in the Depression, his wife lost no time in winkling him out of their beautiful eighteenth-century house and her life. "He was reduced to living alone in a single room in London," Stove comments, "where in due course he died. This saddened Marie, who wrote a little poem about it, deploring the housing shortage."

Stove is not always convincing. It seems peremptory, to say the least, to dismiss religion, as he does in "Idealism: A Victorian Horror-Story (Part One)," as little more than a psychological "deprivation-effect"—especially since, as he puts it elsewhere, "not to understand religion is . . . not to understand nine-tenths of human history." (There is a lot to be said, however, for his description of Victorian idealism as "a sickening evasion, forever restoring religious consolation while pretending to take it away.") Similarly, Stove's intolerance for balderdash sometimes led him drastically to undervalue the achievements of other philosophers. It is understandable that he should despise deliberately mystifying writers like Hegel and Heidegger—whatever their virtues, both were addicted to opacity. But it will hardly do to dismiss Plato ("that scourge of the human mind") and Kant (for example) as little more than overrated poseurs. In such cases, Stove's impatience led him into caricature. "Plato's discovery," he wrote, "went as follows":

It is possible for something to be a certain way and for something else to be the same way.

So,

There are universals.

Who Was David Stove?

(Tumultuous applause, which lasts, despite occasional sub-sidences, 2,400 years.)

Amusing, yes; worth recalling whenever someone starts talking about "the problem of universals," perhaps; but not *quite* fair to the author of *Phaedrus*, the *Symposium*, *Theaetetus*, and the *Republic*.

Stove was not usually so cavalier. But he clearly enjoyed tweaking the intellectual and moral complacencies of his readers. Consider the following paragraph, with which he opens "'Always Apologize, Always Explain': Robert Nozick's War Wounds," Stove's review of the late Harvard philosopher's book *Philosophical Explanations*:

> An unprecedented expansion of Communism took place immediately after the Second World War. For the next twenty-odd years, any possibility of resistance to Communist expansion depended almost entirely upon America: no other country possessed both the requisite military capacity and the willingness to use it. But the outcome of the Vietnam war showed that, while America's capacity for such resistance remained intact, her willingness did not. For that war was lost, not through defeat of American armies in the field, nor yet through treachery among them, but through a massive sedition at home. The nation showed that it had become utterly opposed to any further armed resistance to Communism.

All true, but that wasn't the story one got from Jane Fonda, *The Nation*, *The New York Review of Books*, or professors of philosophy at Harvard University. Such a "revolution in national sentiment," Stove argues, was naturally reflected in the tenor of intellectual life. He examines as Exhibit A Nozick's call for a "non-coercive philosophy."

The completeness of Nozick's composition is remarkable: he touches somewhere in the book, however lightly, almost every note of American decadence. Gandhi is there. The necessary deference to feminism is there. The necessary reproof to "racism" is there. Carlos Castaneda is there, referred to as though he were a thinker, which he is not. . . . Drugs of course are there, and in no unfavorable light: drugs may have their place, Nozick thinks, in "the treatment for philosophical parochialism." Has he left anything out? Is there anyone in post-Vietnam America who needs to be placated, whom he has not placated? This was obviously a worry, and there is a nervous catch-all reference to "children's rights, the treatment of animals, domination and ecological awareness."

Nozick looked forward to a new version of philosophy that would replace *arguments* with a kinder, gentler alternative—*explanations*—because arguments, after all, attempt "to get someone to believe something, whether he wants to believe it or not." Stove is withering about all this, noting among other things that "no ideal could be more destructive of human life than the ideal of non-coerciveness." The only way, he writes, "of producing a non-coercive human being is to produce an autistic one. But then, autism is really the conclusion to which Nozick's conception of philosophy tends, just as it is the conclusion to which American foreign policy in the same period has tended."

THERE IS SOMETHING to offend nearly everyone in Stove's essays. One can imagine the reaction of his colleagues at the University of Sydney when, in 1986, he published "A Farewell to Arts: Marxism, Semiotics, and Feminism." This bombshell begins: "The Faculty of Arts at the Univer-

sity of Sydney is a disaster-area, and not of the merely passive kind, like a bombed building, or an area that has been
flooded. It is the active kind, like a badly-leaking nuclear
reactor, or an outbreak of foot-and-mouth disease in
cattle." Stove went on to quote from, and ridicule, the
work of several of his colleagues. He cheerfully identified
one egregious offender by name, concluding that, intellectually, "the sum of Marxism, semiotics, and feminism is
$0 + 0 + 0 = 0$." Again, he is quite right about this, but such
observations are not a balm to collegiality. It was around
that time that university administrators spoke of bringing
nebulous "disciplinary proceedings" against Stove. In the
end, nothing happened, but one imagines that the threat
must have hardened his resolve and possibly hastened his
departure from academic life.

Stove probably would have had to leave soon anyway.
There are few universities in the United States, at any rate,
at which his life would have been easy after he got around
to writing "The Intellectual Capacity of Women" and
"Racial and Other Antagonisms" (both of which are
reprinted in *Against the Idols of the Age*).

I have noted with some amusement that even the title of
Stove's essay on women tends to elicit a frisson of anxiety.
"He is not going to . . . He wouldn't dare . . . You don't
mean to say that he actually argues . . ." Well, yes. "I
believe," Stove wrote in his first sentence, "that the intellectual capacity of women is on the whole inferior to that
of men." He offered as his main reason for this belief the
uncomfortable observation that "the intellectual *performance* of women is inferior to men." In other words, he
explains, it is the same sort of reasoning as that which
convinces us that "Fords are on the whole inferior to Mer-
cedes; or as that which convinces dog-fanciers that Irish
setters are not as smart as labradors; or as that which con-

vinces everyone that the intellectual capacity of seven-year-old children is on the whole inferior to that of nine-year-olds. They do not do as well, and we infer from this that they cannot do as well." Of course, this is not, Stove readily acknowledges, *proof*: "performance is no infallible guide to capacity." Still, "it is, in the end, the only guide we have or can have."

Stove deals patiently with all the usual objections—that women haven't been given sufficient opportunities, that "patriarchy" has kept them down, etc.—and concludes with an interesting thought experiment. Suppose that the historical evidence had been the reverse and that the intellectual performance of men had been "uniformly inferior, under the widest variety of circumstances, to that of women." Would "those people who are at present equality-theorists be as confident then as they are now of the equal intellectual capacity of the two sexes? To ask this question," Stove writes, "is to answer it. The fact is, our egalitarians treat evidence on a basis of heads-I-win-tails-you-lose."

I am regularly assured, by people who have not actually read Stove's essay but have absorbed the title and possibly the first couple of sentences, that "The Intellectual Capacity of Women" is a misogynistic rant. It challenges the received liberal opinion on a sensitive issue. Ergo it *must* be wrong—more, it must be declared unworthy of discussion. In fact, whether or not one agrees with Stove's conclusions, his essay is a humane and carefully argued piece of work that has as much to do with probability theory as the debate over "affirmative action." Read it and see.

Then read "Racial and Other Antagonisms," a similarly emollient production. Stove begins by noting that some degree of friction is the common if not indeed inevitable result when "two races of people have been in contact for long." Only in the twentieth century, however, has such antagonism been described as a form of "prejudice." Why? Earlier ages had the concept of prejudice, and the word. Part of the reason, Stove suggests, is that by christening racial animosity "racial *prejudice*" we transform it into an *intellectual* fault, i.e., a false or irrational belief that might be cured by education—and this, Stove observes, "is a distinctly *cheering* thing to imply." Alas, while it is certainly true that racial antagonism is often *accompanied by* false or irrational beliefs about the other race, it is by no means clear that it *depends upon* them. And if it doesn't, education will be little more than liberal window dressing.

Stove's essay on race is full of discomfiting observations. He defines "racism"—a neologism so recent, he points out, that it was not in the OED in 1971—as the belief that "some human races are inferior to others in certain respects, and that it is sometimes proper to make such differences the basis of our behavior towards people." Although this proposition is constantly declared to be false, Stove says, "everyone knows it is true, just as everyone knows it is true that people differ in age, sex, health, etc., and that it is sometimes proper to make *these* differences the basis of our behavior towards them." For example,

if you are recruiting potential basketball champions, you would be mad not to be more interested in American Negroes than in Vietnamese. . . . Any rational person, recruiting an army, will be more interested in Germans than in Italians. If what you want in people is aptitude for forming stable family-ties, you will prefer Italians or Chinese to American Negroes. Pronounced mathematical ability is more likely to occur in an Indian or a Hungarian than in an Australian Aboriginal. If you are recruiting workers, and you value docility above every other trait in a worker, you should prefer Chinese to white Americans. And so on.

Stove readily admitted that some of these traits may be culturally rather than genetically determined. But he went on to observe that "they are still traits which are *statistically associated with race*, well enough, to make race a rational guide in such areas of policy as recruitment or immigration." As I say, David Stove would not have been made to feel welcome at many American universities.

THERE IS a certain amount of calculated outrage in Stove's polemical essays. Whatever the subject, he finds the tenderest spot of the most sensitive nerve; then he presses. At the very least, his arguments issue a challenge to (as Kant said about Hume's work) the "dogmatic slumbers" of his readers. When he turns his attention to irrationalism in the philosophy of science or the unthinking acceptance of certain Darwinian propositions about human nature, he manages a great deal more.

Today, the late Karl Popper is generally regarded as a venerable figure whose 1934 book *Logik der Forschung* ("The Logic of Scientific Discovery") deserves its honored place among the classics of the philosophy of science. Popper's influence is enormous; his ideas long ago became part of the intellectual atmosphere, taken-for-granted assumptions even for those who hadn't read him. (The idea that a proposition isn't really scientific unless it is "falsifiable" is an especially popular bit of Popperism.) But as Stove shows in *Anything Goes* and "Cole Porter and Karl Popper: the Jazz Age in the Philosophy of Science," Popper's philosophy of science is actually an efficient engine for generating irrational beliefs about what counts as scientific knowledge.

By the time Popper began writing in the 1920s, the long struggle of empiricism since Bacon had yielded a straightforward but powerful conception of science. According to this view, scientific propositions were distinguished from speculative, religious, or pseudo-scientific propositions by the degree to which they were verifiable; the method of science was essentially inductive, which means that it moved from the observed or known to the unobserved or unknown; the procedures of science were marked by caution; its results were held to be certain or at least highly probable.

Popper stood all this on its head. At the center of Popper's thinking about the philosophy of science is a profound scepticism, derived from David Hume, about the rationality of inductive reasoning: "I agree with Hume's opinion," Popper wrote, "that induction is invalid and in no sense justified." Like the young Hume, Popper concluded from the fact that inductive reasoning was not logically valid—that inductive evidence did not yield absolute certainty—that it was therefore incapable of furnishing compelling reasons for belief.

Popper was a deductivist. He dreamt of constructing a philosophy of science based solely on the resources of deductive logic. He was also an empiricist: he admitted no source of knowledge beyond experience. As Stove shows, the combination of empiricism and deductivism—in Hume as well as in Popper—is a prescription for irrationalism and cognitive impotence. An empiricist says that no propositions other than propositions about the observed can be a reason to believe a contingent proposition about the unobserved; an empiricist who is also a deductivist is forced to conclude that there can be no reasons *at all* to believe any contingent proposition about the unobserved. Hume himself, in his posthumously published *Dialogues Concerning Natural Religion*, ridiculed this "pretended scepticism" as a juvenile affectation. Throughout the nineteenth and early twentieth centuries, Hume's hyperbolic scepticism was generally regarded as little more than an intellectual curiosity, like the ancient scepticism of Pyrrho, which indeed it resembles.

Popper resuscitated Hume's brand of scepticism, dressing it up in a new vocabulary. In Popper's philosophy of science, we find the curious thought that *falsifiability*, not verifiability, is the distinguishing mark of scientific theories. This means that, for Popper, only theories that are *dis-provable* are genuinely scientific. It follows that—amazing thought!—that "irrefutability is not a virtue of a theory . . . but a vice." Popper denied that we can ever legitimately infer the unknown from the known; audacity, not caution, was for him of the essence in science; far from being certain, the conclusions of science, he said, were never more than *guesswork* ("we must regard all laws and theories," he wrote, ". . . as guesses"); and since for Popper "there *are* no such things as good positive reasons" to believe a scientific theory, no theory can ever be more probable than another; indeed, he says that the truth of any scientific proposition is exactly as improbable as the truth of a self-contradictory proposition—or "in plain English," as Stove puts it, "it is impossible."

WHAT WAS NOVEL about Popper's famous doctrine of "falsifiability" was not the idea that negative instances disconfirm or "falsify" a theory. The fact that the proposition "All ravens are black" is disconfirmed by the appearance of one white raven is a logical truism. What was novel was the breathtaking contention that positive instances do not—in principle *cannot*—act to confirm a proposition or theory. For Popper, if every raven anyone has ever seen is black, that fact gives no rational support for the belief that all ravens, in fact, are black. Scientific laws, he says, "can never be supported, or corroborated, or confirmed by empirical evidence." He goes even further: of two hypotheses "the one which can be *better corroborated*, is always *less probable*." Whatever else these statements may be, they are breathtakingly irrationalist. Bertrand Russell was quite right that "the growth of unreason throughout the nineteenth century and what has passed of the twentieth is a natural sequel to Hume's destruction of empiricism." Karl Popper was the twentieth century's chief ambassador of Humean scepticism.

Popper was in a peculiar position. He believed that the aim of science is to discover true laws or theories. But he also believed that this was impossible. Indeed, this tension was an important source of his appeal. He wrote *as if* he believed in the project of science. And this—together with the forbidding logical machinery he habitually deployed in his writing—helps to explain why he is widely believed to be a staunch opponent of irrationalism. After all, his magnum opus in its English translation is called *The Logic of Scientific Discovery*: what could be more promising? But for Popper it always turned out that logic was incurably impotent when it came to scientific discovery.

It would be difficult to overstate the radical implications of Popper's irrationalist view of science. Popper was apparently fond of referring to "the soaring edifice of science." But in fact his philosophy of science robbed that edifice of its foundation. Refracted through the lens of Popper's theories, the history of modern science is transformed from a dazzling string of successes into a series of "problems" or (as in a title of one of Popper's books) "conjectures and refutations." On the traditional view, scientific knowledge can be said to be *cumulative*: we know more now than we did in 1802, more then than in 1602. Popper's theory, which demotes scientific laws to mere guesses, denies this: in one of his most famous phrases, he speaks of science as "conjectural knowledge," an oxymoronic gem that, as Stove remarks, makes as much sense as "a drawn game which was won."

If such ideas were merely the idiosyncrasy of a certain Austrian philosopher of science, they wouldn't much matter. But Popper's ideas did not only propound an irrationalist view of science: they also helped to *license* or legitimate irrationalism for an entire generation. Without the solvent of Popper's theories in their armory, the other philosophers of science that Stove discusses—Imre Lakatos, Thomas Kuhn, and Paul Feyerabend—would never have developed their own influential versions of irrationalism. And without the example of these and other such figures, the blasé irrationalism that infects the humanities and social sciences today—and that infects our entire "postmodern" culture—might never have achieved epidemic proportions.

By far the most influential of these modern irrationalists was Thomas Kuhn, whose famous book *The Structure of Scientific Revolutions* (1962) has been a godsend for academics looking for ways of subverting the authority of science. Indeed, by the mid-1980s, *The Structure of Scientific Revolutions* was the most frequently cited twentieth-century book in the *Arts and Humanities Citation Index*. (The honor of being the most cited author went to V. I. Lenin.) Although rather a dull read, *The Structure of Scientific Revolutions* has two important things going for it. One is its policy of deliberately confusing the history and sociology of science with the logic of science. The other is a memorable slogan: "paradigm change." Humanities professors feel about that phrase the way American Express wants you to feel about their charge card: they won't leave home without it.

Like Popper, Kuhn specialized in appearing to defend the

claims of science while actually undercutting them. According to Kuhn, in its heyday every discarded scientific theory possessed "the full integrity of what we now call sound scientific truth." To illustrate this, he asks: "what mistake was made, what rule broken, when and by whom, in arriving at, say, the Ptolemaic system?" For most people, Stove points out, this is not a difficult question. For starters there was the mistake of believing that the sun goes around the earth every day. But Kuhn, impatient with the idea that "successive theories grow ever closer to . . . the truth," professes to find it "difficult to understand" what it might mean to call "that system, or any other out-of-date theory, a mistake." As Stove observes, "You have to be very learned indeed to find things as hard to understand as Kuhn does."

Whenever anyone accused him of advocating a relativist view of science, Kuhn replied that he, too—just like everyone else—believed that science "solves problems." The rub is that on Kuhn's view of science, problems don't *stay* solved. If the traditional view of science as cumulative were true, Kuhn wrote, then "in the evolution of science new knowledge would replace ignorance rather than replace knowledge of another and incompatible sort." Precisely. But with the phrase "incompatible knowledge" Kuhn has scuttled the word "knowledge" almost as effectively as Popper did with his phrase "conjectural knowledge." As Stove points out "knowledge implies truth, and truths cannot be incompatible with one another."

Kuhn insists that we must relinquish the naïve view that science yields truth. For him, the idea that "changes of paradigm carry scientists and those who learn from them closer and closer to the truth" is all wrong. The paradigms under which scientists work, he says, are "incommensurable": they cannot be meaningfully compared with one another. In other words, Kuhn wishes to speak of scientific knowledge and discovery without the impediments of truth and falsity. Stove shows in meticulous detail that, despite Kuhn's occasional protestations to the contrary, his view that science is essentially "paradigm relative" is deeply irrationalist.

Of course, most people remain uneasy about blatant irrationalism when it comes to science. They bristle if told that "no more is known now than in 1699." They balk if informed that "no one ever knows anything." Irrationalism, to be plausible, must be disguised, and Stove devotes considerable attention, both in *Anything Goes* and in "Cole Porter and Karl Popper," to analyzing the literary devices that Popper, Kuhn, and the others used to achieve plausibility.

There are two basic techniques. The first is to neutralize what Stove calls "success words"—words like "knowledge," "discovery," "facts," "verified," "truth," and "proof." Such words carry an implication of cognitive achievement. No philosopher of science can do without them entirely. But the simple addition of scare quotes alters everything: "Galileo discovers x" means something quite different from "Galileo 'discovers' x." (Stove remarks that the best title for Popper's book would have been *The "Logic" of Scientific "Discovery."*) The element of ambiguity is essential: consider the effect of a sign advertising "fresh" fish. Here for example is Imre Lakatos: "Michelson . . . was primarily frustrated by the inconsistency of the 'facts' he arrived at by his ultra-precise measurements. His 1887 experiments 'showed' that there was no ether wind on the earth's surface. But aberration 'showed' there was. Moreover, his own 1925 experiment . . . also 'proved' that there was . . ." Was Lakatos right about Michelson? Or was he only "right"? The same trick can obviously be used with words of cognitive failure: "mistake," "false," "refuted," etc. A "refuted" theory is not at all the same thing as a refuted theory. As Stove comments, by skillfully using such devices, "you can have, as thick as you like on every page, all the optimistic *words* of the old historiography and philosophy of science, reassuring the reader," but without saying anything inconsistent with irrationalism.

THE SECOND TECHNIQUE for making irrationalism plausible involves deliberately conflating the history or sociology of science with the logic of science. Stove focuses especially on what he calls "sabotaging logical expressions." By embedding a logical statement in a historical context, one thereby undermines its logical status while preserving the *impression* that a logical claim has been made. A simple example is the difference between "P entails Q" and "P entails Q according to most logicians." The first is a logical statement; the second is a historical claim; it is what Stove calls a "ghost logical statement": it poaches on the prestige of logical entailment without actually making any logical claim at all: it is therefore completely immune to criticism on logical grounds. As Stove notes, "Once you mix the history with the logic of science, the possibilities of such sabotage are limitless." Indeed, by such means was the entire pseudo-discipline of "science studies" born.

Stove's analysis of how his authors manage to make their irrationalism plausible to their readers is a *tour de force*. So is his analysis of how they made irrationalism plausible to themselves. The key, at least so far as Popper was concerned, was the challenge that the theory of relativity and quantum mechanics issued to Newtonian physics. As Stove points out, these developments "changed the entire climate of philosophy of science," replacing the nineteenth century's blissful confidence about the impregnable certainty of science with a profound scepticism. Stove shows how Popper and his other authors, attempting "to ensure that no scientific theory should ever again become the object of over-confident belief," overreacted and embraced instead a form of deductivism whose philosophical roots go back to Hume. The best literary parallel, Stove suggests, "is given in Aesop's fable of the fox and the grapes. The parallel would be complete if the fox, having been convinced that neither he nor anyone else could ever succeed in tasting grapes, should nevertheless write many long books on the progress of viticulture."

At bottom, Stove shows, his authors embrace irrationalism because of "a certain extreme belief, by which their minds are dominated, about what is required for one proposition to be a reason to believe another." They all acknowledge that absolute certainty is impossible; but they assume that only absolute certainty will do as a warrant for rational belief. They exhibit, in other words, "a variety of perfectionism."

It is, of course, a disappointed perfectionism. Its chief effect has been to introduce an irresponsible levity and what Stove calls *"enfant terriblisme"* into intellectual life. One thinks, for example, of Paul Feyerabend suggesting in his book *Against Method* that scientific laws, like political laws, ought to be decided by popular vote, or his insistence that science is no sounder, no more cognitively respectable, than (for example) astrology, voodoo, or necromancy. The "only one principle that can be defended," Feyerabend wrote, ". . . is *anything goes.*"

Disappointed perfectionism has also led to what Stove describes as "the frivolous elevation of 'the critical attitude' into a categorical imperative." The principal result, he notes, has been "to fortify millions of ignorant graduates and undergraduates in the belief, to which they are already too firmly wedded by other causes, that the adversary posture is all, and that intellectual life consists in 'directionless quibble.'"

STOVE'S DEMOLITION of certain aspects of Darwinian theory, in *Darwinian Fairytales* and related essays, is equally thorough and convincing. Stove is unusual among anti-Darwinians. He is not a creationist; indeed, he is careful to point out that he is "of no religion." Moreover, he admires Darwin greatly as a thinker, placing him at the top of his personal pantheon, along with Shakespeare, Purcell, Newton, and Hume. Stove furthermore believes that it is "overwhelmingly probable" that our species evolved from some other and that "natural selection is probably the cause which is principally responsible for the coming into existence of new species from old ones." Indeed, he believes that

> the Darwinian explanation of evolution is a very good one as far as it goes, and it has turned out to go an extremely long way. Its explanatory power, even in 1859, was visibly very great, but it has turned out to be far greater than anyone then could have realized. And then, in the 1930s, the Darwinian theory received further accessions of explanatory strength through its confluence or synthesis with the new knowledge of genetics. And this "new synthesis," or "neo-Darwinism," has been itself growing rapidly in explanatory power ever since.

At the same time, Stove maintains that "Darwinism says many things, especially about our species, which are too obviously false to be believed by any educated person; or at least by an educated person who retains any capacity at all for critical thought." Some examples: that "every single organic being around us may be said to be striving to the utmost to increase its numbers"; that "of the many individuals of any species which are periodically born, but a small number can survive"; that it is to a mother's "advantage" that her child should be adopted by another woman; that "no one is prepared to sacrifice his life for any single person, but . . . everyone will sacrifice it for more than two brothers, or four half-brothers, or eight first cousins"; that "any variation in the least degree injurious [to a species] would be rigidly destroyed."

All of these quotations are from Darwin or his orthodox disciples. A moment's reflection shows that none is even remotely true, at least of human beings. Take the last named: that anything in the least injurious to a species would be "rigidly destroyed" by natural selection. What about abortion, adoption, fondness for alcohol, or anal intercourse, just to start with the "A"s? As Stove notes, "each of these characteristics [tends] to shorten our lives, or to lessen the number of children we have, or both." Are any on the way to being "rigidly destroyed"? Again, if Darwin's theory of evolution were true, "there would be in every species a constant and ruthless competition to survive: a competition in which only a few in any generation can be winners. But it is perfectly obvious that human life is not like that, however it may be with other species." Priests, hospitals, governments, old-age homes, charities, police: these are a few of the things whose existence contradicts Darwin's theory.

Some of Darwinism's defenders respond by arguing that although human life may not *now* exhibit the brutal struggle for subsistence that Darwin's theory postulates, it *once did*. This is what Stove calls the "Cave Man" attempt to solve "Darwinism's Dilemma." (The other attempts he calls the "Hard Man" and the "Soft Man" gambits.) But the problem is that Darwin's theory is not meant to be something that was true yesterday but not today. It claims to be, as Stove puts it, "a universal generalization about all terrestrial species at any time." And this means that "if the theory says something which is not true *now* of our species (or another), then it is not true—finish." Stove writes:

> If Darwin's theory of evolution is true, no species can *ever* escape from the process of natural selection. His theory is that two universal and permanent tendencies of all species of organisms—the tendency to increase in numbers up to the limit that the food supply allows, and the tendency to vary in a heritable way—are together sufficient to bring about in any species universal and permanent competition for survival, and therefore universal and permanent natural selection among the competitors.

But this is clearly not true of our species now. Nor, Stove points out, can it *ever* have been true of our species. "It may be possible, for all I know, that a population of pines or cod should exist with no cooperative as distinct from competitive relations among its members. But no tribe of humans could possibly exist on those terms. Such a tribe could not even raise a second generation: the helplessness of the human young is too extreme and prolonged."

Stove shows in unanswerable detail that, despite its enormous explanatory power regarding "cods, pines, flies," etc., Darwin's theory of evolution is "a ridiculous slander on human beings." He is particularly good at exposing the "amazingly arrogant habit of Darwinians" of "*blaming the fact, instead of blaming their theory*" when they encounter contrary biological facts. Does it regularly happen that increasing prosperity leads to lower birth rates? And does this directly contradict Darwinian theory? No problem, just announce that the birth rates in such cases are somehow "inverted."

Stove is also very good at exposing the mind-boggling claims of sociobiology, a school of neo-Darwinism whose fundamental tenet is that an organism is epiphenomenal to its genes: that a human being, for example, is nothing more than a puppet manipulated by his genetic makeup. If this seems like an exaggeration, consider the statement by the eminent sociobiologist E. O. Wilson that "an organism is only DNA's way of making more DNA." It is worth pausing to ponder the implications of that "only." Or consider Richard Dawkins, another eminent sociobiologist and author of *The Selfish Gene*, a hugely popular book whose basic message is that (this is a direct quote from Dawkins) "we are . . . robot-vehicles blindly programmed to preserve the selfish molecules known as genes." (Yes, this is a direct quotation.) Of course, as Stove points out, "genes can no more be selfish than they can be (say) supercilious, or stupid." The popularity of Dawkins's book lies in the powerful appeal that puppet-theories of human behavior always exercise on those who combine cynicism with credulousness; but genetic puppet theories are no more convincing than those propounded by Freudians, Marxists, or astrologers.

In the end, Stove's discussion of Darwinian theory shows that, when it comes to the species *H. sapiens*, Darwinism "is a mere festering mass of errors." It can tell you "lots of truths about plants, flies, fish, etc., and interesting truths, too. . . . [But] if it is *human* life that you would most like to know about and to understand, then a good library can be begun by leaving out Darwinism, from 1859 [when *On the Origin of Species* was published] to the present hour." It is not a pretty picture that Stove paints; but then the exhibition of gross error widely accepted is never a comely sight.

Part Three

Tocqueville Today

What saddens me is, not that our society is democratic, but that the vices which we have inherited and acquired make it so difficult for us to obtain or to keep well-regulated liberty. And I know nothing so miserable as a democracy without liberty.
—Alexis de Tocqueville, in a letter of 1857

A serious life means being fully aware of the alternatives, thinking about them with all the intensity one brings to bear on life-and-death questions, in full recognition that every choice is a great risk with necessary consequences that are hard to bear.
—Allan Bloom, *The Closing of the American Mind*

Men do not receive the truth from their enemies, and their friends scarcely offer it to them; that is why I have spoken it.
—Alexis de Tocqueville, *Democracy in America*

ALEXIS DE TOCQUEVILLE was about a month shy of his twenty-sixth birthday when he and his friend and fellow French magistrate Gustave de Beaumont (1802–1866) landed in Newport, Rhode Island, in May 1831. Both were so to speak refugees from French politics. When the Bourbon dynasty fell the previous summer, the two men swore fealty to the new government of Louis-Philippe. But neither felt in sympathy with the heavy-handed policies of the "citizen king" whom Daumier parodied to such hilarious effect. The lack of sympathy was reciprocated. Tocqueville was demoted and required to take the oath of allegiance a second time. It was then that he hit upon the scheme of going to America. He and Beaumont petitioned the government for an eighteen-month leave to travel to the United States and study its penal system. After much red tape (there is a reason that "bureaucracy" is a French word), permission was granted, though in the event their trip was cut short and they were obliged to return after only nine months. Their work on the American penal system and its application to France was duly published in 1833. But from the beginning, as Tocqueville noted in a letter, the penal system had been merely a "pretext." The real reason that he and Beaumont went to America was to see firsthand "what a great republic is": to immerse themselves in the world's preeminent democratic regime and ponder its lessons.

They were indefatigable travelers. After disembarking at Newport, Tocqueville and Beaumont went by steamer from Providence to New York City. From there, they traveled to Buffalo, traversed the Great Lakes to what was then the frontier in Michigan and Wisconsin. They spent two weeks in Canada, then wended their way down to Baltimore, stopping along the way in Boston and Philadelphia. They went to Pittsburgh and Cincinnati, to Nashville, Memphis, and New Orleans. The final leg of their journey brought them back through Washington to New York. They rode on horses, in coaches, and in steamboats (one of which sank); they stayed in a log cabin; they observed many plain folk and met many eminent personages, including John Quincy Adams, Andrew Jackson, Daniel Webster, and Sam Houston. They devoured newspapers and broadsheets, and Tocqueville, at any rate, absorbed the lessons of *The*

Federalist and Judge Story's famous commentaries on the Constitution.

Although Tocqueville later said that he did not go to America with the idea of writing a book about his experiences, it is clear from his correspondence that he and Beaumont initially had some sort of collaborative project in mind. Both kept journals (Tocqueville's was published as *Journey to America*). At some point, the idea of collaboration fell by the wayside. They traveled together, but they kept to separate mental itineraries. In 1835, Beaumont came to the end of his when he published a didactic novel on race called *Marie, ou l'esclavage aux Etats-Unis: Tableau des moeurs américaines*.

Tocqueville spoke warmly about the work of his friend. But whatever the virtues of Beaumont's book, when it comes to insight into *moeurs américaines* there are few, if any, books that rival Tocqueville's own contribution to the subject, *De la démocratie en Amérique. Marie* is a period piece; *Democracy in America* is a masterpiece. It is, as Harvey C. Mansfield and Delba Winthrop note in the introduction to their sparkling new translation (University of Chicago Press, 2001), "at once the best book ever written on democracy and the best book ever written on America."

High praise. But Tocqueville inspires superlatives. Lord Acton wrote that "of all writers, [Tocqueville] is the most widely acceptable, and the hardest to find fault with. He is always wise, always right, and as just as Aristides." Well, Tocqueville was wrong about some things. Not all of his predictions have come to pass. One may be amazed, for example, at his judgment that the influence of *lawyers* forms one of "the most powerful barriers today against the lapses of democracy." Still, one may endorse the spirit of Lord Acton's remarks. John Stuart Mill wrote in a review that *Democracy in America* had "at once taken its rank among the most remarkable productions of our time." And in our own day, Russell Kirk praised Tocqueville as "the best friend democracy has ever had, and democracy's most candid critic."

The two go together, friend and critic. In his classic study, *Tocqueville and the Nature of Democracy* (1982; English translation, 1996), the French philosopher Pierre Manent noted that democracy has always had two sorts of enemies: the declared enemies who wish to abolish democracy outright and restore aristocracy or some other regime that enshrines political inequality; and the "immoderate friends" who seek to extend the central democratic imperative of equality into every realm of life, thus assuring oppressive new inequalities. Both are dangerous; the activities of both shackle freedom, one by design, the other unwittingly. Manent is right that, today, the immoderate friends of democracy are "incomparably more numerous than its enemies." To love democracy well, he concludes, "it is necessary to love it moderately."

It is a paradox—I almost said a "Tocquevillean paradox"—of human life that the highest excellences are nearly always achieved through moderate, not extreme, zeal. There is something blinding about zealousness, something that overshoots the mark. Eagerness attracts; over-eagerness repels. "Moderation"—what the Greeks called σωφροσύνη—is an aristocratic as well as an ancient virtue. It is not, Tocqueville thought, a virtue native to democracy, though he hoped that it might become, by art, democracy's second nature. That, I believe, is part of what he meant when he said that "a new political science is needed for a world altogether new." *Democracy in America* is the basic textbook of that new political science.

Tocqueville personally instantiated the conundrum that he wrote about. The Comte Alexis-Henri-Charles-Maurice

Clérel de Tocqueville—to give him his full complement of syllables—was himself an aristocrat, the scion of a venerable Norman family. One of his ancestors fought at Hastings with William the Conqueror. Tocqueville remained an aristocrat in temperament; in conviction, he early on became a liberal. "Readers of *Democracy in America*," Professors Mansfield and Winthrop observe, "have always disagreed over how democratic he was in mind and heart, but it is fair to say that he directed much of his energy to warning reactionaries in his country that democracy was irreversible as well as irresistible." Tocqueville looked about him and saw that democracy, the wave of the present, was also the fate of the future, at least in the West, in what could then still be called Christendom. Indeed, Tocqueville more than once dilates on his belief that there was something capital "P" Providential about the march of democracy, so that to oppose it would be not merely bootless but impious. (To wish to stop democracy, he wrote, would be "to struggle against God himself.")

Yet if Tocqueville was a passionate democrat, he was also a circumspect one. He knew what enormities could be perpetrated in its name. His own father had been imprisoned during the Terror, that irrational access of immoderately rational egalitarianism. He was one of the lucky ones: he escaped with his life, though his experiences in prison are said to have turned his hair snow-white at the age of twenty-two. The key to the new political science that Tocqueville envisions is the binocular insight that the democratic revolution is 1) irresistible and 2) "not yet rapid enough to despair of directing it." There was still time to "attenuate its vices and make its natural advantages emerge."

To instruct democracy, if possible to reanimate its beliefs, to purify its mores, to regulate its movements, to substitute little by little the science of affairs for its inexperience, and knowledge of its true interests for its blind instincts; . . . such is the first duty imposed on those who direct society in our day.

Democracy in America is an attempt to instruct those entrusted with directing society in the rudiments of that duty. The book, Tocqueville explicitly says, is not a "panegyric" to democracy; but it is an invitation to rethink democracy, to make the inevitable palatable. Tocqueville spoke like Edmund Burke when he noted that "it seems that in our day the natural bond that unites opinions to tastes and actions to beliefs has been broken . . . the laws of moral analogy have been abolished." But he sounds more like one of Burke's opponents when he warns against those men, even noble souls, whose "idea of evil is indissolubly united with the idea of the new."

Like Tocqueville himself, *Democracy in America* is irretrievably Janus-faced, which is one reason that it speaks to people across the ideological spectrum. As the editors note, "it is striking that both Left and Right appeal to *Democracy in America* for support of" their contrary policies. The Left sees in Tocqueville a critic of the bourgeois addiction to material well-being and an apostle of civic engagement (at the very end of the book, in his last endnote, Tocqueville names "*general apathy*" the greatest danger of the age); the Right sees in him a prophet admonishing us about the dangers of big government and doctrinaire egalitarianism. Both are right, but wrong to think they tell the whole story. Tocqueville's wide appeal, the editors conclude, "should not mask the controversial and unsettling character of the work."

Of course, "controversial" is a debased word today; it

encompasses little more than a certain species of headline-making clichés. Tocqueville is controversial and unsettling in a more permanent sense. He does not shock or outrage us, like the latest "cutting-edge" art offering; on the contrary, like all thinkers who ask fundamental questions, he induces a mood of calm solicitude. If he is "unsettling" it is because he poses important questions for which there are no pat, no settled, answers. What Tocqueville wrote was not a manifesto but an essential reflection on political life—which is to say *our* life in so far as we exist as social creatures. The questions he asks remain our questions: "On What Tempers the Tyranny of the Majority in the United States," "Why Democratic Peoples Show a More Ardent and More Lasting Love for Equality than for Freedom," "How the Americans Understand the Equality of Men and Women," "Why the Americans Show Themselves So Restless in the Midst of Their Well-Being." At the end of his introduction to the first volume of *Democracy in America*, Tocqueville notes that his

> book is not precisely in anyone's camp; in writing it I did not mean to serve or contest any party; I undertook to see, not differently, but further than the parties; and while they are occupied with the next day, I wanted to ponder the future.

His success in that endeavor accounts for what the editors describe as the "discomfiting sagacity of Tocqueville, always more sensitive than reassuring."

The first volume of *Democracy in America* was published, to great acclaim, in 1835; Tocqueville wrote it very rapidly, some 180,000 words in under a year. The second volume—which was less of a public success—was not published until 1840. The delay was caused by many things, including Tocqueville's courtship of and marriage to Mary Mottley, an Englishwoman, and several bouts of illness. (Tocqueville was sick much of his adult life; he died, probably of tuberculosis, in 1859, in his fifty-fourth year). The first volume of *Democracy in America* describes the physical situation of the United States, traces the origins of American democracy in Puritan New England, analyzes the Constitution and the powers it sets forth, and warns about the "tyranny of the majority," a leitmotif in Tocqueville's discussion of democracy. Along the way, Tocqueville has many sobering things to say about the sad fate of the American Indian ("the ruin of these peoples began on the day when Europeans landed on their shores") and blacks under slavery. (Tocqueville is not so much condemnatory as rueful; and his ruefulness is not confined to the whites of America: "Would not one say," he asks, that "the European is to men of other races what man himself is to the animals? He makes them serve his use, and when he cannot bend them, he destroys them.")

In the second volume, Tocqueville is more meditative. He steps back to describe the way democracy has affected intellectual life, manners and morals, and political society. In the famous opening section, "On the Philosophic Method of the Americans," he writes that although there is "no country in the civilized world where [people] are less occupied with philosophy than in the United States," one can nevertheless descry a distinctively American—and by implication, distinctively democratic—outlook and "philosophic method."

> To escape from the spirit of system, from the yoke of habits, from family maxims, from class opinions, and, up to a certain point, from national prejudices; to take tradition only as information, and current facts only as a useful

study for doing otherwise and better; to seek the reason for things by themselves and in themselves alone, to strive for a result without letting themselves be chained to the means, and to see through that to the foundation: these are the principal features that characterize what I shall call the philosophic method of the Americans.

"America," he concludes, "is therefore the one country in the world where the precepts of Descartes are least studied and best followed." Tocqueville is by turns impressed and made anxious by this unwitting "Cartesianism"; it helps account for the vitality of American democracy; perhaps it also helps to account for its roughness, superficiality, and lack of communal spirit. Much of the second volume is concerned with the implications of this tension.

There have been essentially three translations of *Democracy in America*. I say "essentially three" because the first, undertaken by Tocqueville's English friend Henry Reeve, was twice recast and corrected, first by Francis Bowen in 1862, then by Phillips Bradley in 1945. The Reeve work is fluent, engaging, and subtly at odds with Tocqueville's complex championship of democracy. "Without wishing to do so," Tocqueville admonished his friend in a letter, "you quite vividly colored what was contrary to Democracy and almost erased what could do harm to Aristocracy." The second translation, by George Lawrence, was published in 1966; it, too, is fluent and engaging, but is far more interpretive than literal. The new translation by Professors Mansfield and Winthrop (who, incidentally, have also collaborated on marriage) strikes just the right balance between the demands of literal accuracy and readability. They have given us a Tocqueville for today; but what they have given us today is *Tocqueville*, with all his richnesses and stylistic idiosyncrasies (his penchant for short

283

paragraphs, for instance, which was not respected by earlier translators). The editors have also provided a detailed subject index and have intelligently annotated the text. Especially in his second volume, Tocqueville tended to let his thoughts spill forth without bothering to enumerate his sources; this gives his text a peculiar brilliancy, but it obscures the vast amount of scholarship that went into *Democracy in America*. The editors discreetly supply the lack, not only citing Tocqueville's sources but also noting important marginal notes in the author's drafts. (The manuscript given to the printer has not survived, but Tocqueville's working manuscripts, these two Harvard professors tell us, "are preserved at the Beinecke Library at a university located in New Haven, Conn.")

The Mansfield-Winthrop work will henceforth be the preferred English version of *Democracy in America* not only because of the superior translation and critical apparatus, but also because of its long and masterly introductory essay, itself an important contribution to the literature on Tocqueville. I have only two nits to pick. One is that the index does not include the text of the editors' introduction—a pity because in that remarkable essay they cite many writers and works that Tocqueville's readers will wish to have a handy reference for.

I am also sorry that the editors choose to translate *inquiet* and its cognates as "restive" ("restiveness," etc.) instead of the more usual "restless." As they note, *inquiet* is a crucially important term in Tocqueville. It describes the essential condition of the democratic soul, as contrasted with the "natural immobility" of aristocratic nations.†

---

† Tocqueville took the term, the editors show, from Pascal, who together with Rousseau and Montesquieu was one of the three men with whom he "live[d] a little every day." In a famous aphorism

Commenting on their decision, the editors say that "restive," "with its connotation of rebelliousness and intent," seemed better than "the more random 'restless.'" The problem is that "restive" is not a special form of restlessness but something closer to its opposite. It derives from the Latin *restare*, meaning "to remain where one is, linger, 'stay put.'" In a usage note, *The American Heritage Dictionary* tells us that "restive" and "restless" are "now commonly used as equivalent terms" (though it adds that "restive" "implies resistance to some sort of restraint"). But this is merely to codify a solecism. *The Oxford English Dictionary* underscores the problem with its definition of "restive": "1. Inclined to rest or remain stationary"; "2. Persistent, obstinate, settled or fixed in an opinion or course of action." This is not what Tocqueville meant by *inquiet*. In this essay, I have exercised the commentator's privilege and have silently substituted "restless" for "restive."

Modern readers who first encounter *Democracy in America* are almost always amazed by Tocqueville's contemporaneity, his relevance to America *now*. One example: although the stability of American democracy means that elections present "no real danger," Tocqueville notes that one "can still consider the election of the president as a period of national crisis."

Long before the appointed moment arrives, the election becomes the greatest and so to speak sole business preoc-

---

from the *Pensées*, Pascal described the human condition as *inconstance, ennui, inquiétude*. In *Democracy in America*, Tocqueville *seems* to present *inquiétude* in a largely positive light; it is interesting to ponder, therefore, the extent to which Tocqueville shared Pascal's dour estimation of this trait.

285

cupying minds. The factions at that time redouble their ardor; in that moment all the factitious passion that the imagination can create in a happy and tranquil country become agitated in broad daylight. . . .

The entire nation falls into a feverish state; the election is then the daily text of the public papers, the subject of particular conversations, the goal of all reasoning, the object of all thoughts, the sole interest of the present.

And then? "As soon as fortune has pronounced . . . this ardor is dissipated, everything becomes calm, and the river, one moment overflowed, returns peacefully to its bed."

How does he do it? How does he manage to sound like a contemporary pundit, only better? After all, when Tocqueville wrote, Andrew Jackson was president; there were only twenty-four states; the nation-defining events of the Civil War and the end of slavery lay decades in the future, to say nothing of the events of the twentieth century. How is it that so much of what Tocqueville has to say seems to apply as well to the United States at the dawn of the twenty-first century as to the United States *circa* 1830? Tocqueville himself would not have been surprised. Toward the beginning of the first volume of *Democracy in America*, in a chapter called "On the Point of Departure and Its Importance for the Future of the Anglo-Americans," he writes that "peoples always feel the effects of their origins." Just as one can predict a man's "prejudices, habits, and passions" by contemplating his situation as an infant—"the man," Tocqueville says, "is so to speak whole in the swaddling clothes of his cradle"—so, too, with nations. In America, "there is not one opinion, one habit, one law, I could say one event, that the point of departure does not explain." The early experiences of the colonies—their relatively prosperous and well-educated citizenry, their political independence, their common language, above all their stalwart yoking of what Tocqueville calls the *spirit of religion* and the *spirit of freedom* (elements that elsewhere are often opposed to each other)—forecast much of their future. Some things never change; some recur. Tocqueville notes with astonishment that among the "bizarre or tyrannical laws" promulgated early on in the colonies was one that "prohibits the use of tobacco." *Plus ça change.*

THE CHIEF intellectual drama of *Democracy in America* is the struggle between freedom and equality. Equality works to level differences; freedom to increase them. In the name of justice, equality requires us to forgo rank, privilege, even excellence: what is more discriminatory than talent? More unfair than ability? More divisive than brilliance? Freedom, too, appeals to justice: the justice due to achievement, not entitlement. What makes Tocqueville indispensable is his unparalleled appreciation of the fact that the health of democracy—the regime whose "primary fact" is the "equality of conditions"—requires not the triumph of equality but the careful perpetuation of this struggle: victory lies precisely in forsaking conquest. Speaking as the friend of democracy, Tocqueville constantly warns about elements inherent in democracy that, unchecked, make it inhospitable to freedom. Tocqueville's admonitions can mostly be grouped under two main headings: warnings about superficiality, and warnings about oppression.

Tocqueville discusses at some length the fact that democracies tend to champion material well-being to an unusual degree. He is not hostile to material well-being—far from it—but he notes that a single-minded pursuit of well-being tends to be curiously self-defeating. "It is a strange thing to see with what sort of feverish ardor Americans pursue well-being and how they show themselves constantly tormented by a vague fear of not having chosen the shortest route that can lead to it." In part this has to do with that restlessness, that *inquiétude*, that characterizes democratic man. In part it has to do with the fact that the desire for material well-being, when it degenerates into material*ism*, tends to exacerbate rather than satisfy man's cravings. Tocqueville speaks of "self-interest well understood" as one antidote to the poison of materialism: it turns out that self-interest is "well understood" only when it encompasses more than the self. Early on in *Democracy in America*, Tocqueville warns about those "who, in the name of progress, striving to make man into matter, want to find the useful without occupying themselves with the just, to find science far from beliefs, and well-being separated from virtue." It is an integral part of Tocqueville's task, not always noticed, to insinuate the transcendent—justice, faith, virtue—into a society whose fundamental constitution both depends upon it and yet tends to discount or repudiate it.

Tocqueville writes that it was "the religious aspect of the country" that first struck him on his visit to America. In France, the Enlightenment had opposed religion to freedom; in America the two were inextricably joined. This yoking of freedom and religion, Tocqueville believes, is truer to man's essential nature:

> The short space of sixty years will never confine the whole imagination of man; the incomplete joys of this world will never suffice for his heart. Alone among all the beings, man shows a natural disgust for existence and an immense desire to exist: he scorns life and fears nothingness. These different instincts constantly drive his soul toward contemplation of another world, and it is religion that guides it there. Religion is therefore only a particular form of hope,

and it is as natural to the human heart as hope itself. Only by a kind of aberration of the intellect and with the aid of a sort of moral violence exercised on their own nature do men stray from religious beliefs; an invincible inclination leads them back to them. Disbelief is an accident; faith alone is the permanent state of humanity.

Equality, the central democratic imperative, brings "great goods." But it also encourages a kind of spiritual isolationism (Tocqueville calls it "individualism") that tends to erode the binding force of religion. The result is a moral vertigo that exchanges freedom for unanchored worldliness.

> When authority in the matter of religion no longer exists . . . men are soon frightened at the aspect of this limitless independence. This perpetual agitation of all things makes them restless and fatigues them. . . . I doubt that man can ever support a complete religious independence and an entire political freedom at once; and I am brought to think that if he has no faith, he must serve, and if he is free, he must believe.

Religion was an essential leavening ingredient in American democracy; the development of democracy encourages an unwitting "Cartesian" isolation that cuts men off not only from one another but also from their spiritual roots. What seems at first like the progress of freedom threatens to be a march into sterility. The origins of democracy thus not only allow us to predict its mature features but also supply an indispensable source of renewal.

Tocqueville's analysis of the superficialities to which democracy is heir has its complement in what we might call the masterpiece of his masterpiece, his analysis of democratic forms of oppression. There are two main forms, the tyranny of the majority and democratic despotism.

Majority rule is practically synonymous with democracy. But the majority can tyrannize not only over minorities, but also, more insidiously, over itself. The idea, Tocqueville writes, that "in matters of government the majority of a people has the right to do everything" is "impious and detestable." Although the origin of all political power in a democracy lies ultimately with the will of the majority, "justice . . . forms the boundary of each people's right." This means, for example, that one should not obey an unjust law. The "sovereignty of the human race" trumps the "sovereignty of a people" and provides a moral measure for majority rule.

In American society, the tyranny of the majority shows itself above all in the tendency to delegitimize ideas not sanctioned by majority opinion. People are often surprised that Tocqueville should have remarked that "I do not know of any country where, in general, less independence of mind and genuine freedom of discussion reign than in America." After all, is not America the land of the free? But this restrictiveness, now as much as in the 1830s, is a predictable coefficient of the tyranny of the majority. "In America," Tocqueville notes, "the majority draws a formidable circle around thought. Inside those limits, the writer is free; but unhappiness awaits him if he dares to leave them. It is not that he has to fear an auto-da-fé, but he is the butt of mortifications of all kinds of persecutions every day." Here we have, *avant la lettre*, a definitive description of political correctness.

It was in his analysis of "democratic despotism" that Tocqueville, in Russell Kirk's words, made "his supreme achievement as a political theorist, a sociologist, a liberal, and a conservative." In two key chapters toward the end of volume two of *Democracy in America*, Tocqueville discusses the novel ways in which despotism would be likely to establish itself in democratic regimes. It would, he writes, be different from tyrannies of the past, which tended to be "violent but restricted." In democracies, despotism "would be more extensive and milder, and it would degrade men without tormenting them." The "individualism" that encourages democratic man to eschew political engagement and withdraw into himself and his private concerns—that "makes a public virtue of indifference"—also makes him susceptible to a "tutelary" despotism whose most insidious feature is its mildness.

> It would resemble paternal power if, like that, it had for its object to prepare men for manhood; but on the contrary, it seeks only to keep them fixed irrevocably in childhood; it likes citizens to enjoy themselves provided that they think only of enjoying themselves. . . It willingly works for their happiness; but it wants to be the unique agent and sole arbiter of that; it provides for their security, foresees and secures their needs, facilitates their pleasures, conducts their principal affairs, directs their industry, regulates their estates, divides their inheritances; can it not take away from them entirely the trouble of thinking and the pain of living? . . . [This power] extends its arms over society as a whole; it covers its surface with a network of small, complicated, painstaking, uniform rules through which the most original minds and the most vigorous souls cannot clear a way to surpass the crowd; it does not break wills, but it softens them, bends them, and directs them; it rarely forces one to act, but it constantly opposes itself to one's acting; it does not destroy, it prevents things from being born; it does not tyrannize, it hinders, compromises, ener-

vates, extinguishes, dazes, and finally reduces each nation
to being nothing more than a herd of timid and industrious
animals of which the government is the shepherd.

If Tocqueville's analysis of the tyranny of the majority
seems like a proleptic warning about political correctness,
his discussion of democratic despotism sounds a pertinent
tocsin about the encroachments of the nanny state. But
here, too, Tocqueville's doubleness of vision reasserts itself.
He is doubtless correct that, because "it is easier to establish an absolute and despotic government in a people
where conditions are equal than in any other," despotism is
particularly to be dreaded in democratic ages. Nevertheless, attempts to counter democratic despotism by resus-
citating aristocracy are bound to fail. The task is not to
struggle against the egalitarian imperative but to make
"freedom issue from the bosom of the democratic society
in which God makes us live." Equality is our fate, but it is
up to us whether that equality "leads to servitude or
freedom, to enlightenment or barbarism, to prosperity or
misery." In this sense, the greatest danger we face is neither
license nor tyranny, but the indifference, the "general
apathy," that democracy nurtures but cannot long abide.

Anthony Trollope:
A Novelist Who Hunted the Fox

*Imaginary evil is romantic and varied; real evil is gloomy,
monotonous, barren, boring. Imaginary good is boring, real
good is always new, marvellous, intoxicating. "Imaginative
literature," therefore, is either boring or immoral or a mixture
of both.*
—Simone Weil

O F ALL the great nineteenth-century novelists, perhaps
none has suffered more from the obloquy of intellectuals than Anthony Trollope. Writing in the early 1990s in
the London *Sunday Telegraph*, the English academic John
Casey expressed dismay that John Major, then Prime Minister, should have exhibited a fondness for Trollope's
novels. Conjuring up the spectacle of "that deadly thing—a
Trollopian," Casey assured his readers that "Trollope is
overrated. His prose, adequate enough for his purposes, is
undistinguished. His physical descriptions are flat. You
rarely *see* anything vividly through his writing." Moreover,
Casey added, "most confirmed Trollopians do not much
like literature."

Such strictures have dogged Trollope from the beginning. Trollope has no "ideas"; he is too "comfortable"; his
novels, with their abundance of clerics, cabinet ministers,

and happy endings, are insufficiently dramatic, passionate, challenging. Thomas Carlyle, than whom a less Trollopian figure can scarcely be imagined, sneered that the novelist was "irredeemably embedded in the commonplace, and grown fat upon it." And Henry James—in his own, very different, way as un-Trollopian as Carlyle—dismissed *The Belton Estate* (1866) as "a work written for children; a work prepared for minds unable to think; . . . a *stupid* book." "Life is vulgar," James wrote in another early essay on Trollope, "but we know not how vulgar it is till we see it set down in his pages." In the handful of pieces that he wrote about Trollope in the 1860s, James allowed himself a certain admiration—Trollope was, he admitted, a "born story-teller"—but the admiration was always hedged with disparaging qualifications: Trollope's work was essentially "superficial," his dramatic situations "trivial." If he felt an undeniable "partiality" for Trollope's novels, he was nonetheless "somewhat ashamed" of that partiality.

James later responded more warmly to Trollope's achievement, placing him below Dickens, Thackeray, and George Eliot, to be sure, yet insisting that "he belonged to the same family" as that great triumvirate of Victorian writers. What had changed was not so much James's judgment about the character of Trollope's work—Trollope must ever lack Jamesian "seriousness"—but his recognition that work of such character was nothing to be ashamed of. "His great, his inestimable merit," James wrote in an appreciative retrospective essay published shortly after Trollope's death in 1882, "was a complete appreciation of the usual."

Trollope's own estimation of his achievement jibed closely with James's final assessment. He, too, reckoned his place below that of George Eliot and Thackeray. And although he did not particularly care for Dickens or for his work, he acknowledged Dickens's dazzling success. "The primary object of a novelist is to please," Trollope wrote in his posthumously published *Autobiography* (1883); "and this man's novels have been found more pleasant than those of any other writer." Trollope would probably also have agreed with James that his own forte consisted in depicting "the commonplace." "A novel," Trollope wrote, "should give a picture of common life enlivened by humour and sweetened by pathos." As N. John Hall points out in *Trollope: A Biography* (Oxford, 1991), Trollope's "genius, while capable of depicting tragic figures, was essentially a comic one." Even his grimmest work, *The Way We Live Now* (1875), ends with a quartet of marriages and general reconciliation. The evil financier Augustus Melmotte, although he comes a cropper and commits suicide, emerges with a certain dignity; many critics have remarked on the "Roman" trappings of his suicide. The other bad eggs are sent packing to the continent or America. Harmony and happiness reign anew.

It is part of Trollope's achievement to have managed this without seeming sappy. His characters are generally decorous, but never prim, unless for comic effect. This is the other, more positive side of that "commonplace" Carlyle disparaged. As Nathaniel Hawthorne, one of Trollope's early admirers, put it in a well-known encomium, Trollope's work is "written on the strength of beef and through the inspiration of ale, and [is] just as real as if some giant had hewn a great lump out of the earth and put it under a glass case, with all its inhabitants going about their daily business, and not suspecting that they were being made a show of." George Eliot, who professed as great an admiration for Trollope's work as he did for hers (and who credited Trollope's example with helping her to persevere with *Middlemarch*), remarked in a letter that his books "are filled with belief in goodness without the slightest tinge of maudlin."†

What we might call the *easiness* of Trollope's novels is all the more remarkable in view of his frankly didactic ambition. "I have ever thought of myself as a preacher of sermons," he notes in the *Autobiography*. The central question an author must ask himself, he reflects later, is "how shall he teach lessons of virtue and at the same time make himself a delight to his readers?" Trollope never provided anything much in the way of theoretical answers to this (or any other) question. But his life and, especially, his dozens of novels stand as eloquent testimony to the strength and, finally, the complexity of his moral vision. At a moment when art seems often to flaunt its distance from virtue as conventionally understood, Trollope's example may provide a welcome perspective not only on contemporary fiction but also, as Trollope put it in one of his most famous titles, on the way we live now.

Today, at any rate, the reaction against the creator of Barsetshire and Plantagenet Palliser is probably easier to understand than is his enduring popularity.‡ Tolstoy ex-

---

† Trollope muted his admiration for Eliot somewhat in his *Autobiography*. Noting that he regarded her as a "gifted woman and among my dearest and most intimate friends," he nonetheless concluded that "It is . . . the defect of George Eliot that she struggles too hard to do work that shall be excellent. She lacks ease."

‡ And there can be no doubt that his popularity is enduring. Not only does Trollope continue to be much in demand among readers but also he has provided attractive provender for numerous books. Apart from myriad critical studies—among which James R. Kincaid's *The Novels of Anthony Trollope* (1977) and Shirley Robin Letwin's *The Gentleman in Trollope* (1982) deserve special mention—the last thirty years have seen a biography by James Pope Hennessy (1971) and an illustrated "appreciation" by C. P. Snow (1975), as well as Robert Super's *The Chronicler of Barset: A Life of Anthony Trollope*

claimed that "Trollope kills me, kills me with his virtuosity." But there can be few writers of Trollope's stature less calculated to appeal to twentieth-century notions— what are still, after all our ironies and disillusionments, essentially Romantic notions—of artistic privilege and authorial preciousness.

For one thing, there was Trollope's politics. He described himself as an "advanced" "Conservative-Liberal." But such terms meant something rather different in the second half of the nineteenth century from what they've came to mean nowadays. One token of Trollope's distance from contemporary pieties is his view of women. His cast of clever, spirited women is rightly regarded as one of his most sympathetic achievements; one thinks especially of Madame Max Goesler, who appears in several novels and whom Shirley Robin Letwin described as "the most perfect gentleman in Trollope's novels." Nevertheless, Trollope is not exactly what one would call a feminist. What is a woman's goal in life, he asks in *Can You Forgive Her?* (1864)? It is to fall in love, marry the man, have two children, and "live happily ever afterwards."

Also calculated to displease was Trollope's attitude toward the whole notion of artistic "inspiration," which he regarded with undisguised scorn. "To me," he wrote, "it would not be more absurd if the shoemaker were to wait for inspiration." What mattered to Trollope was application. His discipline was legendary. According to the famous story recounted in the *Autobiography*, he paid his groom £5 a year extra to wake him at 5:00 A.M. so that he could

---

(1988) and Richard Mullen's *Anthony Trollope: A Victorian in his World* (1990). Hall's scholarly biography is additional testimony to Trollope's abiding attractions, as is Victoria Glendinning's brisker but less scholarly *Anthony Trollope* (Knopf, 1993).

be at his desk by 5:30. "I do not know that I ought not to feel that I owe more to him than to any one else for the success I have had," Trollope reflected. "By beginning at that hour, I could complete my literary labor before I dressed for breakfast."

Nor did Trollope dawdle and "sit nibbling the pen." He spent half an hour reading over and correcting what he had written the day before. Then, with a clock in front of him, he managed 250 words every quarter hour, covering ten pages and producing on average 2,500 words before he set off for a full day's work on Post Office business. His manuscripts suggest that he did virtually no rewriting. Following this regimen, he generally produced about 10,000 words a week, on some occasions as much as 25,000 words. And this was week in and week out, month after month, year after year. In other words, Trollope exhibited in spades the Victorian belief in the transformative power of work. "[I]t's a sheer matter of industry," he declared. "It's not the head that does it—it's the cobbler's wax on the seat and the sticking to my chair!" Trollope admitted that his procedure might not conduce to works of genius. But, he explains, "the idea that I was the unfortunate owner of unappreciated genius never troubled me." Punctuality, though, was of supreme importance to him. "With all the pages that I have written for magazines I have never been a day late," Trollope remarks proudly, "nor have I ever caused inconvenience by sending less or more matter than I had stipulated to supply. But I have sometimes found myself compelled to suffer by the irregularity of others." Even in this age of word processors and the internet, I daresay that there are few writers who can make that worthy boast.

Trollope's working diaries, in which he jotted down the number of pages he wrote each day, show days missed for illness, holidays, and other engagements, but such lacunae are rare. He could write almost anywhere: not only at his desk but also on the railway (he had a special traveling desk built for this purpose) and on shipboard. Once he became an established writer, he was in the habit of going down to consult with the ship's carpenter in order to arrange for suitable writing accommodations before setting sail. Traveling from New York to London in 1875, Henry James recalled meeting Trollope on board. "The season was unpropitious," James wrote,

> the vessel overcrowded, the voyage detestable; but Trollope shut himself up in his cabin every morning for a purpose which, on the part of a distinguished writer who was also an invulnerable sailor, could only be communion with the muse. He drove his pen as steadily on the tumbling ocean as in Montagu Square.

James supposed that Trollope was working on yet another novel; in fact, he was just then beginning work on his *Autobiography.*

THINKING ABOUT TROLLOPE encourages the habit of tabulation. His first book, *The Macdermots of Ballycloran*, was published in 1847 as Trollope approached his thirty-second birthday. "The book," as Hall notes, "did not sell," even when the publisher vainly resorted to advertisements attributing authorship to Trollope's mother, by then a popular novelist in her own right. Trollope's first, albeit exceedingly modest, success came with *The Warden* in 1855. *The Warden*, which inaugurated the Barsetshire series and is widely regarded as one of Trollope's masterpieces, was Trollope's fourth book; *Barchester Towers*, probably the most popular of all his novels, came next, in

1857. Over the next quarter century, he produced some sixty-five books. Altogether forty-seven novels and nearly twenty volumes of travel writing, short stories, criticism, and biography, including a book on Caesar's *De Bello Gallico* (1870) and a life of Cicero (1880), flowed from his pen. Nor were Trollope's novels skimpy two-hundred-page entertainments. *The Warden* appeared in a single, relatively slender volume, but most of his novels were published serially in magazines, appearing between covers only when they had grown into full-fledged, triple-decker productions. *The Way We Live Now*, his longest book, is well over four hundred thousand words long.

Such fertility, combined with what Trollope himself called "mechanical" habits of composition, engenders first astonishment and then suspicion. As early as 1858, contemporary reviewers wondered whether Trollope were not writing too much, whether the "rapid multiplication of his progeny," as the *Saturday Review* put it, must not require a corresponding diminution of quality. Since then it has been a standard, if not adequately examined, assumption that Trollope sacrificed quality to quantity—something, we are given to understand, no serious artist would think of doing.

Then there was Trollope's attitude toward money. Like most authors, he liked it. Unlike many, he frankly admitted that he wrote for it. Moreover, he kept as meticulous tabs on his earnings as he did on his writing, reproducing at the end of the *Autobiography* the sums he received for each of his books through 1879. The total was £68,939 17 s. 5 d., a result that Trollope described as "comfortable" but not "splendid." (According to Hall, the total at the time of his death three years later was some £10,000 more.) He comments caustically that "authors are told that they should disregard payment for their work, and be content to devote their unbought brains to the welfare of the public. Brains that are unbought will never serve the public much. Take away from English authors their copyrights, and you would very soon take away also from England her authors."

More generally, Trollope tended to agree with Dr. Johnson that a man is never so innocently employed as when he is making money. In *Can You Forgive Her?*, the first of the six Palliser novels, Plantagenet Palliser remarks that "there is no vulgar error so vulgar,—that is to say, common or erroneous,—as that by which men have been taught to say that mercenary tendencies are bad. A desire for wealth is the source of all progress. Civilization comes from what men call greed."

Dowries, legacies, "expectations," church livings, and financial speculation play as large a role in the lives of Trollope's characters as they did in the lives of the people Trollope observed in his travels around the British Isles. When Laura Standish tells Phineas Finn that she has become engaged to another man, he asks bitterly whether she might have accepted him had he asked a week earlier.

> "How can I answer such a question, Mr. Finn? Or, rather, I will answer it fully. It is not a week since we told each other, you to me and I to you, that we were both poor,— both without other means than those which come to us from our fathers. You will make your way;—will make it surely; but how at present could you marry any woman unless she had money of her own? For me,—like so many girls, it was necessary that I should stay at home or marry someone rich enough to dispense with fortune in a wife."

Not all Trollope's characters are mercenary; few, not even the saintly Septimus Harding in *The Warden*, are blind to the importance of money in affecting life's possibilities. "A man must live," reflected Phineas Finn, "even though his heart be broken, and living he must dine." "Of all novelists in any country," W. H. Auden remarked in "A Poet of the Actual," his aptly titled review of James Pope Hennessy's biography of the novelist, "Trollope best understands the role of money. Compared with him, even Balzac is too romantic." Aldous Huxley sounded a similar note when he remarked that, should his library suddenly be destroyed, he would "repossess [himself] of quite a lot of Trollope; for his bourgeois shrewdness is so great as to be positively titanic, his common sense, Victorian Britishness intense to the point of being almost supernatural."

One of Trollope's most famous characters is the appalling Mrs. Proudie, wife and faithful tormentor of Dr. Proudie, Bishop of Barchester. Mrs. Proudie is a frightful busybody and scheming harridan, the real force behind the bishop's throne. Yet she is not stupid, nor is she entirely without feeling. In *Barchester Towers*, Mrs. Proudie arranges—well, she connives and maneuvers—for the poor and beleaguered Mr. and Mrs. Quiverful, who have fourteen children ("fourteen *living*," as Mrs. Quiverful plaintively puts it), to receive a church position that will double their income.† Mrs. Proudie's beneficence was far from wholly altruistic: she was pursuing her own political objectives as much as she was aiding the distressed curate and his fruitful wife. But while Mrs. Quiverful understands some of this and rightly regards Mrs. Proudie as "stiff and

---

† "Quiverful"? Alas, yes. Among others one encounters in Trollope's pages are Dr. Pessimist Anticant (a crude caricature of Carlyle), Mr. Popular Sentiment (Dickens), the rich parvenu Sir Damask Monogram, a musician named Blowhard, and a doctor named Fillgrave. Sometimes such fanciful names are amusing; more often, one feels that Trollope was not as subtle as he might have been in naming his characters.

hard and proud as piecrust," she nevertheless concludes that the bishop's wife is "right at bottom." Trollope notes dryly that "people when they get their income doubled usually think that those through whose instrumentality this little ceremony is performed are right at bottom."

BUT IT IS NOT ONLY Trollope's severely pragmatic attitude toward his literary endeavors (how he would have loathed the term "creative writing"!) that sets him apart from the idealized image of literary culture; nor is it simply his candid acknowledgment that money constituted an important spur to writing; there was also his whole mode of life. Contrasting Trollope with such "sedentary" French novelists as Flaubert and Zola, James described Trollope, not *altogether* nastily, as "a novelist who hunted the fox." And indeed, among the three chief occupations of Trollope's life—writing novels, working for the British Post Office, and "hunting the fox"—writing certainly came in third. "Nothing has ever been allowed to stand in the way of hunting," Trollope declared, "neither the writing of books, nor the work of the Post Office, nor other pleasures." From the time that he could afford it, in the 1840s, Trollope habitually rode to hounds three times weekly for the entire season, November through April. Although increasingly heavy and dangerously near-sighted—Trollope never rode particularly well—he did not give up the sport until 1876 when he was sixty-one.

It would be also a mistake to think that Trollope regarded his position at the Post Office as a sinecure. He had an absolute horror of seeming to receive public money without earning it. As he often took pains to point out, he devoted vastly more time and energy to his career as a civil servant, which lasted from 1834 until September of 1867, than he did to his writing. He prosecuted his job as Surveyor for the British Post Office with unflagging energy. He probably logged more miles riding over Ireland (where he spent more than fifteen years) and England to investigate complaints and improve service than any other individual. "I became intensely anxious," he noted, "that people should have their letters delivered to them punctually." It is characteristic that some of his most critical remarks about the United States concern its postal system, whose service he described as "absolutely barbarous." In any event, if Trollope's novels can be said to lack innovation, not so his work for the Post Office. Probably his most important innovation came in 1851, when he proposed erecting letter boxes (which were already being used in France) to make the collection of mail more convenient and efficient. By the mid-1850s, letter boxes were in widespread use in Britain. Not only did Trollope work at the Post Office for more than thirty years, but long after he had become a successful writer he applied for a position that he knew would sharply curtail his literary activities. His disappointment on not receiving the job was intense. When he resigned a couple of years later, the rebuff still rankled.

The fact is, Trollope strove mightily to embody the nebulous ideal epitomized in the word "gentleman"—what the critic James Kincaid called "the most common standard for moral behaviour in Trollope." Fox hunting could clearly be accommodated by this standard, as indeed, for Trollope, could a career in the civil service. An excessive devotion to writing novels was perhaps more problematic. In the event, Trollope's effort to join these activities under the rubric "gentleman" was not accomplished seamlessly. As W. H. Auden pointed out, Trollope was "a very eccentric character who might well, though he would have hated to admit it, have come straight out of a novel by Dickens."

Contemporary recollections of the novelist are pretty much of a piece. Trollope was a bluff, kind-hearted, slightly uncouth man, rough, sociable, and above all loud. James Russell Lowell recalls meeting Trollope in Boston. "Dined the other day with Anthony Trollope; a big, red-faced, rather underbred Englishman of the bald-with-spectacles type. A good roaring positive fellow who deafened me . . . till I thought of Dante's Cerberus." "Anthony's outer and inner selves," Victoria Glendinning notes in her biography, "confused many who met him. How could this loud, obstreperous man be the Anthony Trollope who wrote with such extraordinary insight into the hearts of men and, even more extraordinary, of women?" The relation between this comic, whist-playing monster and the delicate delineator of nineteenth-century English manners is perhaps difficult to fathom until we recognize that in addition to being bluff Trollope was painfully shy and fundamentally lonely. The nineteenth century was full of famously unhappy childhoods; but few were memorialized with as much quiet pathos as Trollope brought to the memory of his early wretchedness. "My boyhood was, I think," he writes at the beginning of his *Autobiography,* "as unhappy as that of a young gentleman could well be."

Trollope's father, Thomas Anthony, was an intelligent though failed barrister who suffered from migraines and a foul temper. He was modestly prosperous when Trollope was born, in 1815, the fifth of seven children. But by the time young Anthony went to school, his father was well on his way to the poverty and unshakable depression that dogged him for the rest of his life. "Everything went wrong with him," Trollope noted sadly of his father. "The touch of his hand seemed to create failure." After he had driven away all his clients and failed thoroughly in his attempt to farm, Trollope *père* turned to compiling an *Encyclopedia*

LIVES OF THE MIND

Ecclesiastica, meant to define all the ecclesiastical terms that had ever existed. It was the perfect vehicle to complete his futility. By the time he died he had gotten only to the letter D.

In Trollope's early years, however, Thomas Anthony was still cogent enough to oversee his children's education. "From my very babyhood," Trollope recalled,

> I had to take my place alongside of him as he shaved at six o'clock in the morning, and say my early rules from the Latin Grammar, or repeat the Greek alphabet; and was obliged at these early lessons to hold my head inclined towards him, so that in the event of guilty fault, he might be able to pull my hair without stopping his razor or dropping his shaving-brush. No father was ever more anxious for the education of his children, though I think none ever knew less how to go about the work.

Trollope's real misery began when, like his older brothers Thomas Adolphus and Henry, he was sent as a day boy to Harrow. The Trollopes' poverty had taken firm hold by the time young Anthony matriculated, and he was ragged mercilessly by his fellow students. "I suffered horribly!" Trollope writes. "I was big, and awkward, and ugly, and, I have no doubt, skulked about in a most unattractive manner. Of course I was ill dressed and dirty." Nor did the young Trollope find much solace among the masters; he was a poor student, irremediably slovenly and remiss in his studies. Trollope recalls encountering Dr. Butler, headmaster at Harrow, who would stop him in the street and ask whether it was possible that Harrow should be disgraced by so dirty and unkempt a boy. "He must have known me," Trollope remarks, "for he was in the habit of flogging me constantly. Perhaps he did not recognize me by my face."

Trollope's mother, Frances, was the antipode of his father: bright, sociable, and like Anthony graced with extraordinary energy. It was she who pulled the family through after all her husband's schemes collapsed. Not that Frances was exactly a practical woman. She hit upon one of her most notorious schemes when making a protracted visit to the States (leaving poor Anthony alone in the "care" of his father). With a combination of capital that she could ill-afford to spend and credit she could not repay, she built a bazaar in Cincinnati, stocked with the tawdry trinkets her husband insisted on sending her from England. "[W]ithin half a year the building was put into receivership," Hall notes; "everything, even Mrs. Trollope's own belongings, was seized."

AND YET, the sojourn in America was not entirely wasted, for it sparked her own career as a writer. *Domestic Manners of the Americans*, a wry and caustic account of American foibles, was published in 1832 when Mrs. Trollope was fifty-three. It instantly became a *succès de scandale*, immensely popular in Britain, loudly detested in the States. While the money she made from *Domestic Manners* staved off disaster for only a couple of years, it did provide her with a vocation and a means to feed her family. From that moment forward she was a writer, turning out with extraordinary fluency a prodigious number of novels and travel books, even as she nursed her sick husband and children, four of whom were eventually to die of consumption. She continued writing until 1856, when she was seventy-six, producing all told over one hundred volumes. "Her career," Trollope remarks, "offers great encouragement to those who have not begun early in life, but are still ambitious to do something before they depart hence."

Despite Mrs. Trollope's efforts, the bailiff continued to

threaten. Finally, in March 1834, he could be put off no longer: the family fled to Bruges to escape creditors. Mrs. Trollope managed to secure a teaching position for Anthony, but within a few months a vacancy opened up in the General Post Office in London. In the autumn of 1834, he started work as a clerk for £90 per year. Trollope's early years at the Post Office were not a success. His salary was inadequate, so he was always in debt; his work was poor, his habits irregular, his attitude obstreperous. He was several times on the verge of being dismissed.

But then, in 1841, he applied for and was appointed to the position of Deputy Postal Surveyor in King's County, Ireland. Somehow, Ireland changed everything. Poverty, ignominy, loneliness: all were suddenly banished. "From the day on which I set my foot in Ireland all these evils went away from me," Trollope recalled. "Since that time, who has had a happier life than mine?" Within a year, he was engaged to Rose Heseltine, a quiet Englishwoman he met at a watering place near Dublin and whom he married in 1844. Not only did he pursue his new postal duties avidly, to the astonishment of his superiors in London, but he finally set about realizing his dream of becoming a writer, beginning work on *The Macdermots of Ballycloran* in 1843.

It was a dream that he had cultivated carefully since childhood. Partly in an effort to relieve his loneliness, Trollope had early on fallen into the habit of daydreaming. "Thus it came to pass," he confided in the *Autobiography*, "that I was always going about with some castle in the air firmly built within my mind."

> For weeks, for months, if I remember rightly, from year to year, I would carry on the same tale, binding myself down to certain laws, . . . I myself was of course my own hero.

Such is a necessity of castle-building. . . . There can, I imagine, hardly be a more dangerous mental practice; but I
have often doubted whether, had it not been my practice, I
should ever have written a novel. I learned in this way to
maintain an interest in a fictitious story, to dwell on a work
created by my own imagination, and to live in a world altogether outside the world of my own material life.

By the late 1840s, Trollope's daydreams had begun to take
on a semblance of reality; by the late 1850s, he might as
well have stepped out of the pages of one of his novels: the
final installments of the romance had begun, and early sufferings and complications were resolved in neat if homely
harmonies.

In fact, many commentators have wondered whether the
picture that Trollope presents in the *Autobiography* isn't a
little too neat: whether the childhood miseries were quite
as severe or the later triumphs quite so unruffled as Trollope presents. While Hall corrects a few dates and other
minor lapses, he does not argue substantially with the self-
portrait which Trollope provides for us in the *Autobiography*. Nor does Victoria Glendinning. Indeed, for those
familiar with the *Autobiography* none of the recent
biographies of Trollope offers much in the way of revelation. This can hardly be a criticism, perhaps, since there
are precious few revelations about Trollope to be had.
Some youthful indiscretions are hinted at in the *Autobiography*. There was a bit of drinking and the occasional
sticky romantic entanglement. (Trollope recounts an
episode in which one girl's mother marched into the Post
Office, basket on her arm, loudly demanding to know
when Anthony Trollope was going to marry her daughter.)
But Trollope tells his own story with as much decorum
as he brings to his novels. What he presents is not the

309

record of his inner life but a chronicle of his endeavors. His discussion of his marriage is a case in point: "My marriage was like the marriage of other people, and of no special interest to anyone except my wife and me." Hall, like Trollope's other biographers, cannot do much better. About Rose, for example, he tells us simply that "she remains the great unknown in Trollope's life." Victoria Glendinning adverts to Rose's "shrewdness," fondness of novels, and poor spelling, but does not coax her out of nebulousness. Apparently, it was the same for Trollope's friends. George Henry Lewes, having spent a night at the Trollopes' house in 1861, wrote in his journal that "Mrs Trollope did not make any decided impression on me, one way or the other." And it was the same, too, for many other aspects of Trollope's life. Discussing *The Small House at Allington* (1864)—the fifth of the six Barsetshire novels—Hall notes that the hero, Johnny Eames, was hopelessly in love with the inaccessible Lily Dale. Both in *The Small House at Allington* and in *The Last Chronicle of Barset* (1867), Eames is recognizably a self-portrait of the young Trollope. (Mrs. Oliphant said that she could not read Trollope's book on Caesar without laughing: "It is so like Johnny Eames.") But, Hall concedes, "whether there was ever a Lily Dale in Trollope's early life, a woman he worshipped for years but, for whatever reason, could never win, is beyond discovery."

"Beyond discovery," as it happens, describes almost everything of importance about Trollope's life that is not contained in his *Autobiography*. This means that a biographer, especially one coming on the heels of several recent accounts of the novelist's life, labors at a marked disadvantage. What will infuse his redaction with new life and interest? Hall, who teaches English at Bronx Community College and who has edited an edition of Trollope's letters

(1983), has probably done as well as one could have hoped. He has brought the habits of a meticulous scholar as well as the passion of an enthusiast to his task. His book proceeds in deliberate steps through every important episode of Trollope's life, taking us from Trollope's unhappy school days through his place at the heart of literary London. He dutifully recounts the signal events of Trollope's career, his rise in the Post Office, the publication of his books, his association with the *Cornhill Magazine*, the *Fortnightly Review*, and *St. Paul's Magazine*, and his failed bid to win a seat in Parliament; he has sifted through contemporary reviews and provides a kind of running score card on Trollope's popularity; he follows him as eagerly to America, Australia, and South Africa as to the Garrick Club, the Cosmopolitan Club, and the Athenaeum. Above all, perhaps, he stresses the fundamental Trollopian achievement: that "no one is thoroughly virtuous or thoroughly evil, and Trollope engages a qualified sympathy for almost everyone."

Hall also reminds us of just how droll Trollope's *Autobiography* can be. For example, when passing through Salt Lake City in 1872, Trollope recounted his brief encounter with Brigham Young. Having sent up his card, he waits to be received. "I did not achieve great intimacy with the great polygamist of the Salt Lake City," Trollope confesses.

> He received me in his doorway, not asking me to enter, and inquired whether I were not a miner. When I told him that I was not a miner, he asked me whether I earned my bread. I told him I did. "I guess you're a miner," said he. I again assured him that I was not. "Then how do you earn your bread?" I told him that I did so by writing books. "I'm sure you're a miner," said he. Then he turned upon his heel, went back into the house, and closed the door.

Throughout his long book, Hall is utterly responsible, competent, and not infrequently a bit dull. His basic procedure, once Trollope has gotten around to publishing books, is to insert a potted summary of the latest volume every dozen pages or so. This is a perfectly normal operation, of course, but *en masse* and without much effort to "place" Trollope in a larger literary context, it soon becomes tedious. If one has read the book, the summary is superfluous; if one hasn't, it is opaque. Then, too, Hall has allowed himself a great deal of repetition: readers encounter the same points, even some favorite quotations, again and again. Perhaps he would have done well to trim his manuscript by eighty or one hundred pages. Victoria Glendinning's book is a more allegro effort: not, perhaps, as thorough or as scholarly, but possessed of greater narrative velocity.

HALL REMARKS in his introduction that he has not attempted to write a "'thesis' biography." That is certainly all to the good. But those familiar with the lineaments of Trollope's life are nonetheless likely to find Hall's book most engaging when he steps back from his chronicle and offers an opinion. He is particularly good on the nature of Trollope's religious belief. It has often been remarked that Trollope's clergymen are longer on amenity than theology. Even the dreamy Mr. Harding, for all his charm, doesn't get beyond asking himself what "can a man's religion be worth, if it does not support him against the natural melancholy of declining years?" In fact, Trollope specialized in what Henry James called "the full-fed worldly churchman," men like Archdeacon Grantly: canny, political, vigilant. "Unlike Homer," Trollope writes, Dr. Grantly "never nods." But this is not to say that Trollope regarded religion as a species of applied hypocrisy. As Hall notes,

Trollope, like so many Victorians, wanted to believe, but belief itself was so much a mystery to him that . . . he hardly knew, precisely, what he believed. That segment of the Church of England informally denominated "broad" suited Trollope nicely; he could pretty much dismiss the Old Testament, admire the moral teachings of Christ, and keep up an ill-defined belief in a supreme being and a vague hope of some kind of immortality.

Victoria Glendinning came to a similar conclusion about Trollope's religious sentiments. "No close reader of his work," she writes,

> can doubt that his own beliefs were painfully vague, and that this troubled him. Equally, no one can doubt that he clung to a strong sense of God, something he also called Providence, or a "superior power," which had to do with the natural law, and purpose and rightness, the grandeur of mountains and torrents and the immortality of the soul.

Many modern commentators, reading themselves back into Trollope, have depicted him as a kind of closet atheist. But as Hall's and Victoria Glendinning's comments imply, this is to misunderstand the complexity of Trollope's situation and the religious milieu of his time. "It is very hard," Trollope wrote at the end of a collection of essays called *The Clergymen of England* (1866),

> to come at the actual belief of any man. Indeed how should we hope to do so when we find it so very hard to come at our own? How many are there among us who, in this matter of our religion, which of all things is the most important to us, could take pen in hand and write down even for their own information exactly what they themselves believe?

Whatever religious doubts Trollope entertained, they did not capsize his spiritual equanimity. And why should they have? We may be reasonably certain he would have regarded the deliberate *cultivation* of doubt—something we take more or less for granted—as a culpable self-indulgence. In this respect, his spiritual outlook, if we can call it that, differs markedly from ours. It may indeed be one of the chief glories of such serious-minded Victorians that they were able to sustain doubt without jettisoning their faith. Where the modern, secular world begins by assuming doubt, the Victorians had the luxury of beginning from the assumption of faith. Certainly, there were plenty of Victorians assailed by radical doubt; but this was regarded—as much by themselves as by those around them—more as a catastrophe than a liberation. If that dampened their appetite for irony and sometimes rendered their earnestness naïve, well, there are virtues beyond irony and faults beyond naïveté.

Among the virtues that Trollope practiced in his novels was unstinting honesty to the fundamentals of human experience. As he stressed repeatedly, in the *Autobiography* and elsewhere, it was a matter of "deep conscience" with him how he portrayed his characters. To be sure, "the writer of stories must please, or he will be nothing." But, for Trollope, the novelist must not sacrifice truth for effect. In this respect, the novelist's task resembles the poet's: both work toward "the same end": "By either, false sentiments may be fostered; false notions of humanity may be engendered; false honour, false love, false worship may be created; by either, vice instead of virtue may be taught." One way that Trollope sought to avoid "false sentiments" was by reminding his readers that the tale they were reading was just that, a tale. For example, in *Barchester Towers*, when Eleanor Bold is pursued by a clutch of undesirable suitors, Trollope lets us know early on that Eleanor will choose wisely in the end. "But let the gentle-hearted reader be under no apprehension whatsoever. It is not destined that Eleanor should marry Mr. Slope or Bertie Stanhope." James recoiled from such passages, describing them as "suicidal." But in the context of Trollope's moral purpose, they may be seen as salutary disenchantments.

And what, finally, was Trollope's "moral purpose"? It is of course hard to say. Trollope is not a writer from whom one can easily extract formulas. But in her unjustly neglected essay "Trollope For Grown-Ups" (1962), the critic Clara Claiborne Park comes close to the heart of the matter when she describes the novelist as "the laureate of compromise." Trollope is almost alone, she notes, in telling us "what we need to hear: be reasonable, be moderate, in action, in desire, in expectation, and you will be fairly happy." This may seem like small beer. But it can be powerful compensation for what Park calls "the desolation caused by naked principle among people." If Trollope lacked a doctrine to impose as virtue, he came armed with an abundance of experience and psychological insight. Shirley Robin Letwin, quoting the philosopher Michael Oakeshott, observes that "a gentleman feels obliged to reconcile himself to 'the unavoidable dissonances of a human condition' and his ability to achieve such a reconciliation makes him gentle." Such was Trollope's ambition and his teaching. As his narrator puts it in *Barchester Towers*, "Till we can become divine we must be content to be human, lest in our hurry for a change we sink to something lower."

G. C. Lichtenberg:
A "Spy on Humanity"

We may use Lichtenberg's writings as the most wonderful dows-
ing rod: wherever he makes a joke, there a problem lies hidden.
—Goethe

Lichtenberg digs deeper than anyone. . . . He speaks from the
subterranean depths. Only he who himself digs deep hears him.
—Karl Kraus

[T]here are truths that are singularly shy and ticklish and cannot
be caught except suddenly—that must be surprised *or left alone.*
—Nietzsche

IN THE EXACTING LEDGER of posterity, the aphorist Georg Christoph Lichtenberg rates high but is undeniably a specialty item. He is not a household name. He is something rarer: a name savored by household names. Goethe, who corresponded with Lichtenberg, admired him greatly (even though Lichtenberg disputed his theory of color). Arthur Schopenhauer, not someone addicted to dispensing praise glibly, reserved his highest compliment for Lichtenberg, declaring him to be a *Selbstdenker*, someone who genuinely thought for himself. Likewise, Nietzsche, whose powers of contempt often outshone his talent for appreciation, repeatedly cited Lichtenberg with agreement and respect. (Nietzsche might have had Lichtenberg in mind when, in *The Gay Science*, he defended his own method of handling philosophical problems: "I approach deep problems like cold baths: quickly into them and quickly out again. That one does not get to the depths that way, not deep enough, is the superstition of those afraid of the water.") Kierkegaard, too, regularly cited or alluded to Lichtenberg, and in fact prefaced his book *Stages on Life's Way* with a version of one of Lichtenberg's most famous aphorisms: "Such works are mirrors: when an ape looks into them, no apostle looks out." Wittgenstein, with his weakness for sudden enthusiasms, made Lichtenberg one of his causes, recommended him to various correspondents, and pressed copies of his work on friends, including Bertrand Russell. Lichtenberg's influence on Wittgenstein's work went deeper than mere content: the gnomic form of the *Tractatus* and *Philosophical Investigations* owes a great deal to the example of Lichtenberg's aphorisms. Scratch an important nineteenth- or twentieth-century thinker and the chances are good that you will find a warm word or two for the work of G. C. Lichtenberg.

Nevertheless, what Jacques Barzun said of the English essayist Walter Bagehot is also true of Lichtenberg: he is well known without being known well. A healthy slice of his most enduring work has been translated into English, but that was some years ago and—such is the fickleness of intellectual fashion—Lichtenberg's reputation has diminished into a name flanked by a handful of witty remarks:

He swallowed a lot of knowledge, but it seemed as if most of it had gone down the wrong way.

He who is enamored of himself will at least have the advantage of being inconvenienced by few rivals.

Not only did he not believe in ghosts, he wasn't even afraid of them.

A handful of soldiers is always better than a mouthful of arguments.

The fly that does not want to be swatted is safest if it sits on the fly-swatter.

There is a lot of gold in Lichtenberg. The casual negligence of presumed familiarity has assured that it remains buried for most American and English readers. We hear the name, remember an epigram or two, and leave it at that. The republication of R. J. Hollingdale's translation of a selection of Lichtenberg's aphorisms (New York Review Books, 2001) may serve as a welcome corrective. First published by Penguin in 1990, Hollingdale's translation of 1,085 aphorisms amounts to perhaps a quarter of the material that Lichtenberg collected in the nine volumes of his notebooks (two of which went missing in the nineteenth century, along with portions of two others). Lichtenberg began keeping his notebooks in his student days in the mid-1760s and he kept scribbling in them until a few days before his death, at fifty-seven, in 1799.

As Hollingdale observes in his introductory essay, these notebooks are not diaries. Lichtenberg did keep a diary—a voluminous one—where he recorded the itineraries of his domestic and social life. But the notebooks were something else, a general repository, an intellectual clearinghouse, "a Book wherein I write everything, as I see it or as my thoughts suggests it to me." Lichtenberg's notebooks are a sort of omnibus. As J. P. Stern put it in *Lichtenberg: A Doctrine of Scattered Occasions* (1959)—the best book in English on Lichtenberg—they consist of "jottings, extracts, calculations, quotations, autobiographical observations, platitudes, witticisms, drafts as well as polished aphorisms." Lichtenberg considered publishing at least portions of his notebooks but never did. His feelings about their value seemed to vacillate with his moods, which themselves vacillated wildly. Sometimes he referred to their contents as *Pfennigs-Wahrheiten*—"penny-truths"—at other times he waxed grandiloquent: "I have scattered seeds of ideas on almost every page which, if they fall on the right soil, may grow into chapters and even whole dissertations."

The first German edition of Lichtenberg's notebooks, published early in the nineteenth century, bore the title *Bemerkungen vermischten Inhalts* ("Remarks on Miscellaneous Subjects"). It was an accurate if understated title. Later editions have been known by the picturesque word that Lichtenberg himself occasionally employed: *Sudelbücher*, Lichtenberg's translation of the disused English term "Waste Books." According to the OED, a "waste book" is "A rough account-book . . . in which entries are made of all transactions (purchases, sales, receipts, payments, etc.) at the time of their occurrence, to be 'posted' afterwards into the more formal books." Substitute the words "thoughts, musings, observations, quotations, etc." and you have the "waste book"—the rough draft—of the soul's economy that Lichtenberg produced. Hollingdale speaks in this context of the "variegated inconsequentiality" of the *Sudelbücher*. They have a little of everything, but what they present is not so much a system as a sensibility, a take on the world.

Lichtenberg did not think of himself as an aphorist. I am not sure that the word *Aphorismus* even appears in the *Sudelbücher*. By training, he was an academic and a man of science. He was born in Oberramstadt, near Darmstadt, in 1742, the youngest of seventeen children, five of whom survived childhood. His father, who died when Lichtenberg was nine, was a prominent clergyman, part of the reformist Lutheran movement called Pietism, which stressed Bible-study and the ideal of simple Christian living. Lichtenberg tells us that he lost his Christian faith when he was sixteen, though he retained a somewhat amorphous belief in God inspired less by the Bible than by Leibniz's vision of a pre-established, divinely ordered harmony that suffuses the cosmos. Although popular with other children, Lichtenberg was a weak and sickly child. He suffered from a malformation of the spine, caused probably by tuberculosis, which resulted in his being a hunchback. Not surprisingly, this physical fact influenced his entire life and outlook. Still, Lichtenberg was not without a sense of humor about his condition. "My head," he explained, "lies at least a foot closer to my heart than is the case with other men: that is why I am so reasonable." Later he mused that "If Heaven should find it useful and necessary to produce a new edition of me and my life I would like to make a few not superfluous suggestions for this new edition chiefly concerning the design of the frontispiece and the way the work is laid out."

Lichtenberg's malady did not prevent his having many erotic attachments. Hollingdale describes his private life as "very irregular." Lichtenberg's executors destroyed the more intimate portions of his diaries, so posterity has been spared many details, but it is clear that he preferred his women simple and he preferred them young. In 1777 he met Maria Stechard, a poor weaver's daughter who was then twelve or thirteen. Lichtenberg employed her as a housekeeper, and she soon became his mistress. They lived together from 1780 until her early death in 1782. He was affected by her death, Hollingdale notes, "as by nothing before or afterwards." The relationship provided Lichtenberg's neighbors with something to gossip about, much to his chagrin. It also brought him much happiness. "She reconciled me," Lichtenberg sadly recalled, "to the human race." In 1784, Lichtenberg met Margarete Kellner, a daughter of a whitewasher, who was then in her early twenties. From 1786 they lived together and were married in 1789. Although the relationship was stormy, Margarete gave Lichtenberg seven children. She survived him by forty-nine years.

Life was not easy for Lichtenberg. One early critic described him as "the Columbus of hypochondria." The fact that not all his maladies were imaginary made his situation all the more painful. J. P. Stern speaks of the "indefinable mixture of illness and hypochondria, sloth and fits of depression, indolence and fear" that ruled intermittently over Lichtenberg's life. In one note, he bitterly announced his plan to write an autobiography called "The Story of My Mind, as well as of My Wretched Body."

Lichtenberg's career unfolded at the University of Göttingen, where he studied mathematics and science and, from 1770, held a succession of academic positions. He was an immensely popular teacher, one of the first to weave experiments into his lectures. Students came from far and wide not so much to study with as to witness, to "hear Lichtenberg." A man of prodigious but unfocused curiosity, Lichtenberg dabbled everywhere but persevered nowhere. In science, his primary interests were in astronomy and electricity. Some of his scholarly work in astronomy was recognized by later astronomers who named a lunar crater after him. In 1780, to the consternation of his neighbors, he erected the first lightning rod in Göttingen ("That sermons are preached in churches," Lichtenberg observed, "doesn't mean the churches don't need lightning rods.") In 1784, Alessandro Volta came to watch Lichtenberg's experiments with electricity. We still speak of "Lichtenberg figures," the star-shaped patterns formed in dust by certain electrical discharges. ("Lightning flowers" are Lichtenberg figures etched in the capillaries just beneath the skin when someone is hit by lightning.) Although he was elected to the Royal Society in 1788, Lichtenberg made no important scientific discoveries. "A physical experiment which makes a bang," he noted, "is always worth more than a quiet one. Therefore a man cannot strongly enough ask of Heaven: if it wants to let him discover something, may it be something that makes a bang. It will resound into eternity." Much to his regret, Lichtenberg made no bangs in the world of science.

He did, however, generate an enthusiastic following. At the beginning of his teaching career, Lichtenberg tutored the sons of some English aristocrats. So popular was he that, in 1770, he was invited to England by his former pupils. It was the first of two visits. (The second, longer, one was from September 1774 until just before Christmas 1775.) It was love at first sight. Like the better sort of German then and later, Lichtenberg became a ferocious Anglophile. He moved in the highest social circles. He met Priestley, who performed experiments for him, and many other men of science. The King and Queen delighted in his company and in speaking German with him. (Göttingen, as it happened, was one of George III's Hanoverian dominions.) So conspicuous was the royal favor—the King caused great commotion by coming to Lichtenberg's lodging one morning at 10:00 AM and asking for "Herr Professor"—that a rumor briefly circulated that Lichtenberg was George II's illegitimate son. Lichtenberg became an avid theater-goer in London. He was mesmerized especially by Garrick's acting ("he appeared wholly present in the muscles of his body") and said that it was from Garrick that Germans could learn most about what the word "man" really means. (Garrick for his part told Lichtenberg that he had never met a foreigner who spoke English so well.)

Lichtenberg's other great discovery in London was Hogarth (who had died in 1764). Beginning in 1794, he published a series of meticulously detailed "explanations" (Lichtenberg called it an *Ausfürliche Erklärung*) of Hogarth's engravings. Not a belt-buckle or button, barely a speck of dust, is left uninventoried. Lichtenberg's English translator described that work, which remained incomplete at Lichtenberg's death, as "a unique and sometimes bizarre excursion" into the textual recapitulation of the visual.

It is not surprising that Lichtenberg found in Hogarth a congenial spirit. Quite apart from their artistic merit, Hogarth's engravings are masterpieces of social observation. And it was to this above all that Lichtenberg devoted himself. "Chief employment of my life," he minuted in his diary in 1771, "to observe people's faces." One commentator described him as a "spy on humanity." It was almost literally true. Lichtenberg delighted in observing the street scene with a telescope from the eyrie of his window. "When an acquaintance goes by I often step back from my window, not so much to spare him the effort of acknowledging me as to spare myself the embarrassment of seeing that he has not done so." Lichtenberg was the faculty of *menschenbeobachterisch*—human observing— made flesh. The fruit of that passion was a collection of aphorisms united not by theme or tone but by a sensibility that was at once generous and disabused.

He who says he hates every kind of flattery, and says it in earnest, certainly does not yet know every kind of flattery.

If people should ever start to do only what is necessary millions would die of hunger.

Wine is accredited only with the misdeeds it induces: what is forgotten is the hundreds of good deeds of which it is also the cause. Wine excites to action: to good action in the good, to bad in the bad.

The detection of small errors has always been the property of minds elevated little or not at all above the mediocre; . . .

Lichtenberg once said that he would give part of his life to know what was the average barometric pressure in paradise. He never discovered that quantum, but in his aphorisms we have an extraordinary register of the barometric pressure of the human heart.

As a literary form, aphorisms have the liability of their strength. Aphorisms are insights shorn of supporting ratiocination. Sometimes they are arrived at in an instant, in a sudden illumination; sometimes, as Lichtenberg's draftings and redraftings of the same phrase or idea reveals, they are arrived at through a process of intellectual and rhetorical honing. Bertrand Russell, we have seen above, reported that when he told Wittgenstein that he should not simply *state* what he thought was true but should provide arguments, Wittgenstein replied that arguments spoil the beauty of insights and that "he would feel as if he was dirtying a flower with muddy hands." Just so, aphorisms are the blossoms of thought. They may depend on stalk and soil, but their beauty is independent of those prerequisites.

Whether arrived at instantly or through patient refinement, the defining characteristic of the successful aphorism is what we might call its *suddenness*. Some good aphorisms are obvious truths stated neatly. "You can make a good living from soothsaying [*vom Wahrsagen*] but not from truthsaying [*vom Wahrheit-sagen*]." The best are truths that only seem obvious after they have been stated neatly.

(They inspire the thought: "Now why didn't I think of that?") Many aphorisms have an enigmatic or double-sided character: they cut both ways and depend upon some essential ambiguity or equivocation for their power, their poetry. Whether they are *true* often seems secondary or beside the point: they are piquant, they *feel* revelatory and thought-provoking, and that is enough. "The roof tile," Lichtenberg says, "may know many things the chimney doesn't know." I would hate to part with that mot. But is it true? It would take an intrepid man to say.

Many people discount aphorisms, partly because so many are ambiguous, partly because they are episodic, isolated, and compressed. They seem too pat to be pertinent. Those traits can be liabilities, depending on the subject at hand. One would be ill-advised, for example, to trust a manual for bridge-builders or heart surgeons that was composed of aphorisms. But in other contexts the very characteristics that rob aphorisms of discursive strength endow them with other sorts of intellectual power. Nietzsche was quite right to defend the aphorism against its detractors. ("It is aphorisms!" he wrote with mock contempt. "Is it aphorisms?—May those who would reproach me thus reconsider and then ask pardon of themselves.")

But Nietzsche was also right that the aphorism, though it can reach deep, must do so quickly. A ponderous aphorism is a failed aphorism. It follows that, considered as intellectual nourishment, aphorisms are best taken sparingly; their very concentration makes them hard to digest *en masse*. Like an electric flash on a camera, they require time between discharges if they are to be fully illuminating. When Lichtenberg says that "The most dangerous untruths are truths slightly distorted," we nod in agreement. He has encapsulated an entire theory of heresy in a handful of words. When he goes on to say in another aphorism that

"With most people disbelief in a thing is founded on a blind belief in something else," we nod again. Here we have the mechanics of some forms of atheism in a nutshell. When we read further that "This was the handle by which you had to grip him if you wanted to pour him out; if you gripped him anywhere else you burned your fingers," we may nod again—here is an astute observation about a familiar character type. But how many more such nuggets can we take on board at a sitting? My own recommendation is that aphorisms be taken in doses of no more than a few pages a day. Any more, and the mind begins skipping.

Many aphorisms appeal not so much to the truth as to our prejudices. We tend to think too poorly of prejudice, confusing it with its unpleasant cousin, bigotry. "Prejudices," Lichtenberg wrote in an early notebook entry, "are so to speak the mechanical instincts of men: through their prejudices they do without any effort many things they would find too difficult to think through to the point of resolving to do them." (Compare Burke, who observed that prejudice "makes a man's virtue his habit.")

Often, the appeal of an aphorism is a function of its cynical knowingness: "If I should ever produce an edition of his life," Lichtenberg wrote of we know not whom, "go straight to the index and look up the words *bottle* and *conceit*: they will contain the most important facts about him." We all know people like that, just as we know what Lichtenberg means when he observes that "Sometimes men come by the name of genius in the same way that certain insects come by the name of centipede; not because they have a hundred feet, but because most people cannot count above fourteen."

Still, the element of cynicism can be overdone. "What is called an acute knowledge of human nature," Lichtenberg writes, "is mostly nothing but the observer's own weaknesses reflected back from others." Well, sometimes, perhaps. But sometimes an acute knowledge of human nature is just that: an acute knowledge of human nature. "What they call 'heart,'" Lichtenberg tells us, "lies much lower than the fourth waistcoat-button." Well, yes, there is such a thing as sex. But is "heart," is romance, to be entirely explained as a cover or front for sex? Freud thought so. Maybe Lichtenberg did, too. Were they right?

Having a low opinion of human nature may not be a prerequisite for being a good aphorist. But it helps. (It also, *nota bene*, aids in one's appreciation of aphorisms.) Chamfort, Pascal, Gracián, Vauvenargues, La Rochefoucauld: none of these master aphorists was burdened by an overly sunny view of humanity, though each was gloomy in his own way. Pascal's observation that all a man's troubles begin when he leaves his room is of quite a different character from La Rochefoucauld's thought that "In the misfortunes of our best friends we always find something that does not displease us." But both proceed from the assumption that things are always worse than they seem.

The cynical nature of many aphorisms is one reason the genre is so popular. Many people, especially many intellectuals—the most ardent customers for the aphorism—pride themselves above all on their disillusionment. They see themselves "seeing through" manners, pretensions, morals, whatever, and what they see is seldom edifying. (As a class, intellectuals are rarely—to use Wordsworth's phrase— "surprised by joy.") Aphorists are by profession debunkers. That is a large part of their power. It also points to a limitation. Untempered by elements of affirmation, debunking generates its own species of bunk. Take the aphorism by La Rochefoucauld quoted above. It is one of his most famous, and was well-known already in Lichtenberg's day. Lichtenberg himself thought well of it, noting that "It sounds peculiar, but he who denies the truth of it either doesn't understand it or does not know himself." But mightn't it also be that it sounds peculiar because it *is* peculiar, and that the misfortunes of our best friends generally stir pity, empathy, and compassion?

Many of Lichtenberg's aphorisms are more ruminative than scarifying. "There is a great difference," he observes, "between *still* believing something and *again* believing it." Anyone who has reflected on the seasons of faith will know what Lichtenberg means. Some of his aphorisms have pointed relevance to the contemporary cultural scene: "It requires no especially great talent to write in such a way that another will be very hard put to understand what you have written." Others, alas, have been overtaken by events: "It is easy to construct a landscape out of a mass of disorderly lines, but disorderly sounds cannot be made into music." John Cage? Rock music? Who could have foreseen it? But Lichtenberg was unfailingly acute about the follies that intellectual life falls prey to—about the use and abuse of intelligence. "Nowadays," he notes, "we everywhere seek to propagate wisdom: who knows whether in a couple of centuries there may not exist universities for restoring the old ignorance." He proffered several aphorisms and observations about books, reading, and their relation to insight. "There are," he observes, "very many people who read simply to prevent themselves from thinking."

> When a book and a head collide and a hollow sound is heard, must it always have come from the book?

> I forget most of what I have read, just as I do most of what I have eaten, but I know that both contribute no less to the conservation of my mind and my body on that account.

There can hardly be stranger wares in the world than *books*: printed by people who do not understand them; sold by people who do not understand them; bound, reviewed and read by people who do not understand them; and now even written by people who do not understand them.

Lichtenberg's late encounter with the philosophy of Kant had a profound effect on him, though in the end he seems to have been more impressed than convinced. One finds him asking silly questions like "How do we arrive at the concept of *outside us*? Why do we not believe that everything is *within us*?" (How much intellectual damage the little word "in" has perpetrated!) But Lichtenberg soon extricates himself from such futilities. Kant's philosophy is so difficult, he notes, that "once we have finally succeeded in understanding it there is a great temptation to regard it as true": so much effort must not go unrewarded.

Do Lichtenberg's aphorisms add up to a coherent philosophy? I doubt it. J. P. Stern suggests that Lichtenberg promulgated a doctrine of "scattered occasions" (the phrase is Bacon's), a sort of "inverted Categorical Imperative" that invests the moment, not the moral maxim, with absolute value. Perhaps. But that is simply to elevate the absence of doctrine into a doctrine. Lichtenberg's acts of espionage on mankind were unsystematic even about being unsystematic. They were raids on the interesting, conducted as time, mood, and inspiration permitted. There is no unifying thread, though there are recurrent themes. One familiar theme is part description, part admonition: "It is almost impossible to bear the torch of truth through a crowd without singeing somebody's beard." If you decide to bear that torch, Lichtenberg seems to say, be wary.

The Genius of Wodehouse

A LTHOUGH IT IS shocking to report, candor requires that I begin by acknowledging that it was not until 1982, when I was in my late twenties, that I first acquainted myself with the sublime work of Sir Pelham Grenville Wodehouse.

I remember the occasion vividly. I was recovering from the effects of oral surgery after a botched root canal. Thanks to some tablets prescribed by my doctor, I passed a few days draped bonelessly over a sofa in a not unpleasant sort of semi-coma. I almost managed to forget the excavation site on the gum above my abused molar. Leafing through *The Times Literary Supplement* as I mended, I paused over a review of Frances Donaldson's biography of Wodehouse. It sounded like good stuff.

It was (as Wodehouse himself might have put it) the work of a moment to nip down to the local bookstore, latch on to a volume or two, and nip back to my bed of modified woe. Anyone inclined to doubt the workings of Providence should attend closely to what happened next. Of the dozens of Wodehouse titles lining the bookshelves, the one I chanced to open first was *Carry On, Jeeves* (1925), a masterly collection of stories whose first chapter explains how that unsurpassable valet, the brainy and omni-competent Jeeves, came into the employ of the feck-less chump Bertie Wooster:

> Lots of people think I'm much too dependent on him. My Aunt Agatha, in fact, has even gone so far as to call him my keeper. Well, what I say is: Why not? The man's a genius. From the collar upward he stands alone. I gave up trying to run my own affairs within a week of his coming to me.

Wodehouse (the name, by the way, is pronounced "Woodhouse") was amazingly prolific; as Frances Donaldson notes, no one knows the exact extent of his output because, when young, he often wrote under other people's names or noms de plume. But we do know that over the course of his ninety-three years he wrote at least ninety-six books, wrote or collaborated on sixteen plays, and composed at least some of the lyrics and/or the book for twenty-eight musicals. The man was a writing machine. And although he often wrote at or near the top of his form, surely it was (as the Marxists say) no accident that I should have stumbled onto one of his supreme master-pieces right off the bat. These things must be fated. When St. Augustine was going through a rough patch and he heard some children chanting *tolle lege*—"take and read" —he picked up the Bible and it changed his life.

I won't say that my discovery of Wodehouse was quite so earth-shaking, but it was serendipitous. After two or three pages I was hooked. Had my doctor seen me then, convulsed as I was with laughter, he doubtless would have looked askance and confiscated those tablets. But Wode-house, if addictive, is an innocent, indeed a beneficent, ad-diction. Although I came to him late, I have made up for that tardiness with unwavering devotion. No writer has given me more merriment and delight. It was naturally with great pleasure, then, that I greeted the announcement in the year 2000 that the Everyman Library was bringing out a hardcover edition of Wodehouse's novels and stories. The first batch included three masterpieces, *Right Ho, Jeeves* (1934), *The Code of the Woosters* (1938), and *Pigs Have Wings* (1952). This is the first uniform—well, almost uniform—edition† of Wodehouse to appear, and it is long overdue.

Oscar Wilde said that he put his genius into his life and only his talent into his work. Wodehouse upped the ante and put everything into his work. Everyone who knew Wodehouse described him as excessively shy. When his wife set out to get a flat in New York, Wodehouse asked her to be sure it was on the ground floor because he never knew what to say to the lift boy. In 1939, Oxford gave him an honorary degree; when at a dinner following the ceremony the crowd began to shout "We want Wodehouse," he just barely managed to get to his feet and mumble "thank you."

Wodehouse was kindly and well-meaning; he was also irretrievably dull. And definitely not funny. Donaldson says Wodehouse was "a genuine recluse and socially incompetent." "I loathe clubs," said the inventor of the Drones Club in 1956. In matters of haberdashery, the creator of the impeccably turned out Psmith took after the shabby Lord Emsworth. When he suffered a small stroke in 1951, Wodehouse wandered in a dazed state into a doctor's office on Park Avenue. "A bum came into my office," the doctor reported: arrangements were being made to have him sent

---

† The publishers have not, alas, taken particular care with the typography of these otherwise handsome volumes. In several of the titles published so far, running headers and footers are printed incorrectly. Jeeves would be aghast.

to Bellevue when a secretary, going through his pockets in an effort to identify the mystery man, announced, "He's not a bum, he's an Englishman!" Bellevue was scratched in favor of Doctor's Hospital, a private institution. Donaldson concluded that the key to Wodehouse's character lay "in his inability to feel strong emotions." Wodehouse might well have agreed. "I haven't got any violent feelings about anything," he said in a 1961 interview. "I just love writing." (Hence, perhaps, his native inclination to contentment: "Nothing," the aphorist G. C. Lichtenberg wrote, "can contribute more to peace of soul than the lack of any opinion whatever.")

As it happens, Donaldson—the daughter of the playwright Frederick Lonsdale—came to Wodehouse even later than I did. She knew the master personally, having been a close friend of Leonora, Wodehouse's beloved stepdaughter (who died in her late thirties in 1943). But it was not until Donaldson was seventy that she "got" Wodehouse. She then sat down and read through virtually the entire corpus in a couple of years. Her biography (Weidenfeld & Nicolson, now out of print) is simply splendid. It is well-written, well-informed, admiring but by no means hagiographical. Donaldson claims that of ten confirmed Wodehouse addicts, only one will be a woman; "women as a whole," she says, do not care for the sort of "masculine fantasy" he specialized in. My own informants take issue with that judgment. But it is hard to imagine a better biography of this peculiar man.†

Wodehouse's father was a magistrate in Hong Kong. His mother was staying with a sister in Guildford when P. G.,

---

† Nevertheless, the English writer Robert McCrum is even now working on another biography of Wodehouse that, as of this writing, is scheduled to appear in 2003 from Penguin.

the third of her four sons, was born in 1881. There were some glittering antecedents. The family could trace itself back to the sister of Anne Boleyn; and Cardinal Newman was a great uncle on his mother's side. There had, however, been a considerable falling off. Donaldson describes Wodehouse's mother as a "stupid woman" whose "actions continually suggest that her emotions were as undeveloped as her intellect." She certainly seems not to have been overly burdened by the maternal instinct. The infant Wodehouse returned with her to Hong Kong, but was shipped back to England with his older brothers two years later to be brought up by a Miss Roper, a complete stranger. Wodehouse grew up being passed from aunt to aunt, a fact that has been made much of by those seeking personal correlatives for the formidable aunts who populate his books. "It is no use telling me that there are bad aunts and good aunts," we read in *The Code of the Woosters*. "At the core they are all alike. Sooner or later out pops the cloven hoof." And from elsewhere in that volume:

> "If I had my life to live again, Jeeves, I would start it as an orphan without any aunts. Don't they put aunts in Turkey in sacks and drop them in the Bosphorus?"
> "Odalisques, sir, I understand. Not aunts."

Wodehouse went to school at Dulwich College, where he did well at games, especially cricket. At first he worked hard at his studies, but when it transpired that there would not be enough money to send him to university, his attention drifted. But he had loved Dulwich: "To me, the years between 1894 and 1900 were like heaven." After leaving school, he worked briefly at the Hong Kong and Shanghai Bank in London: it was an uncongenial experience. He had begun writing at the age of seven (in one recollection he says he started "turning out the stuff" at five): it was the thing he was born to do. He began contributing to numerous papers and magazines and had published his first book by 1902.

IN LATER LIFE, Wodehouse was universally known as "Plum" or "Plummie." As he explained in the preface to *Something Fresh* (1915), the first of the Blandings Castle novels, in those days a writer in America who "went about without three names was practically going around naked." So the Pelham Grenville, he thought, helped his early career. But he never liked the names: "I have my dark moods when they seem to me about as low as you can get. At the font I remember protesting vigorously when the clergyman uttered them, but he stuck to his point. 'Be that as it may,' he said firmly, having waited for a lull, 'I name thee Pelham Grenville.'"

Fans of the Blandings Castle stories will be interested to learn that after Dulwich, Plum spent time visiting a friend at a school called Emsworth House in a village of the same name; the friend was Herbert Westbrook, an inveterate sponger who was the model for Ukridge (pronounced to rhyme with "Duke-ridge"). Wodehouse rented a house there called Threepwood—Lord Emsworth's family name —and in 1905 acquired a car with what amounted to a year's wages. Like one of his characters, he promptly succeeded in driving it into a ditch. "He left the car there," Donaldson tells us, "and never drove again." Jeeves, we learn, is named for a Warwickshire cricketer called Percy Jeeves, though Wodehouse first thought of his most famous character after reading Harry Leon Wilson's *Ruggles of Red Gap*, which features a super-competent butler.

Wodehouse made his first trip to America in 1904 and by 1909 was coming regularly. In August of 1914, Wodehouse met a young widow named Ethel Newton in New York. By the end of September, they were married—quick service for a shy chap, you might say, but the merger was probably instigated more by Ethel than the retiring Plum. Ethel was not the brains of the family, exactly, but she was clearly its senior management: treasurer, executive secretary, and CEO. She took entire charge of Wodehouse's affairs, and, Donaldson observes, "stood between him and the rest of the world in all things, except those which most immediately concerned his work."

Sex is conspicuous by its absence in Wodehouse's work. (Some of his early stories attempt to include a love interest: the effort is always embarrassing.) As Richard Usborne, author of the excellent *Wodehouse at Work* (1961)† noted, "There is no suggestion that either clubman or girl would recognize a double bed except as so much extra sweat to make an apple-pie of." How far this attitude extended into Wodehouse's life is uncertain. Donaldson rightly observes that "Wodehouse may or may not have been inhibited sexually as well as emotionally and this inhibition may have been partial or complete. Not a matter on which one is ever likely to have exact evidence, it is in this case not one which matters very much."

In 1914, Wodehouse had yet to hit his stride. When he married Ethel, he had exactly $100 in the bank. By the 1920s he was earning $100,000 per annum from his books and his work in the theater. (Although not much noticed today, Wodehouse's theater work, much of it done in collaboration with Guy Bolton and Jerome Kern, was extraordinarily successful.) In 1929, he went to Hollywood, where he was paid $2000 a week to be a rewrite man—money for jam, as he might have put it. He was socking

---

† Revised and republished in 1976 as *Wodehouse: At Work to the End.*

the stuff away. Wodehouse himself was the opposite of mercenary. As long as he had some pipe tobacco and could be left alone with his typewriter he was happy. But, then as now, the Internal Revenue Service couldn't look at a pile of money without wanting a good bit of it, and in 1932 the first of several tax imbroglios ensued. Donaldson notes that in all his tangles with the IRS and England's Inland Revenue, Wodehouse "either won or achieved a compromise settlement in his favor." In 1934, partly to escape the badgering tax authorities, he and Ethel acquired Low Wood, a villa in Le Touquet on the coast of France, which became their home base for several years. They were there in 1939 when World War II started. They were still there the next year when the Germans rolled through and appropriated the villa, confiscated much of their property, and interned Wodehouse.

Wodehouse was in various German camps for about a year; he was released in 1941 just shy of his sixtieth birthday and was allowed to go to Berlin. It was there that he recorded five radio talks to be broadcast to America and England. The talks themselves were completely innocuous:

> Young men, starting out in life, have often asked me "How can I become an Internee?" Well, there are several methods. My own was to buy a villa in Le Touquet on the coast of France and stay there until the Germans came along. This is probably the best and simplest system. You buy the villa and the Germans do the rest.

But the response back home was not at all amused. It was first put about that Wodehouse had agreed to do the broadcasts in exchange for his release; this turned out not to be true. It didn't matter. William Connor, writing as "Cassandra" in the *Daily Mirror*, excoriated Wodehouse as a quisling. Broadcasting later on the BBC, Connor began: "I have come to tell you tonight the story of a rich man trying to make his last and greatest sale—that of his own country." Donaldson devotes about a third of her book to these broadcasts and their aftermath. Her conclusion was the conclusion of the officials who investigated the episode after the war: The broadcasts were ill-advised, certainly, but "Wodehouse did not betray his country: he spoke no word of propaganda, he did no deal."

Again, it didn't matter. Wodehouse was awarded a knighthood in 1975, two months before he died (on Valentine's Day, which seems somehow appropriate for so merry an author). But many who faulted him for the broadcasts never forgave him. After the war, Wodehouse settled permanently in America, first in New York City, then in Remsenburg, Long Island. There was no assurance, had he returned to London, that he would not have been prosecuted. In 1953, Wodehouse was induced to give lunch to William Connor. It tells us a lot about Wodehouse's character that he became fast friends with a man who had caused him so much damage. "We got on together like a couple of sailors on shore leave," Wodehouse reported in a letter. "We parted on christian name terms, vowing eternal friendship."

Donaldson is doubtless right that Wodehouse was "socially incompetent." He was also one of the most accomplished prose writers of the last century. High praise. But it is entirely in keeping with the encomia Wodehouse's work has elicited over the years. In a radio broadcast from 1934, Hilaire Belloc called him "the best writer of English now alive . . . the head of my profession." That remark loosed an avalanche of inquiries: What could Belloc have meant by such extravagant commendation for a writer of what, after all, are only light comedies? A few years later, in a preface for a chrestomathy called *Week-end Wode-house* (1939, and still in print), Belloc elaborated:

> Writing is a craft, like any other: playing the violin, skating, batting at cricket, billiards, wood carving . . . ; and master-ship in any craft is attainment of the end to which that craft is devoted. . . . The end of writing is the production of a certain image and a certain emotion. And the means towards that end are the use of words in any particular language; and the complete use of that medium is the choosing of the right words and the putting of them into the right order. It is *this* which Mr. Wodehouse does better, in the English language, than anyone else alive.
>
> In all the various departments of his skill Mr. Wode-house is unique for simplicity and exactitude. . . . He gets the full effect, bang!

Belloc particularly admired Wodehouse's similes, citing as an example his description of Honoria Glossop as "one of those robust, dynamic girls with the muscles of a welter-weight and a laugh like a squadron of cavalry charging over a tin bridge."

EVELYN WAUGH shared Belloc's high opinion. Reviewing *Week-end Wodehouse*, he praised Belloc for treating Wodehouse "as he deserves, soberly and seriously, as a prose stylist and as the expression of a culture for the safety of which Mr. Belloc feels anxiety." Waugh admired Wodehouse partly for "the exquisite felicity of his lan-guage," partly for the incorrigible innocence of his vision. Quoting Wodehouse's remark that "Jeeves knows his place, and it is between the covers of a book," Waugh un-derscored the purely literary quality of Wodehouse's characters and the world they inhabit.

We do not concern ourselves with the economic implications of their position; we are not skeptical about their
quite astonishing celibacy. We do not expect them to grow
any older, like the Three Musketeers or the Forsytes. We
are not interested in how they would "react to changing
social conditions" as publishers' blurbs invite us to be interested in other sagas. They are untroubled by wars
(Jeeves first appeared . . . in 1917, and Bertie Wooster, then
unquestionably of military age, was "in the dreamless" at
11:30 A.M.). . . . They all live, year after year, in their
robust middle twenties; their only sickness is an occasional
hangover. It is a world that cannot become dated because it
has never existed.

In "An Act of Homage and Reparation to P. G. Wodehouse" (1961), Waugh came back to this point. (The
"reparation," of course, was for the calumny that people
like William Conner had directed at Wodehouse.) Bertie
Wooster, like other Wodehouse characters, "inhabits a
world as timeless as that of *A Midsummer Night's Dream*
and *Alice in Wonderland*." Waugh stressed that Wodehouse characters are not, as is sometimes said, "survivals
of the Edwardian age. They are creations of pure fancy. . . .
The Drones [Club], with its swimming bath and its
smoking concerts, its 'Old Beans' and 'Old Crumpets'
touching one another for fivers, has no correspondence at
all with any London club of any period."

The central oddity of Wodehouse's artistry is its purity,
which means in part its distance from the cares and concerns of ordinary human life. In her biography, Donaldson
observes that "no humour is consistently funny which is
not related to human life." Perhaps so. But Wodehouse
reminds us of the irony that one way of being related to
human life is by bracketing its everyday imperatives. To

some extent, that is something all art does. Wodehouse does it more radically, and with greater virtuosity, than almost anyone. In a memorial piece from 1975, Bernard Levin observed that "it is difficult to find comparisons that do not jar, because [Wodehouse's] matter was so utterly unlike that of his true peers of manner, and none of those whose matter was recognizably similar to his could write like him." It is silly to compare him to Shakespeare or Swift or Rabelais (to pick a few favorite analogues from the literature on Wodehouse). But lesser touchstones seem somehow unfair to his excellences.

What are those excellences? For one thing, Wodehouse had a genius for concocting absurd but apposite names. Every Wodehouse aficionado has his favorites. Among mine are Gussie Fink-Nottle ("a fish-faced pal of mine who on reaching man's estate had buried himself in the country and devoted himself entirely to the study of newts"); Madeline Basset ("a droopy, soupy, sentimental exhibit, with melting eyes and a cooing voice. . . . I remember her telling me once that rabbits were gnomes in attendance on the Fairy Queen and that the stars are God's daisy chain"); and Cyril "Barmy" Fotheringay-Phipps (pronounced Barmy Fungy-Phipps).

Wodehouse was also a master phrase-maker. He was not a coiner of epigrams, exactly, but he produced many memorable one-liners: "Slice him where you like, a hellhound is always a hellhound." "I could see that, if not actually disgruntled, he was far from being gruntled." "Unseen, in the background, Fate was quietly slipping the lead into the boxing glove." And this gem about understanding the gist of an argument: "He followed me like a leopard."

But the full extent of Wodehouse's excellence as a writer does not emerge in short snippets. His real genius lay in his ability to endow patently absurd situations with momen-

tary conviction. Many of the Bertie and Jeeves stories involve extricating Bertie from a matrimonial engagement
that he (or sometimes Jeeves) deems inadvisable. A frequent subplot involves some article of Bertie's clothing that
doesn't pass muster with Jeeves. In "Jeeves Takes Charge,"
Bertie is more or less happily engaged to Florence Craye, a
frightful bluestocking with a "wonderful profile" who was
"particularly keen on boosting [Bertie] up a bit nearer her
own plane of intellect." Bertie's usual reading matter, insofar as he has any, does not depart far from mystery
novels of the pulpier sort. But Florence has him ploughing
through a book called *Types of Ethical Theory*.[†] Still,
"seen sideways," as Bertie says, she was "most awfully
good looking."

Florence threatens to break off their engagement unless
Bertie can destroy the manuscript of his Uncle Willoughby's "Recollections of a Long Life," a gossipy trove
with horrid things about everyone he knew when young,
including Florence's father. "You may look upon it as a
test, Bertie." she says, "If you have the resource and
courage to carry this thing through, I will take it as
evidence that you are not the vapid and shiftless person
most people think you. If you fail, I shall know that your

---

† I was pleased to discover that this tome actually exists. It is a work of
inadvertently comical pedantry in two volumes by the English
Platonist James Martineau, D.D., S.T.D, D.C.L., LL.D. *Types of Ethical
Theory* was published by Oxford University Press under their most
prestigious imprint, the Clarendon Press. My edition, which I have
filed together with the works of Wodehouse under Humor, is the
third, revised edition and was published in 1901. The passage that
Wodehouse quotes (beginning "Of the two antithetic terms in the
Greek philosophy, one only was *real and self-subsisting* . . .") occurs
in volume I, page 124. Martineau, an eminent personage in his time,
was also the brother of the social commentator Harriet Martineau.

Aunt Agatha was right when she called you a spineless invertebrate.'"

Bertie fails, of course, largely because Jeeves sees to it that the manuscript finds its way to the publisher. At first, he is so outraged that he fires Jeeves. Gradually, however, he changes his mind. "It was her intention," Jeeves had told him, "to start you almost immediately upon Nietzsche. You would not like Nietzsche, sir. He is fundamentally unsound." The story ends with this exchange:

"Oh, Jeeves," I said; "about that check suit."
"Yes, sir?"
"Is it really a frost?"
"A trifle too bizarre, sir, in my opinion."
"But lots of fellows have asked me who my tailor is."
"Doubtless in order to avoid him, sir."
"He's supposed to be one of the best men in London."
"I am saying nothing against his moral character, sir."
I hesitated a bit. I had a feeling that I was passing into this chappie's clutches. . . . "All right, Jeeves," I said, "You know! Give the bally thing away to somebody!"
He looked down at me like a father gazing tenderly at the wayward child.
"Thank you, sir. I gave it to the under-gardener last night. A little more tea, sir?"

Silly. Preposterous. Absurd. But as Wilde's Algernon said about a similar absurdity, perfectly phrased.

To canvass Wodehouse for quotable scenes is to be in the position of a child in a candy store. And I don't mean one of those small, village operations, with only a shelf of sweets. I mean a large, multi-storied emporium stuffed to the gills with toothsome morsels. Consider, for example, the golf stories, the character of Monty Bodkin, or

Frederick Altamount Cornwallis Twistleton, the fifth Earl of Ickenham. Consider—what some knowledgeable observers consider to be Plum's best work—the many tales spun by Mr. Mulliner at the bar parlour of the Anglers' Rest. One of my favorite Mulliner stories is "The Man Who Gave Up Smoking." The story opens with "a flushed Lemon Squash and a scowling Tankard of Ale" falling foul of each other at the Anglers' Rest.

> A Tankard of Ale pointed the stem of his pipe accusingly at his adversary. One could see that he was deeply stirred.
>
> "He's talking rot about smoking."
>
> "I am talking sense."
>
> "I didn't hear any."
>
> "I said that smoking was dangerous to the health. And it is."
>
> "It isn't."
>
> "It is. I can prove it from my own personal experience. I was once," said the Lemon Squash, "a smoker myself, and the vile habit reduced me to a physical wreck. My cheeks sagged, my eyes became bleary, my whole face gaunt, yellow and hideously lined. It was giving up smoking that brought about the change."
>
> "What change?" asked the Tankard.

The Lemon Squash leaves in a huff and Mr. Mulliner, the narrator, breathes a sigh of relief:

> I look upon tobacco as life's outstanding boon and it annoys me to hear these faddists abusing it. And how foolish their arguments are, how easily refuted. They come to me and tell me that if they place two drops of nicotine on the tongue of a dog the animal instantly dies; and when I ask them if they have ever tried the childishly simple device of

not placing nicotine on the dog's tongue, they have nothing to reply. They are nonplussed. They go away mumbling something about never having thought of that.

Clearly the anti-smoking fanatics who litter the landscape these days have paid insufficient attention to the teachings of Wodehouse.

In my opinion, one of Wodehouse's greatest novels is *Leave it to Psmith* (1924). Many friends agree. Unaccountably, though, the book is somewhat slighted in The Literature. It is accorded respect but not the wild enthusiasm it deserves. Perhaps its reappearance in the Everyman series will correct that error. When we are introduced to Ronald (or Rupert—Wodehouse wasn't quite sure) Eustace Psmith in this account of his adventures, he has fallen on hard times. Nevertheless the "very tall, very thin, very solemn young man" cuts a striking figure in his "speckless top hat and a morning-coat of irreproachable fit." He is on his way through a run-down neighborhood to visit the wife of his school friend Mike Jackson.

A small maid-of-all-work appeared in answer to the bell, and stood transfixed as the visitor, producing a monocle, placed it in his right eye and inspected her through it.

"A warm afternoon," he said cordially.

"Yes, sir."

"But pleasant," urged the young man. "Tell me, is Mrs. Jackson at home?"

"No, sir."

"Not at home?"

"No, sir."

The young man sighed.

"Ah, well," he said, "we must always remember that

these disappointments are sent to us for some good purpose. No doubt they make us more spiritual. Will you inform her that I called. The name is Psmith. P-smith."

"Peasmith, sir?"

"No, no. P-s-m-i-t-h. I should explain to you that I started life without the initial letter, and my father always clung ruggedly to the plain Smith. But it seemed to me that there were so many Smiths in the world that a little variety might well be introduced. Smythe I look on as a cowardly evasion, nor do I approve of the too prevalent custom of tacking another name on in front by means of a hyphen. So I decided to adopt the Psmith. The p, I should add for your guidance, is silent, as in phthisis, psychic, and ptarmigan. You follow me?"

"Y-yes, sir."

"You don't think," he said anxiously, "that I did wrong in pursuing this course?"

"N-no, sir."

"Splendid!" said the young man, flicking a speck of dust from his sleeve. "Splendid! Splendid!"

After various vicissitudes, Psmith winds up at Blandings Castle impersonating the young poet Ralston McTodd, author of *Songs of Squalor* and other scaly specimens of modern poetry. (One of his efforts begins: "Across the pale parabola of Joy . . .") A diamond necklace worth £20,000 has been stolen. The efficient Baxter, Lord Emsworth's secretary and Psmith's nemesis, suddenly has the idea that it may be hidden in one of the flowerpots on the terrace. It is after 2:00 A.M. when he starts digging, strikingly attired in lemon-colored pyjamas; it is getting on to dawn when he realizes that he is locked out of the castle and inadvertently wakes his employer by hurling flowerpots through his bedroom window. Suspecting that his secretary has gone off his rocker, Lord Emsworth rouses Psmith and brings him along to confront Baxter.

> Lord Emsworth adjusted his glasses.
> "Your face is dirty," he said, peering down at his dishevelled secretary. "Baxter, my dear fellow, your face is dirty."
> "I was digging," replied Baxter sullenly.
> "What?"
> "Digging!"
> "The terrier complex," explained Psmith. "What," he asked kindly, turning to his companion, "were you digging for? Forgive me if the question seems an impertinent one, but we are naturally curious."

Well, Baxter is eventually sent packing, but not before he exposes Psmith as an impersonator. Psmith explains that he did it to save Lord Emsworth embarrassment. When Emsworth mistook him for McTodd at the Senior Conservative Club in London, Psmith decided to step into the breach and save the dreamy peer from the "inconvenience of having to return here without a McTodd of any description."

> His lordship digested this explanation in silence. Then he seized on a magnificent point.
> "Are you a member of the Senior Conservative Club?"
> "Most certainly."
> "Why, then, dash it," cried his lordship, paying to that august stronghold of respectability as striking a tribute as it had ever received, "if you're a member of the Senior Conservative, you can't be a criminal. Baxter's an ass!"
> "Exactly."

When Psmith suggests that he stay on and take over Baxter's position as secretary, Lord Emsworth asks if he has had any experience. Psmith admits that he hasn't, adding that until recently his family was well-to-do and owned a local pile called Corfby Hall.

> "Corfby Hall! Are you the son of the Smith who used to own Corfby Hall? Why, bless my soul, I knew your father well."
> "Really?"
> "Yes. That is to say, I never met him."
> "No?"
> "But I won the first prize at the Shrewsbury Flower Show the year he won the prize for tulips."
> "It seems to draw us very close together," said Psmith.

In many ways, Wodehouse accomplished what Flaubert aspired to do: to write a novel about nothing.

WODEHOUSE achieved his effects through a combination of flawless diction and fastidious plotting. Not that there is anything original about his plots. On the contrary, he tells the same handful of stories over and over again. Even many of his characters are interchangeable. In his preface to *Summer Lightning* (1929), Wodehouse mentions "a certain critic" who "made the nasty remark about my last novel that it contained 'all the old Wodehouse characters under different names.'" Wodehouse cheerfully owned the charge; that critic, he wrote,

> has probably by now been eaten by bears, like the children who made mock of the prophet Elisha: but if he still survives he will not be able to make a similar charge against *Summer Lightning*. With my superior intelligence, I have outgeneralled the man this time by putting in all the old

Wodehouse characters under the same names. Pretty silly it will make him feel, I rather fancy.

In fact, Wodehouse's success in retelling the same few stories is a further testimony to his skill. It is a matter of success through limitation. As the English critic Ernest Newman observed in 1956, Wodehouse was "the last perfect representative of a once great race of artists—the practitioners of the commedia dell'arte."

> These people did not trouble about anything so easy as inventing new forms, new settings, new characters. They took the standardized characters of Pulcinella, Scaramouche, Harlequin, the Captain, the Doctor, the Notary, and so on and re-created them afresh each time out of the abundance of their own genius. This was really a much harder thing to do than to invent quasi-new beings with names and place them in new situations.

Wodehouse's mastery is equally evident in his superb light verse. Consider "Good Gnus (A Vignette in Verse)" which appears in the Mulliner tale "Unpleasantness at Bludleigh Court." Charlotte Mulliner, a confirmed animal lover and poetess of the droopiest sort, finds that the blood-sporting atmosphere of Bludleigh Court is doing strange things to her verse. Asked to provide a poem for the *Animal-Lovers Gazette* she produces the following masterwork:

> When cares attack and life seem black,
> How sweet it is to pot a yak,
> Or puncture hares and grizzly bears,
> And others I could mention:
> But in my Animal's "Who's Who"

No name stands higher than the Gnu;
And each new gnu that comes in view
Receives my prompt attention.

When Afric's sun is sinking low,
And shadows wander to and fro,
And everywhere there's in the air
A hush that's deep and solemn;
Then is the time good men and true
With View Halloo pursue the gnu:
(The safest spot to put your shot
Is through the spinal column).

To take the creature by surprise
We must adopt some rude disguise,
Although deceit is never sweet,
And falsehoods don't attract us.
So, as with gun in hand you wait,
Remember to impersonate
A tuft of grass, a mountain-pass,
A kopje, or a cactus.

A brief suspense, and then at last
The waiting's o'er, the vigil past:
A careful aim. A spurt of flame.
It's done. You've pulled the trigger,
And one more gnu, so fair and frail
Has handed in its dinner-pail:
(The females all are rather small,
The males are somewhat bigger).

Light verse doesn't get much better than this.

Yet another measure of Wodehouse's skill was the expert way he handled clichés. He knew just how to deploy them for maximum humor. Typically, he cut them in two. Like Caesar, his motto was divide and conquer.

It is pretty generally recognised in the circles in which he moves that Bertram Wooster is not a man who lightly throws in the towel and admits defeat. Beneath the thin-gummies of what-d'you-call-it, his head, wind and weather permitting, is as a rule bloody but unbowed, and if the slings and arrows of outrageous fortune want to crush his proud spirit, they have to pull their socks up and make a special effort.

Wodehouse's mastery of the cliché was inseparable from his celebrated use of literary quotations: primarily from Shakespeare and the Bible, but also from Burns, Kipling, Omar Khayyám, Bret Harte, and others. Wodehouse's penchant for literary allusion has led some people to commend his erudition. In fact, as Donaldson notes, his stock of references was actually quite small. Wodehouse did have a classical education, but he himself drew attention to the importance of Bartlett's *Familiar Quotations*, "that indispensable adjunct to literary success." When Jeeves expresses his distaste about a ghastly china vase Bertie picked up on his peregrinations, Bertie tells us that he "ticked him off with no little vim. *Ne sutor ultra* whatever-it-is, I would have said to him, if I'd thought of it." As Richard Usborne observed, what we find again and again in Wodehouse is "a pleasant skid on the banana skin of education," a humorous mix of quotation, half-quotation, and pure whimsy. Wodehouse was not a scholar. Much less was he an intellectual: a class of people that he rather feared and disliked but that he nevertheless managed to entertain mightily.

Wodehouse understood perfectly what he was about. In a late and unduly neglected gem called *Ice in the Bedroom* (1961), Wodehouse portrays a successful romance novelist who determines to give up the fluff and settle down to write "an important novel."

"But can you?"

"Can I what?"

"Write an important novel."

"Of course I can. All you have to do is cut out the plot and shove in plenty of misery."

Wodehouse cut out the misery and shoved in plenty of delight. "I believe," he remarked in an oft-quoted letter to his friend William Townend, "there are only two ways of writing a novel. One is mine, making the thing a sort of musical comedy without music, and ignoring real life altogether; the other is going down deep into life and not caring a damn." Most great artists plumb the depths; Wodehouse remained fixed, gloriously, on the surface. That was both his limitation and his achievement. What he lacked in profundity he made up for in verbal dexterity. His province was humor: he didn't trespass into other realms. He came bearing pleasure, not insight. A master of incongruity, Wodehouse left anguish and betrayal, self-knowledge and social awareness to other, generally lesser, talents.

The Mystery of Charles Péguy

A great philosophy is not that which passes final judgments,
which takes a seat in final truth. It is that which introduces
uneasiness, which opens the door to commotion.
—Charles Péguy, "Note on M. Bergson"

Truth's pedagogue, braving an entrenched class
of fools and scoundrels, children of the world,
his eyes caged and hostile behind glass—still
Péguy said that Hope is a little child.
—Geoffrey Hill, *The Mystery of the Charity of Charles Péguy*

I N THE INTRODUCTION to his *Essays on European Litera-*
ture (1950), E. R. Curtius remarked on his good fortune
in having been a contemporary and an interpreter of "men
like Gide, Claudel, Péguy, Proust, Valéry, Hofmannsthal,
Ortega, Joyce, Eliot." Greatness calls forth greatness, so it
is easy to understand Curtius's gratitude. But what about
his list? Joyce and Eliot are self-explanatory. Likewise
Proust and Valéry, Ortega and Hofmannsthal. Gide and
Claudel are at least plausible, even if their reputations have
declined in the years since Curtius wrote. But Péguy? How
did that unfamiliar name find its way onto the distinguished critic's "A-list"?

In the English-speaking world, the French poet and intermittently Catholic polemicist Charles Péguy is barely even a name today. Until recently, I knew him only as the author of the penetrating observation (found in a 1905 essay called "Notre Patrie") that "It will never be known what acts of cowardice have been motivated by the fear of not looking sufficiently progressive." Having gained in pertinence for nearly a century, that remark by itself is worth a modest sort of literary immortality.

From about 1910 until around the time Curtius composed his tabulary homage, Péguy was regularly invoked as a modern master—a peculiar master, to be sure, but a master nonetheless. He was, as the sociologist Irving Louis Horowitz noted in a book about Péguy's friend-turned-enemy Georges Sorel, "perhaps the most significant voice in French social Christianity since Proudhon." Writing in *The New Statesman* in 1916, two years after Péguy's death in action at the beginning of World War I, T. S. Eliot commended him as "one of the most illustrious of the dead who have fallen in this war," "a national, a symbolic figure, the incarnation of the rejuvenated French spirit." The philosopher Henri Bergson, whom Péguy knew and whose work he wrote about, said that "he knew my most secret thought, such as I have never expressed it, such as I would have wished to express it." Similar encomia abound.

In our own day, enthusiasts for Péguy's work are much rarer. One of them is the French philosopher Pierre Manent. In "Charles Péguy: Between Political Faith and Faith" (1984), Manent extolled Péguy as "one of the most penetrating critics of the historical and sociological points of view which dominate modern consciousness." High praise. Manent acknowledges the "violently personal" character of Péguy's work, his habit of lacing considered arguments with *ad hominem* attacks, of ending lyrical expostulations with "an insult." But Manent discerned a "luminous mind, eager to understand and to think," behind the self-obsession and often bitter polemics. Péguy, Manent argues, continues to be "of capital importance," above all because of his insights into the distinctive hubris of modernity: the curious modern tendency to substitute faith in technique for the cultivation of wisdom, the belief that a perfect administration of life could somehow relieve the burden, the unpredictable adventure, of living.

Another of Péguy's recent admirers is the British poet Geoffrey Hill. Hill not only devoted a long poem to Péguy in 1984—*The Mystery of the Charity of Charles Péguy* evokes the title of Péguy's most famous poem *Le Mystère de la Charité de Jeanne d'Arc* (1909)—but also wrote an enthusiastic appreciation of Péguy, whom he clearly regards as a kindred spirit. Péguy was, Hill admitted, a man of violent emotions ("violent" and "passionate" are words that inevitably turn up whenever Péguy is on the menu), but also "a man of the most exact and exacting probity," "one of the great souls, one of the great prophetic intelligences, of our century." Reflecting on Péguy's return to an unorthodox Catholicism after a period of loudly declared atheism, Hill speaks of Péguy's having "rediscovered the solitary ardors of faith but not the consolations of religious practice. He remained self-excommunicate but adoring." Students of Hill's poetry will recognize the terrain.

I would not myself place Péguy in the exalted company of Proust, Eliot, and Co. His genius was too idiosyncratic, his achievement too diffuse. Even Péguy's admirers—most of them, anyway—acknowledge this. Eliot, for one, stressed Péguy's genuineness and lack of "affectation"; he also noted that "one would hardly call him a 'thinker.'" Péguy's style, Eliot said, "is not a style to think in; it is too emphatic, too insistent." In 1928, writing about Péguy's friend Julien

Benda, Eliot noted in passing that Péguy was "a remarkable example of a writer who managed to influence many people, largely because he had so confused a mind that there was room for everything in it somehow." One misunderstands Eliot, I believe, if one misses the element of admiration in that deflationary remark. Order is admirable—Eliot wouldn't want us to do without that—but capaciousness, too, he suggests, is an intellectual strength.

In any event, if Péguy has occasionally been rated rather too highly, he is unduly neglected today. One reason for this is the temperament of Péguy's work. His combination of spiritual earnestness and rhetorical ferocity is currently out of fashion. There is also the pedestrian fact that so little of Péguy's work is readily available in English. Translations of a good deal of his poetry were made in the 1940s. And in 1943 a miscellany of prose snippets and poems was published under the title *Basic Verities*. That volume went through several printings but has long been out of print.

IT IS WELCOME news, then, that Liberty Fund has undertaken republication of *Temporal and Eternal*, an "adaptation" of two long essays by Péguy that were first published in English in 1958. The book, with a new foreword by Pierre Manent, contains abbreviated and edited versions of *Notre Jeunesse*, Péguy's 1910 meditation on the Dreyfus Affair, and "Clio I," a posthumously published reflection on history, the clergy, and the modern world. *Notre Jeunesse* (translated as "Memories of Youth") is generally regarded as one of Péguy's most important essays. "Clio I," although it develops some themes introduced in *Notre Jeunesse*, is also (as Péguy's translator comments) "among the most turgid of his works."

In some respects, Péguy was very much a period piece.

Immersed in the controversies, prejudices, and emotional
weather of his day, he took on their coloring. This boosted
his contemporary relevance. It also assured that he would
soon seem dated. In intellectual matters as in hemlines,
nothing seems more out-of-fashion than yesterday's rage.
But Péguy was not only a creature of his time. As Manent's
comments suggest—and as passages in *Temporal and Eternal* demonstrate—he was also a writer whose insights continue to resonate today. Péguy was above all an apostle of
the firsthand, the present reality, the rootedness in lived
experience. Hence his repudiation of all efforts to deal with
things by proxy. "The modern idea," he wrote in a passage
on historiography that Manent quotes,

> the modern method comes down essentially to this: given a
> work or given a text, how do we proceed to know it? Let
> us start by ignoring the text; above all let us be careful not
> to pick up the text or even to look at it, that would come at
> the end, if it were ever to happen. Let us begin at the
> beginning or rather because we must be complete, let us
> begin by the beginning of the beginning; the beginning of
> the beginning is to find in the vast, moving, universal, total
> reality, the exact vantage point which, though bearing some
> relation to the text, is the farthest removed from the text.

Anyone who has followed the divagations of contemporary
literary criticism or museological practice will know what
Péguy means.

That much of what he had to say about the modern
world is unwelcome and falls on deaf ears is naturally
another element in Péguy's neglect. The criticisms he formulated are unflattering to modern vanities, especially our
apparently unassailable sense of self-importance and self-sufficiency. But of course that is precisely why Péguy's

work is valuable and worth recalling. "If Péguy is susceptible to looking bizarre in our contemporary eyes,"
Manent notes, "it is only because he was much more con-
crete and real than we ordinarily care to be."

I would argue only with Manent's "only." Let us grant
Péguy's vividness and "reality," qualities that when overdone do seem bizarre. There is also the matter of Péguy's
style. Eliot regretted its being "too emphatic, too insistent." But that's only part of the problem. One of Péguy's
critics tartly remarked that Péguy "lacked the one talent
that would have made him a great pamphleteer: brevity."

His poem *Eve*, written in 1914, begins with what have
become among Péguy's most famous lines:

> *Heureux ceux qui sont morts pour la terre charnelle*
> *Mais pourvu que ce fût une juste guerre.*

("Happy are those who die for the carnal earth/ but only if
it be for a just war.") Péguy embroiders his theme for 1911
quatrains—that is 7643 alexandrine lines and a concluding
hemistich, making *Eve* one of the longest poems in French.

In both his poetry and his prose, Péguy favored repetition. A word, a line, an image would be taken up over and
over again, slightly varied, often repeated outright. His
style was at once accretive, like a pearl, and relentless, like
a tidal wave. It doesn't work for everyone. When François
Mauriac was told that someone was translating *Le Mystère
de la Charité de Jeanne d'Arc* into English, he said "What
a pity someone does not translate him into French." Not
entirely fair, but having sampled a bit of Péguy in French I
know what he means.

Musing in 1910 on Péguy's style, André Gide produced
a baroque correlative:

Péguy's style is like that of very ancient litanies. It is like Arab chants, like the monotonous chants of heath and moor; it is comparable to the desert; a desert of esparto, a desert of sand, a desert of stone. . . . Péguy's style is like the pebbles of the desert which follow and resemble each other so closely, one so much like the other, but yet a tiny bit different; and with a difference which corrects itself, recovers possession of itself, repeats itself, seems to repeat itself, stresses itself, and always more clearly.

And so on. Gide had intended to be flattering. But what might be extraordinary and exotic in a verbal construct is not necessarily readable.

Thanks to the chaperoning of translators, readers of Péguy in English encounter this aspect of his work in much diluted form. (Alexander Dru, noting the "plodding gait" of Péguy's prose, claimed that he attempted "to prune the style in order to reveal the fruit.") One result is that Péguy is mostly known—to the extent that he is known at all—as the author of one-liners. I have already mentioned his marvelous observation about acts of cowardice motivated by the fear of not looking sufficiently progressive. He has many others nearly as good:

Tyranny is always better organized than freedom.

Surrender is essentially an operation by means of which we set about explaining instead of acting.

Homer is new and fresh this morning, and nothing, perhaps, is as old and tired as today's newspaper.

A word is not the same with one writer as with another. One tears it from his guts. The other pulls it out of his overcoat pocket.

He who does not bellow the truth when he knows the truth
makes himself the accomplice of liars and forgers.

The last two, especially, are characteristic of Péguy's—what
to call it?—his style, his outlook, his personality.

But Péguy was more than a coiner of epigrams. No one
would accuse him of being a systematic thinker, but he was
an unusually candid one. He was born in modest circumstances in 1873 in Orléans, where, in 1429, Joan of
Arc was instrumental in raising the siege of the city by the
English. Péguy's father, a carpenter, died several months
later, and Péguy was raised by his mother and grandmother. They eked out a living recaning chairs, a craft that
Péguy also practiced occasionally in his youth to help
maintain the family coffers. Péguy later paraded his
"peasant" background—rather overstating (or perhaps I
mean "understating") his origins, but he regarded an ear-
thy provenance as a patent of authenticity. (It was an attitude that underlay his ardent nationalism.) Péguy early
on displayed academic promise, won a scholarship to the
Ecole normale supérieure, but failed part of his examina-
tion and left without taking a degree. Overall, his academic
performance was indifferent. By the time he was twenty,
Péguy had ceased practicing his native Roman Catholicism,
declared himself a socialist, and worked running a socialist
bookshop in the Latin Quarter. When his closest friend
died in 1896, Péguy determined that duty required him to
marry his friend's sister, which he did the following year.
They had four children, the youngest of whom was born in
1915, after Péguy's death. In 1898, Péguy used his wife's
inheritance to open his own bookshop, located near the
Sorbonne, which he studiously mismanaged and brought
to the brink of bankruptcy within a year.

In 1900, he started the *Cahiers de la Quinzaine*

("Fortnightly Notebooks"), the journal that he ran until his death and in which most of his work first appeared. As F. C. St. Aubyn writes in his book on Péguy,

> his editorial policy was idealistic. No advertising was to be accepted for fear of inhibiting the freedom of expression. Those interested in the review would support it financially according to a sliding scale of ability to pay. All points of view were welcome. No manuscript would be censored although the author might later find himself the object of a strongly worded rebuttal if his ideas differed from those of Péguy.

Péguy's journal was a distinguished but not quite indispensable publication—though to call it a publication tells only half the story. It was almost a way of life. Contributors included Maurice Barrès, Julien Benda, Anatole France, Daniel Halévy, Romain Rolland, André Suarès, and Jean Juarès—a respectable roster of semi-luminaries that, one notes, does not include such incandescent names as Gide, Proust, and Apollinaire. At any one time there were only a few hundred subscribers, but the *Cahiers* seem to have formed the center of their intellectual universe. Thursdays Péguy was "at home" to a dozen or so friends who dropped by to discuss the events of the day. Controversy and contention were always in order. "A review only continues to have life if each issue annoys at least one-fifth of its readers," Péguy wrote. "Justice lies in seeing that it is not always the same fifth."

In 1908, Péguy startled his friends by announcing his return to the Catholic faith (but not quite to the Catholic church: he remained hostile to the institution). Péguy continued to regard himself as a socialist, but here, too, his allergy to "parties" and institutions made him an unreliable ally. One admirer said that Péguy's socialism was "far more akin to the socialism of Saint Francis than to that of Karl Marx."

Perhaps. He liked to remind his readers that he was pursuing "none other than The Eternal Salvation of France," etc. Alexander Dru is probably right to argue that attempting to label Péguy politically is "a waste of time." He was too idiosyncratic, not to say erratic. Or perhaps it would be better to say that he was too stalwart in following his own conscience to make a good member of any party. Until the last four or five years of his life, the vast majority of Péguy's writing was polemical. There was always a lyric strain in his sensibility. But until 1910, when he fell in love with Blanche Raphaël, a longtime friend, that lyricism showed itself sporadically. Péguy remained faithful to his wife, but his new emotional attachment probably helps explain the huge outpouring of poetry in his last years. Péguy was a lieutenant in the reserves; it is said that when war was declared in August 1914, he left off writing in mid-sentence to join the mobilization. On the first day of the first battle of the Marne, about twenty-five kilometers from Paris, Péguy was felled by a bullet through the head. "For God's sake, push ahead!" are said to have been his last words. He was forty-one.

At the center of *Notre Jeunesse*, as at the center of Péguy's life, was the Dreyfus affair. It is difficult for us to comprehend the riveting importance of this episode for French life at the turn of the century. In its divisiveness, it was like the Vietnam War in American society, only more so. The fate of Alfred Dreyfus, a Jewish army captain on the French general staff who was falsely accused of spying, was a lightning rod, a catalyst, a test of will and political good faith. Everyone took sides. And, as Proust noted midway through *A la recherche*, "The waves of the two currents of Dreyfusism and anti-Dreyfusism divided France from top to bottom." The affair officially lasted from 1894, when Dreyfus was first courtmartialed and sent to prison on Devil's Island, until 1906, when he was finally reinstated. In fact, its repercussions lasted decades. The army, the old guard of society, the Catholic church hierarchy were adamantly against Dreyfus; enlightened opinion was tirelessly on his side. It was not simply a matter of anti-Semitism, a virulent species of which erupted throughout France. The Dreyfus Affair was one of those world-defining, world-changing occurrences whose ramifications are all the more surprising because unexpected. "There is nothing," Péguy noted, "so unforeseen as an event."

Péguy was from the beginning of the affair a passionate Dreyfusard. By 1910, when he wrote *Notre Jeunesse*, he had invested the event with nearly cosmic significance. For him the Dreyfus Affair did not merely dramatize an instance of justice violated and set right. It was the stage upon which the soul of modern man struggled for significance. The Dreyfus Affair was bound up with the future of the French Republic and the future of France as a Christian society. He saw in the Dreyfus Affair and its aftermath an emblematic movement of history in which the fate of society was at stake. "Everything," Péguy wrote in one of his most quoted aphorisms, "begins in mysticism [*la mystique*] and ends in politics [*la politique*]."

Péguy wrote *Notre Jeunesse* as a response to—and an attack upon—a long essay by his friend Daniel Halévy about the Dreyfus Affair in the *Cahiers*. Halévy, too, was a staunch Dreyfusard. But he did not, as Péguy saw it, understand that the terms of the debate had been transformed utterly in the years following Dreyfus's reinstatement. Over the years, supporters of Dreyfus had hardened into the party of Dreyfus. They had lost the spontaneity and faith

LIVES OF THE MIND

that had originally fueled their cause. The division was no longer between Dreyfusards and anti-Dreyfusards, but between those who had succumbed to the inert, tabulating spirit of modernity and those who understood that culture was something deeper and more vital. "Dreyfusism triumphant" had capitulated to the sterility of party domination just as thoroughly as had the anti-Dreyfusards years before.

For Péguy, it was not enough to be on the right side of the debate, because the debate was fundamentally about more than choosing the right side. It was about the direction of the modern world. He was "horrified," he wrote, to discover that what was "to us an instinct has for the young become a matter of *propositions* . . . a matter of logic." Péguy hoped to show "what culture is, and how utterly different from (infinitely more precious than) science, archaeology, a doctrine, erudition, and, of course, a system. You will see what culture was like before the professors crushed it."

In Péguy's mind, the Dreyfus Affair had originally called forth a kind of heroism that had been sadly depleted by the institutionalization of its own success. He lamented

the world we call . . . the modern world. The world that tries to be clever. The world of the intelligent, of the advanced, of those who know, . . . who have nothing more to learn. The world of those who are not had on by fools. Like us. *That is to say:* the world of those who believe in nothing, not even in atheism, who devote themselves, who sacrifice themselves to nothing. *More precisely* the world of those without a *mystique*. And who boast of it.

As far as I know, Péguy never attempted to define what he meant by *la mystique*. Doubtless he would have regarded the exercise as an example of precisely the sort of degradation he was warning against: the movement of "organic" (a favorite word) plenitude to lifeless rationalism. In part, I suppose, Péguy was issuing the same sort of admonition that Walter Bagehot, writing about the English monarchy, made about the fragile but indispensable charisma of the throne: "We must not," Bagehot wrote, "let in daylight upon magic." Warning about the extent to which politics was "devouring" *la mystique*, Péguy was calling attention to the non-rational currents of life that nourish healthy institutions and preserve reason from rationalism.

Clearly, Péguy was a kind of romantic. Much that he had to say about the differences among nations, the French "race," etc., seems curiously dated, even odious, to our twenty-first-century ears. As Manent noted, "Péguy did not go so far as to say that a German saint was an impossibility, a contradiction in terms, but it must be said that he came close to it." Perhaps Péguy's notion of *la mystique* is similar to what Kant meant by an "aesthetical idea": a "representation of the imagination which occasions much thought, without however any definite thought, i.e., any *concept* being capable of being adequate to it." But I think there was more to it than that. It is easy to dismiss a figure like Péguy. His enthusiasms are embarrassingly frank, his rhetoric volatile, his categories clumsy. But he saw something essential about the spiritual aridity of modern rationalism, the attempt to reduce life to a calculus of competing interests. We live in a world increasingly determined by the administrative imperative Péguy recoiled from. In such a world, Péguy's ambition to "introduce uneasiness" and open the door to "commotion" is a necessary corrective. It is not the whole story. But it is a part of the human mystery that we neglect at the cost of our diminishment.

Index

Index

Index

Index

Index

Kojève, Alexandre, 131
Kokoschka, Oskar, 204
Kolakowski, Leszek, 129
Kraus, Karl, 202, 316
Kristol, Irving, 17
Kuhn, Thomas, 247, 251; *The Structure of Scientific Revolutions*, 264–266

La Rochefoucauld, François, Duc de, 327
Lacan, Jacques, 131
Lakatos, Imre, 264, 266
Lamarckianism, 71
Lambert, J. H., 121
Lawrence, George, 283
Leavis, F. R., 203
Leibniz, Gottfried, 97, 320
Lengenfeld, Charlotte von, 107
Lenin, V. I., 130, 194, 242, 253, 264
Lenoir, Alexandre, 45
Lessing, Gotthold, 20
Letwin, Shirley Robin, *The Gentleman in Trollope*, 296–297, 315
Levin, Bernard, 341
Lewes, George Henry, 310
Lichtenberg, G. C., 316–329, 333; *Sudelbücher*, 319
Lippmann, Walter, 179
Locke, John, 94
Lonsdale, Frederick, 333
Loos, Adolf, 204
Louis Napoleon (later Napoleon III), 41, 46, 54, 67–68, 70
Louis-Philippe, 38, 46–47, 49, 275
Lowell, James Russell, 305
Lowrie, Walter, 166, 168
Lucretius, 189
Lukács, Georg, 110
Lycurgus, 20

Macaulay, Thomas Babington, 54, 76
Macmillan, Harold, 242
Magee, Bryan, *The Philosophy of Schopenhauer*, 142–148, 151, 153–154
Major, John, 293
Malcolm, Norman, 221
Malleson, Lady Constance, 229
Malleson, Miles, 229
Malthus, Thomas, *Essay on Population*, 71

Manent, Pierre, 354–358, 365; *Tocqueville and the Nature of Democracy*, 278
Manet, Edouard, 42
Mann, Thomas, 106, 142–143; *Buddenbrooks*, 140, 152–154; *Death in Venice*, 140; *Doctor Faustus*, 140; *The Magic Mountain*, 140
Mansfield, Harvey C., 5, 277, 279, 283–285
Marcuse, Herbert, *Eros and Civilization*, 110
Maritain, Jacques, 92, 97
Marseille, Walter, 241–242
Martensen, Hans Lassen, 170
Martial, 28
Martineau, James, *Types of Ethical Theory*, 342
Martineau, Harriet, 342
Marx, Karl, 4, 9, 13, 43, 84, 110, 135, 194, 253, 362; *Capital*, 130–131; *The Communist Manifesto*, 13
Marxism, 5, 7, 11–14, 130–131, 251, 256–257, 272, 331
Mather, Cotton, 20
Mauriac, François, 358
McCormick, John, *George Santayana: A Biography*, 178–179, 181, 185, 188, 200
McCrum, Robert, 333
McGuinness, Brian, 202–203, 209–210, 218
Meier-Graefe, Julius, *The Development of Modern Art*, 42–43, 51
Menander, 25
Mendel, Gregor, 71
Mendelssohn, Felix, 122–123
Merleau-Ponty, Maurice, 6, 12, 131
Mersenne, Marin, 93, 95–96
Michelangelo Buonarroti, 40
Michelson, Albert, 266
Mill, John Stuart, 223, 249, 277; *Autobiography*, 225; *On Liberty*, 253
Monk, Roy, 227; *Wittgenstein: The Duty of Genius*, 201–205, 207, 218–220
Monnier, Henri, 46
Montagu, Lady Mary Wortley, 65–66
Montaigne, Michel de, 21, 30

371

Index

Montesquieu, Charles, Baron de, 18, 284
Moore, G. E., 205–206, 208, 210–211, 231
Moorehead, Caroline, 227
Morrell, Lady Ottoline, 180, 207–208, 229, 239–240, 244
Mottley, Mary, 282
Mozart, Wolfgang, 117
Milton, John, 19–20, 54, 58, 184
Mullen, Richard, *Anthony Trollope*, 297
Murray, Gilbert, 231, 235
Musée d'Orsay, 49

Napoleon, 124–125
Nation, The, 255
National Review, 60
Nazism, 117, 194
Negri, Antonio, *Empire*, 13–14
Nero, 21
Nerva, 28
New Science, the, 83
New Statesman, The, 354
New Testament, 160
New York Review of Books, The, 255
New York Times, The, 4, 13
Newman, Ernest, 349
Newman, John Henry, 334
Newton, Ethel, 336–337
Newton, Isaac, 269
Newtonian physics, 214, 267
Nicias, 20
Nietzsche, Friedrich, 13, 84, 98, 110, 141, 143, 155, 196, 316, 325, 343; *Ecce Homo*, 154; *The Gay Science*, 317; *Untimely Meditations*, 140; *The Will to Power*, 196
Nobel Prize, 230
North, Thomas, 26
Nozick, Robert, *Philosophical Explanations*, 255–256

Oakeshott, Michael, 315
Olafson, Frederick, 193
Oliphant, Margaret, 310
Olsen, Regine, 170–172
O'Niel, Colette, 229
Ortega y Gasset, José, 353
Orwell, George, 14, 246
Osiris, 26, 29
Ovid, 29, 97

Palmerston, Henry Temple, Lord, 56
Park, Clara Claiborne, 315
Pascal, Blaise, 175, 284, 327; *Pensées*, 99, 102, 285
Pater, Walter, *Marius the Epicurean*, 198
Peel, Sir Robert, 54
Péguy, Charles, 353–365; *Basic Verities*, 356; *Eve*, 358; *Le Mystère de la Charité de Jeanne d'Arc*, 355, 358; *Notre Jeunesse*, 356, 362; *Temporal and Eternal*, 356–357
Peloponnesian War, 33
Pericles, 19, 35
Perrin, Bernadotte, 27
Petrarch, 184
Phidias, 35
Philipon, Charles, 39, 43, 45–47, 49–50
Phillips, Duncan, 41, 47, 50
Phillips Collection, the, 40, 49
Picasso, Pablo, 42
Pinkard, Terry, *Hegel: A Biography*, 120–125, 127
Plato, 24, 28, 38, 98, 103, 146, 150, 186, 194, 254, 342; *Dialogues*, 102; *Phaedrus*, 255; *Republic*, 245, 255; *Symposium*, 32, 255; *Theaetetus*, 255
Pliny the Younger, 28
Plutarch, 18–36, 130
Pol Pot, 253
Pope Hennessy, James, 296, 302
Popper, Karl, 143, 247, 252, 260–269; *Logik der Forschung*, 260, 263
Positivism, 214
Pound, Ezra, 184, 199
Pragmatism, American, 146
Prichard, James Cowles, 61
Priestley, Joseph, 322
Prospective Review, The, 62
Proudhon, Pierre-Joseph, 354
Proust, Marcel, 143, 181, 353, 355, 361–363
Ptolemy, 265
Purcell, Henry, 269

Quadrant, 253

Rabelais, François, 47, 341
Raphaël, Blanche, 362
Read, Herbert, 110

Index

Roger Kimball is Managing Editor
of *The New Criterion* and an art critic
for the London *Spectator*. His previous
books include *Tenured Radicals: How
Politics Has Corrupted Our Higher
Education*; *The Long March: How the
Cultural Revolution of the 1960s Changed
America*; *Experiments Against Reality:
The Fate of Culture in the Postmodern
Age*; and *Art's Prospect: The Challenge
of Tradition in an Age of Celebrity*.

2 1982 01302 9842